Modernism and...

Series Editor: **Roger Griffin**, Professor in Modern History, Oxford Brookes University, UK.

The series *Modernism and...* invites experts in a wide range of cultural, social, scientific and political phenomena to explore the relationship between a particular topic in modern history and 'modernism'. Apart from their intrinsic value as short but groundbreaking specialist monographs, the books aim through their cumulative impact to expand the application of this highly contested term beyond its conventional remit of art and aesthetics. Our definition of modernism embraces the vast profusion of creative acts, reforming initiatives and utopian projects that, since the late nineteenth century, have sought either to articulate, and so to symbolically transcend, the spiritual malaise or decadence of modernity or to find a radical solution to it through a movement of spiritual, social and political – even racial – regeneration and renewal. The ultimate aim is to foster a spirit of transdisciplinary collaboration in shifting the structural forces that define modern history beyond their conventional conceptual frameworks.

Titles include:

Roy Starrs
MODERNISM AND JAPANESE CULTURE

Marius Turda
MODERNISM AND EUGENICS

Shane Weller
MODERNISM AND NIHILISM

D1003724

Ben Hutchinson
MODERNISM AND STYLE

Thomas Linehan
MODERNISM AND BRITISH SOCIALISM

Forthcoming titles:

Maria Bucur
MODERNISM AND GENDER

Frances Connelly
MODERNISM AND THE GROTESQUE

Elizabeth Darling
MODERNISM AND DOMESTICITY

Matthew Feldman
MODERNISM AND PROPAGANDA

Axle Staehler
MODERNISM AND FUNDAMENTALISM

Ariane Mildenberg
MODERNISM AND EPIPHANY

Mark Antliff and Patricia Leighten
MODERNISM AND PRIMITIVISM

Agnese Horvath
MODERNISM AND CHARISMA

Carmen Kuhling
MODERNISM AND NEW RELIGIONS

Patricia Leighten
MODERNISM AND ANARCHISM

Gregory Maertz
MODERNISM AND NAZI PAINTING

Paul March-Russell
MODERNISM AND SCIENCE FICTION

David Ohana
MODERNISM AND ZIONISM

Anna Katharina Schaffner
MODERNISM AND PERVERSION

Richard Shorten
MODERNISM AND TOTALITARIANISM

Mihai Spariosu
MODERNISM, EXILE AND UTOPIA

Erik Tonning
MODERNISM AND CHRISTIANITY

Veronica West-Harling
MODERNISM AND THE QUEST

Modernism and ...
Series Standing Order ISBN 978–0–230–20332–7 (Hardback)
978–0–230–20333–4 (Paperback)
(*outside North America only*)

You can receive future titles in this series as they are published by placing a standing order. Please contact your bookseller or, in case of difficulty, write to us at the address below with your name and address, the title of the series and the ISBN quoted above.

Customer Services Department, Macmillan Distribution Ltd, Houndmills, Basingstoke, Hampshire RG21 6XS, England

---

Modernism and British Socialism

Thomas Linehan
Lecturer in Modern History, Brunel University, UK

First published 2012 by
PALGRAVE MACMILLAN

Palgrave Macmillan in the UK is an imprint of Macmillan Publishers Limited,
registered in England, company number 785998, of Houndmills, Basingstoke,
Hampshire RG21 6XS.

Palgrave Macmillan in the US is a division of St Martin's Press LLC,
175 Fifth Avenue, New York, NY 10010.

Palgrave Macmillan is the global academic imprint of the above companies
and has companies and representatives throughout the world.

Palgrave® and Macmillan® are registered trademarks in the United States,
the United Kingdom, Europe and other countries.

ISBN 978–0–230–23010–1 hardback
ISBN 978–0–230–23011–8 paperback

This book is printed on paper suitable for recycling and made from fully
managed and sustained forest sources. Logging, pulping and manufacturing
processes are expected to conform to the environmental regulations of the
country of origin.

A catalogue record for this book is available from the British Library.

A catalog record for this book is available from the Library of Congress.

10   9   8   7   6   5   4   3   2   1
21 20 19 18 17 16 15 14 13 12

Printed and bound in Great Britain by
CPI Antony Rowe, Chippenham and Eastbourne

To my children, Ciara and Michael, and my late mother, Margaret Linehan

Contents

Series Editor's Preface   viii

Acknowledgements   xiv

Introduction   1

1   Defining Modernism   9

2   The Spiritual and Epiphanic Modernism of British
    Socialism   24

3   Socialist Utopian Modernism: The Myths of the
    Kingdom and the Golden Age   43

4   Experiments in Social Modernism: The Communities of
    Hope   65

5   Contesting Abstract Space   79

6   The Return to Origins: Modernism, Socialism and
    Childhood   98

7   Fabian Modernism   116

Conclusion   132

Notes   139

Select Bibliography   157

Index   166

Series Editor's Preface

As the title 'Modernism and…' implies, this series has been conceived in an open-ended, closure-defying spirit, more akin to the soul of jazz than to the rigour of a classical score. Each volume provides an experimental space which allows both seasoned professionals and aspiring academics to investigate familiar areas of modern social, scientific, or political history from the defamiliarising vantage point afforded by a term not routinely associated with it: 'modernism'. Yet this is no contrived makeover of a clichéd concept for the purposes of scholastic bravado. Nor is it a gratuitous theoretical exercise in expanding the remit of an 'ism' already notorious for its polyvalence – not to say its sheer nebulousness – in a transgressional fling of postmodern *jouissance*.

Instead this series is based on the *empirically*-oriented hope that a deliberate enlargement of the semantic field of 'modernism' to embrace a whole range of phenomena apparently unrelated to the radical innovation in the arts it normally connotes will do more than contribute to scholarly understanding of those topics. Cumulatively the volumes that appear are meant to contribute to a perceptible paradigm shift slowly becoming evident in the way modern history is approached. It is one which, while indebted to 'the cultural turn', is if anything 'post-postmodern', for it attempts to use transdisciplinary perspectives and the conscious clustering of concepts often viewed as unconnected – or even antagonistic to each other – to consolidate and deepen the reality principle on which historiography is based, not flee it, to move closer to the experience of history of its actors, not away from it. Only those with a stunted, myopic (and actually *unhistorical*) view of what constitutes historical 'fact' and 'causation' will be predisposed to dismiss the 'Modernism and…' project as mere 'culturalism', a term which due to unexamined prejudices and sometimes sheer ignorance has, particularly in the vocabulary of more than one eminent 'archival' historian, acquired a reductionist, pejorative meaning.

Yet even open-minded readers may find the title of this book disconcerting. Like all the volumes in the series, it may seem to conjoin two phenomena that do not 'belong'. However any 'shock of the new' induced by the widened usage of 'modernism' to embrace non-aesthetic phenomena that makes this juxtaposition possible should be mitigated by realising that in fact it is neither new nor shocking. The conceptual ground for a work such as *Modernism and British Socialism* has been prepared by such seminal texts as Marshall Berman's *All That Is Solid Melts into Air. The Experience of Modernity* (1982), Modris Eksteins' *Rites of Spring* (1989), Peter Osborne's *The Politics of Time. Modernity and the Avant-Garde* (1995), Emilio Gentile's *The Struggle for Modernity* (2003) and Mark Antliff's *Avant-Garde Fascism. The Mobilization of Myth, Art and Culture in France, 1909–1939* (2007). In each case modernism is revealed as the long-lost sibling (twin or maybe even father) of historical phenomena from the social and political sphere that is rarely mentioned in the same breath.

Yet the real pioneers of such a 'maximalist' interpretation of modernism were none other than some of the major aesthetic modernists themselves. For them the art and thought that subsequently earned them this title was a creative force – passion even – of revelatory power which, in a crisis-ridden West where *anomie* was reaching pandemic proportions, was capable of regenerating not just 'cultural production', but 'socio-political production', and for some even society *tout court*. Figures such as Friedrich Nietzsche, Richard Wagner, Wassily Kandinsky, Walter Gropius, Pablo Picasso and Virginia Woolf never accepted that the art and thought of 'high culture' were to be treated as self-contained spheres of activity peripheral to – and cut off from – the main streams of contemporary social and political events. Instead they assumed them to be laboratories of visionary thought that were vital to the spiritual salvation of a world being systematically drained of higher meaning and ultimate purpose by the dominant, 'nomocidal' forces of modernity. If we accept Max Weber's thesis of the gradual *Entzauberung*, or 'disenchantment', of the world through rationalism, such creative individuals could be seen as having set themselves the task – each in his or her own idiosyncratic way – of *re-enchanting* and re-sacralising the world. Such modernists consciously sought to restore a sense of higher purpose, transcendence and *Zauber* (magic) to a spiritually starved modern humanity condemned by 'progress' to live in a permanent state of existential exile, of *liminoid transition*, now that the forces of the divine seemed to have withdrawn in what Martin Heidegger's muse, the poet Friedrich Hölderlin, called 'The Flight of the Gods'. If the hero of modern popular nationalism is the

Unknown Warrior, perhaps the patron saint of modernism itself is *Deus Absconditus*.

Approached from this oblique angle modernism is thus a revolutionary force, but is so in a sense only distantly related to the one made familiar by standard accounts of the (political or social) revolutions on which modern historians cut their teeth. It is a 'hidden' revolution of the sort referred to by the 'arch-'aesthetic modernist Vincent van Gogh in his letter of 24 September 1888 to his brother Theo about the sorry plight of the world. In one passage he waxes ecstatic about the impression made on him by the work of another spiritual seeker disturbed by the impact of 'modern progress', Leo Tolstoy:

> It seems that in the book, *My Religion*, Tolstoy implies that whatever happens in a violent revolution, there will also be an inner and hidden revolution in the people, out of which a new religion will be born, or rather, something completely new which will be nameless, but which will have the same effect of consoling, of making life possible, as the Christian religion used to.
>
> The book must be a very interesting one, it seems to me. In the end, we shall have had enough of cynicism, scepticism and humbug, and will want to live – more musically. How will this come about, and what will we discover? It would be nice to be able to prophesy, but it is even better to be forewarned, instead of seeing absolutely nothing in the future other than the disasters that are bound to strike the modern world and civilization like so many thunderbolts, through revolution, or war, or the bankruptcy of worm-eaten states.

In the series 'Modernism and...' the key term has been experimentally expanded and 'heuristically modified' to embrace any movement for change which set out to give a name and a public identity to the 'nameless' and 'hidden' revolutionary principle that van Gogh saw as necessary to counteract the rise of nihilism. He was attracted to Tolstoy's vision because it seemed to offer a remedy for the impotence of Christianity and the insidious spread of a literally soul-destroying cynicism, which if unchecked would ultimately lead to the collapse of civilisation. The term 'modernism' thus applies in this series to all concerted attempts in any sphere of activity that enable life to be lived more 'musically' and that resurrect the sense of transcendent communal and individual purpose being palpably eroded by the chaotic unfolding of events in the modern world, even if the end result could be 'just' to make society physically and mentally healthy.

What would have probably appalled van Gogh is that some visionaries no less concerned than him by the growing crisis of the West sought a manna of spiritual nourishment emanating not from heaven, nor even from an earthly beauty still retaining an aura of celestial otherworldliness, but from strictly secular visions of an alternative modernity so radical in its conception that attempts to enact it inevitably led to disasters of its own following the law of unintended consequences. Such solutions were be realised not by a withdrawal from history into the realm of art (the sphere of 'epiphanic' modernism), but by applying a utopian artistic, mythopoeic, religious or technocratic consciousness to the task of harnessing the dynamic forces of modernity itself in such spheres as politics, nationalism, the natural sciences and social engineering in order to establish a new order and a 'new man'. It is initiatives conceived in this 'programmatic' mode of modernism that the series sets out to explore. Its results are intended to benefit not just a small coterie of like-minded academics but also mainstream teaching and research in modern history, thereby becoming part of the 'common sense' of the discipline even of self-proclaimed 'empiricists'.

Some of the deep-seated psychological, cultural and 'anthropological' mechanisms underlying the futural revolts against modernity here termed 'modernism' are explored at length in my *Modernism and Fascism. The Sense of a Beginning under Mussolini and Hitler* (2007). The premise of this book could be taken to be Phillip Johnson's assertion that 'Modernism is typically defined as the condition that begins when people realise God is truly dead, and we are therefore on our own.' It presents the wellsprings of modernism in the primordial human need for a new metaphysical centre in a radically decentred reality as well as for a new source of transcendental meaning in a godless universe, and in the impulse to erect a 'sacred canopy' of culture which not only aesthetically veils the infinity of time and space surrounding human existence to make existence feasible, but also provides a totalising world view within which to locate individual life narratives, thus imparting it with the illusion of cosmic significance. By eroding or destroying the canopy of culture, modernity creates a protracted spiritual crisis which provokes the proliferation of countervailing impulses to restore a 'higher meaning' to historical time that are collectively termed by the book (ideal-typically) as 'modernism'.

Johnson's statement seems to make a perceptive point by associating modernism not just with art, but with a general 'human condition' consequent on what Nietzsche, the first great modernist philosopher, called 'the Death of God'. Yet in the context of this series his statement requires significant qualification. Modernism is *not* a general historical condition (any more than 'post-modernism' is), but a generalised revolt against even the *intuition* made possible by a secularising modernisation that we are spiritual orphans in a godless and ultimately meaningless universe. Its hallmark is the bid to find a new home, a new community and a new source of transcendence.

Nor is modernism itself necessarily secular. On the contrary: both the wave of occultism, Theosophy and the Catholic revival of the 1890s and the emergence of radicalised, Manichaean forms of Christianity, Hinduism, Islam and even Buddhism in the 1990s demonstrate that modernist impulses need not take the form of secular utopianism, but may readily assume religious (some would say 'post-secular') forms. In any case within the cultural force field of modernism, even the most secular entities are sacralised to acquire an aura of numinous significance. Ironically Johnson himself offers a fascinating case study in this fundamental aspect of the modernist rebellion against the empty skies of a disenchanted, anomic world. A retired Berkeley law professor, some of the books he published, such as *The Wedge of Truth* (2000), made him one of the major protagonists of 'Intelligent Design', a Christian(ised) version of creationism that offers a prophylactic against the allegedly nihilistic implications of Darwinist science.

Naturally no attempt has been made to impose the 'reflexive metanarrative' developed in *Modernism and Fascism* on the various authors of this series. Each has been encouraged to tailor the term modernism to fit their own epistemological cloth, as long as they broadly agree in seeing it as the expression of a reaction against modernity not restricted to art and aesthetics, and as driven by the aspiration to create a spiritually or physically 'healthier' modernity through a new cultural, political and ultimately biological order. Naturally the blueprint for the ideal society varies significantly according to each diagnosis of what makes actually existing modernity untenable, 'decadent' or doomed to self-destruction.

The ultimate aim of the series is to help bring about a paradigm shift in the way 'modernism' is used, and hence stimulate fertile new areas of research and teaching with an approach which enables methodological empathy and causal analysis to be applied even to events and processes ignored by or resistant to the explanatory powers of conventional historiography. I am delighted that Thomas Linehan, an expert on fringe political movements working to transform Britain in the inter-war period, has contributed a volume to this series which presents British Socialism in a refreshingly unfamiliar context.

Roger Griffin
Oxford
January 2012

Acknowledgements

I would like to take this opportunity to express my thanks to Roger Griffin for inviting me to contribute to this important series on modernism. I would also like to express my gratitude to the commissioning and editorial staff at Palgrave Macmillan who provided me with due guidance and support during this project, particularly Michael Strang during its earlier stages and Ruth Ireland throughout the process. It is also a pleasure to acknowledge the assistance of archivists and librarians who assisted me during my visits to their establishments. Special mention here must be made to the wonderfully endowed and ever helpful Bodleian Library in Oxford, UK.

Finally I would like to acknowledge those friends, colleagues and family members who provided support, encouragement and comradeship during the course of writing this book. As always, my wife Janet is deserving of a very special mention. She was responsible for the final arrangement of the book manuscript and her hard work and support in these often trying final stages is greatly appreciated. The love, support and patience of my children, Ciara and Michael, is also much appreciated. I love them dearly, and I partly dedicate this book to them.

Introduction

the age of fellowship had dawned[1]

Beginning in the early 1880s and continuing through to the Edwardian period, there was a quite dramatic, seemingly spontaneous awakening of new socialist political life in Britain. This followed the earlier failures of the Owenite co-operative experiments of the 1820s and 1830s. This rebirth is all the more remarkable given that during the 1860s and 1870s there was virtually no socialist presence in Britain to speak of. This presence was confined to a handful of activists that included Owenite survivors, ageing ex-Chartists or O'Brienite radicals with socialist leanings, socialist émigrés from continental Europe and a small body of Christian socialists linked to J.M. Ludlow, Frederick D. Maurice and Charles Kingsley.[2] In stark contrast, the late Victorian and Edwardian period saw the proliferation of a veritable kaleidoscope of new socialist groups and large numbers of new converts to the socialist faith. A brief mention of these groups will reveal the extent of the socialist awakening. Henry Mayers Hyndman's Democratic Federation was the first to arrive on the political landscape, on 8 June 1881, later mutating into the overtly Marxist Social Democratic Federation (SDF) in 1884 (1884–1909). Late 1881 saw the arrival of the Fellowship of the New Life (dissolved 1898), followed by the Fabian Society in 1883 and the Socialist League (SL) in 1884 (1884–91). The Fabians and the SL were both breakaway groups, from the Fellowship of the New Life and the SDF respectively. The Christian Socialist Society and the Scottish Labour Party were founded shortly afterwards, the former in 1886 the latter in 1888, as was the short-lived Socialist Union (1886–8).[3] Then in 1891 John Trevor's Labour Church and Robert Blatchford's Clarion movement appeared on the scene. The same year also saw the arrival of the Labour Army founded by a former Salvation Army

1

member Frank Smith with its periodical *The Workers' Cry*, and the William Morris-inspired Hammersmith Socialist Society. The next to join the growing socialist camp were the Socialist Sunday Schools in 1892, the Independent Labour Party (ILP) in January 1893 and John Clifford's Christian Socialist League in 1894, the latter evolving into the Christian Social Brotherhood in 1898.[4] In 1906 the Church Socialist League made its appearance, as did Guild Socialism, the latter associated with Alfred Orage, G.D.H. Cole, G.K. Chesterton and the *New Age* journal. The Labour Representation Committee (LRC) must be mentioned as well, of course. Established in February 1900, the LRC changed its name to the Labour Party in 1906. We also have the Socialist Party of Great Britain (1904–present), the Socialist Labour Party (1903–20) and the British Socialist Party (1911–20), the latter two groups being the forerunners of the Communist Party of Great Britain (1920–91). We will become reacquainted with many of these new socialist groups and some of the individuals associated with them during the course of this book. As a postscript to the above, it should be said that the 1890s saw the most spectacular surge in support of socialism. It is estimated that the ILP had over 400 clubs and branches by 1894 and maybe as many as 50,000 members by 1895, while Blatchford's *Clarion* newspaper was selling 80,000 copies per issue by the close of the decade.[5]

If this sudden awakening of socialist sentiment at this particular historical 'moment' was quite striking, so was socialism's ideological makeup during these years. British socialists of the revival era saw nothing wrong with infusing their socialism with ideas, assumptions and moral messages drawn from a range of home-grown and continental sources that included Thomas Carlyle, Charles Dickens, the nature mystic Richard Jefferies, John Ruskin, Prince Peter Kropotkin, Karl Marx and Leo Tolstoy. Ideas could be drawn in from even further afield, as with those emanating from the American 'Single Tax' advocate Henry George, and American Romantic writers like Henry Thoreau and Walt Whitman. Even a particular socialist grouping could exhibit these quite surprising juxtapositions, as with the welding of anarchism and Marxism in the socialism of the SL, or the intermingling of British Romanticism and Protestant Nonconformity in the ILP. The boundaries between the various branches of socialism tended to be quite fluid and blurred during these years as well, with socialist converts moving easily across 'borders'. The experience of Caroline Martyn was not uncommon. During her short spell as a socialist activist during the first half of the 1890s, she was a

Fabian Society member, joined the Guild of St Matthew, served on the National Administrative Council of the ILP, followed the Labour Army, attended the Labour Church and was Editor of *Fraternity*, the journal of the International Society for the Brotherhood of Man.[6]

Another intriguing feature of the socialist revival was the high level of spiritual content within socialist ideology and thinking. Again, this spiritual content did not emanate from a single source. It could have been derived from the Sermons of Christ, the immanentist theological beliefs of the American Romantic Ralph Waldo Emerson, or even from mysticism and occultism. In all this, there was a desire to fuse the spiritual with the material. Caroline Martyn's socialism was a case in point, as we have just seen. The luxuriant socialism of Edward Carpenter provides another example, combining as it did fragments of Eastern mysticism, Emersonian immanentism, and primitive myth, which then fused with a heightened social concern about poverty in late Victorian Britain.[7] Annie Besant's socialism contained a similar fusing of the spiritual and the material, knitting together a desire for social justice with a yearning for personal spiritual transcendence. We can get a sense of this from the following passage from Besant's autobiography, where she describes the nature of her socialist faith c.1886:

Deeper and deeper into my innermost nature ate the growing desire to succour, to suffer for, to save. I had long given up my social reputation, I had now given up with ever-increasing surrender ease, comfort, time; the passion of pity grew stronger and stronger, fed by each new sacrifice, and each sacrifice led me nearer and nearer to the threshold of that gateway beyond which stretched a path of renunciation I had never dreamed of, which those might tread who were ready wholly to strip off self for Man's sake, who for Love's sake would surrender Love's return from those they served, and would go out into the darkness for themselves that they might, with their own souls as fuel, feed the Light of the World.[8]

The freethinker Besant's conversion to socialism had come via a journey which saw her embrace ardent Secularism following an earlier attachment to evangelical Christianity. Given the spiritual content of her socialist thought, it should not surprise us to find Besant continuing her search for ever-deeper sources of spiritual nourishment, which she eventually found in Theosophy and the occultism of Madame Helena Blavatsky. The rather perplexing juxtaposing of socialism with Theosophy could be passed off as a minor idiosyncrasy within the socialist revival if confined to Besant were it not for the presence of a similarly discordant note in the socialism of some of her contemporaries, as we shall see in a later chapter.[9]

The spiritual impulse within contemporary socialism was particularly apparent in that aspiration for human 'fellowship' beyond actually existing capitalist relations which appeared as a strand of thought within the socialist revival. This aspiration was a ubiquitous presence within the revival and can be observed, though with varying degrees of intensity, in a range of phenomena seeking to give expression to the fellowship ideal around a vision of a regenerated socialist man and woman and a regenerated socialist future. The aspiration for socialist fellowship came in a number of organisational guises ranging from the Fellowship of the New Life to the Clarion Fellowship, while its philosophy on life registered a range of influences, including British utopianism and romanticism, Protestant non-conformism, American romanticism and utopianism, Eastern mysticism and even anarchism. The aspiration for socialist fellowship aimed to achieve for the individual and eventually the wider society a sense of transcendent value, meaning and spiritual purpose in the context of a new beginning during a period of late Victorian and Edwardian capitalism perceived as predatory, rapacious, alienating, mechanistic, philistine and spiritually impoverished and decadent.

There were other intriguing features of the socialist revival. There was that tendency to evoke the socialist future not through conventional political declarations or detailed policy formulations but through aesthetics, myth, Christian symbolism and idioms, metaphor and other forms of literary embellishment, dreams and various kinds of utopian imagining. Another interesting feature was the spate of utopian socialist community building that emerged as a significant strand of socialist political activity during the revival years. These applied forms of socialist utopianism mushroomed during these decades and complemented the imagined forms of socialist utopianism which appeared in contemporary socialist writing and other outlets.

How should we account for all this? How should we explain the sudden awakening of socialist sentiment at this particular historical 'moment', and the speed at which it spread? How, too, should we interpret the highly variegated ideological makeup of British socialism in this period, as well as the ubiquitous presence of spiritual elements within this ideology? Additionally, how should we account for that inclination on the part of many contemporary socialists to evoke the socialist future through myth, religious symbolism and idioms, aesthetics, metaphor, dreams and utopian imagining? The 'sudden' appearance of those utopian socialist communities at this juncture needs to be explained as well.

One could follow the trajectory of earlier historiography to explain all this. The onset of the socialist revival itself, particularly in its earliest stages from 1881 through to around 1896, has been put down to a chain of developments leading inexorably towards the emergence of a more secular, mature and representative class-based political party system, a 'tributary' feeding into a political mainstream that was to be eventually filled by the Labour Party.[10] In this interpretation, which clearly exhibits historicist undertones, no particularly unique, novel or special characteristics are ascribed to the sudden awakening of socialist sentiment at this 'moment'. Other accounts go further, even rejecting the view that the sudden emergence of socialist groups in the 1880s represented a 'turning point' or ushered in a new, distinctly socialist era. Rather, it is claimed that there was no sharp break with the past in the 1880s and that account needs to be taken of the strong line of continuity between British socialism and Liberal Radicalism.[11] Again, such accounts are unwilling to ascribe novel or special qualities to the socialist revival. As for the presence of those aesthetic, utopian, religious and other spiritual elements within socialism's ideological makeup during the revival years, this has been the subject of plentiful comment in the scholarship. This being said, this scholarship has tended to employ a particular mode of conceptual language to describe these elements. The widespread use of the concept of 'ethical socialism' is a particular case in point.[12] Though it does shed some light on the strong moral component within the revival, the broad, all-embracing master-narrative of 'ethical socialism' leaves other important areas of socialist ideology relatively unexplored. At the very least, the ethical socialism interpretation has been unable to fully explain why British socialism assumed such a highly variegated, nuanced and luxuriant profile during these decades. Other attempts to view aspects of the revival's spiritual and religious content through the prism of concepts such as the 'religion of socialism' or theological 'primitivism' also lack the necessary precision to fully comprehend the extraordinary richness of socialism at this point in its development.[13] Other comment is less fulsome. These accounts tend to understate or downplay the exotic religious, aesthetic and utopian strands within British socialism, passing them off as aber-rant phenomena, a quirky sub-text to the main story concerning the development of Labour socialism which tends to follow the trajectory of the dominant Fabian narrative or a Marxist narrative associated with Hyndman's SDF or Morris's SL.[14]

In the spirit of *Aufbruch*, of 'breaking out' of established historio-graphical frameworks, this book offers a different interpretation of the socialist revival to those currently available in the existing schol-arship. It attempts this by examining the socialist revival from the standpoint of a concept which usually has a narrower usage and is typically employed in fields of study and disciplines other than modern history. This is the concept of modernism. In so doing, and following the work of Roger Griffin, Modris Eksteins, Marshall Berman and other scholars, this book identifies with a 'maximalist' concept of modernism, seeing the modernist project as extending beyond the realm of the avant-garde, art and literature to embrace political and social manifestations of revolt which were fuelled by an urge to regenerate meaning and forge deeper spiritual bonds in a world thought to be lapsing into decadence.[15] British socialism dur-ing the revival years was a political and social movement of this type. It was always much more than a movement working to bring about greater economic justice. Beyond this economic agenda, socialism was one of the foremost 'revitalisation' movements of the *fin de siècle*, a heavily spiritualised movement for change which sought to counter the deep spiritual and cultural malaise thought to be afflicting mod-ern Britain. Socialists aspired to bring to birth a new age distinguished not by economic justice alone but by a new, more transcendental conception of life based on individuals entering into more intimate spiritual communion with the cosmos, nature and their 'fellows'. As such, British socialism was a species of modernism in its own right. Alongside this broader picture, there were a number of clearly identi-fiable modernist elements within British socialism during the revival years, which the following chapters will seek to bring to the fore. These would include those intriguing mythological, religious, aes-thetic, metaphorical and utopian elements we referred to above. The following chapters will tease out other aspects of modernism within the revival, as in the attempt to build small-scale, self-contained socialist utopias during this period. Modernist elements, too, can be observed in the effort to build self-contained 'utopias' of socialist children during these decades, as well as in those passionate socialist attempts at child rescue in this period.

Modernism and British Socialism, then, spans the period of the socialist revival which, broadly speaking, unfolded between 1880 and 1910 and sets out to identify the links between the revival and modernism. In so doing, this monograph redefines and reconceptualises core features of the revival, including those referred to above, seeing them as so many forms, manifestations and expressions of modernism. In other words, this book seeks to explore what has often been misunderstood, misrepresented, insufficiently considered or even ignored in the existing scholarship on the British socialism of the revival years. In the process, of course, British socialism itself will undergo a re-evaluation. It is necessary at this point to be more precise about the term 'modernism'. While the predominant and overarching strain of modernism present in the socialist revival was 'political modernism', we need to be mindful that the seam of modernism running through British socialism at this stage of its development had many shades of colour. These other shades of modernism would include 'social modernism', 'utopian modernism', 'aesthetic modernism' and what Roger Griffin has referred to as 'epiphanic modernism'.[16] Even this did not exhaust the rich vein of modernism running through the revival. As the final chapter in this book will show, we can even detect a potent strain of 'heroic modernism' within socialist modernism. Though quite distinct within contemporary socialism, these other species of modernism always overlapped and intersected with political modernism and never operated as phenomena separate from it.

In addition to this, modernism is itself, in its broadest sense, a rich, complex and highly contested concept. So, before we can embark on the task of re-evaluating British socialism in the way proposed, demonstrate an affinity between the socialist revival and modernism, it is vitally important to engage with the issue of modernism, as well as its conceptual cousins, modernisation and modernity, and the scholarship on these topics. This is necessary in order to help clarify our definitions, terms and methodology, and to specify how modernism is being interpreted and applied in relation to this book and to existing scholarship in this area. This engagement with the concepts of modernism, modernisation and modernity will form the basis of Chapter 1. Chapter 2 will then go on to explore those aspirations for spiritual regeneration, transcendence and heightened consciousness within the socialist movement, as well as the form of modernism we know as 'epiphanic modernism' as it relates to these aspirations. Chapter 3 will then attempt to uncover the seam of utopian modernism running through the socialist revival, as evident in those metaphoric and aesthetic evocations of the socialist future which socialist propagandists used to delight in conveying to their enthralled audiences, but particularly as manifested in two of the core myths of the revival years: the myth of the Kingdom and the myth of the Golden Age. The other form of modernism, social modernism, will form an important part of the discussion in Chapter 4, in the context of exploring those experiments at building the small-scale, socialist communities outside the mainstream of capitalist life. There was another aspect to these community experiments. They represented efforts to carve out new types of space beyond the mainstream of capitalist space, and this will form a key focus of Chapter 5, bearing in mind that the processes of modernisation, modernity and modernism were all bound up with the question of space. Chapter 6 will then go on to look at the relationship between the socialist revival and childhood, taking into account the importance of childhood and the figure of the child for modernism and modernist attempts to counteract the spiritual crisis engendered by the combined and overlapping processes of modernisation, modernity and progress. Chapter 7 will then examine the strain of heroic modernism within British socialism. It remains, finally, to mention that this book will draw on a range of primary sources, both contemporary and autobiographical, as well as secondary sources, concepts and arguments where relevant and appropriate, to investigate the relationship between modernism and British socialism.

1
Defining Modernism

In order to establish a relationship between the socialist revival and modernism, we must engage with the concept of modernism, as well as the concepts of modernisation and modernity. This preliminary survey will also enable us to clarify our methodology and establish how modernism is being defined in this study. We should begin by noting that, though related, the terms modernism, modernity and modernisation have quite different meanings and applications. Frederic Jameson offers a helpful formulation, which highlights the main distinctions. This formulation posits 'modernity as the new historical situation, modernisation as the process whereby we get there, and modernism as a reaction to that situation and that process alike, a reaction that can be aesthetic and philosophico-ideological, just as it can be negative and positive'.[1] This formulation is quite basic and partial, as Jameson admits, but provides a useful baseline from which to proceed. Given its precursory and preparatory role in relation to the other two concepts, it seems wise to start by providing a definition of modernisation.

More than modernity and modernism, modernisation is a term which refers to a range of processes which unfolded within a chronological framework, though this framework is of a very imprecise nature. There is no consensus within the scholarship as to the date when these modernisation processes began, with some scholars citing the sixteenth century still others the seventeenth century, but there is general agreement that once set in motion modernisation assumed a 'state of perpetual becoming', a juggernaut that went on to shape subsequent centuries, up to the twentieth century and beyond.[2] The geographical birthplace of modernisation can be identified with more certainty, as it initially began as a phenomenon affecting Western Europe but increasingly by the nineteenth century, and certainly by the twentieth century, it had fanned out to take in other parts of the globe. What needs to be understood here, too, is that these ongoing modernisation processes did not unfold uniformly across geographical spaces and social relations within a given society, but that they unfurled and sometimes exploded in accordance with different rhythms and temporal registers. This meant that the impact of modernisation during these centuries was highly uneven. Frederic Jameson claims that even Western Europe, more evidently in some countries than others, was experiencing a situation of 'incomplete modernisation' as late as the twentieth century.[3]

As to the nature of these modernisation processes, they assumed a range of forms. Roger Griffin's list is admiringly helpful here. This partly distinct though self-reinforcing set of processes included – in the realm of intellectual, cultural and ideological developments – the diffusion of rationalism, individualism, positivism, materialism, literacy, secularism, liberalism, the idea of progress, nationalism and imperialism.[4] Add to this list, in the sphere of institutional and technological development, representative democratic forms of government, bureaucracy and advances in science, transport and mass communications. Other modernisation processes associated with material and social developments were industrialisation and the emergence of distinct social-class groupings. To these latter processes we should add the quite dramatic increases in population which characterised the modern era. Whereas the first UK Census in 1801 recorded a population of 10.5 million, for example; by the 1851 Census this had leapt to 21 million. Related phenomena were rapid urban growth and those demographic irruptions which saw millions migrate within and across national boundaries. There were certain key 'drivers' that triggered, nurtured or accelerated these modernisation processes, namely the Enlightenment, the French Revolution and the Industrial Revolution. Capitalism was just as pivotal to modernisation as well, of course, in that, particularly through the eighteenth and increasingly through the nineteenth and early twentieth centuries up to 1917, it was the dominant or at least ascendant mode of production in Western Europe, though its impact varied between individual countries. Indeed, this book, following David Harvey, Frederic Jameson and others, sees the rise of capitalism as crucial to any analysis of modernisation, modernity and modernism, not least because of the extent of its advance in Britain, the geographical focus of this study.[5] Here we should note that the extraordinary inventiveness, dynamism and sheer pace of the modernisation process were generated to a large degree by capitalism's frenetic energy and voracious appetite for new markets and sources of profit.

Though inexorably bound up with modernisation, different features and meanings need to be ascribed to the concept of 'modernity'. As suggested above, it refers to a new historical situation that was brought about by the process of modernisation. This very basic formulation is in need of further elaboration. It might be helpful to begin by emphasising, a theme prominent in Marshall Berman's account of modernity, that at one level modernity was a category of personal experience or consciousness that results from an encounter with the maelstrom engendered by modernisation. Modernity thus denotes a particular *condition* or quality of personal and social experience undergone or felt by those living through the dramatic upheavals generated by modernisation. This 'mode of vital experience', as Berman put it, the condition of modernity, was itself of a quite specific nature. In Berman's conception of modernity, a contention generally accepted by scholars, modern life had its own particular atmosphere and quite specific properties that were internal to it and quite different to those that featured in preceding, more 'traditional' modes of life. Modern life, according to this conception, was, and still is, characterised by an overwhelming and disconcerting sense of the transient, fleeting, ephemeral, contingent and fragmentary. In modernity's unsettling atmosphere, as we attempted to navigate our way through a dynamic, unstable and ever-changing world, as we tried to make sense of the turbulence and 'fragments' thrown at us by the maelstrom of modern life, our subjectivity remained restless, forever troubled and never completely whole. This was the 'secret restlessness' of the modern urban mindset identified by Simmel.[6]

Although the atmosphere and condition of modernity can be traced to the modernisation process in general, particularly the peculiar structural dynamic of capitalist modernisation, one of modernity's key philosophical determinants was the Enlightenment. One reason for this was that the Enlightenment 'grand narrative' aimed to create a *project* of modernity that sought to universalise the experience of modernity and underpin what would become a homogenising world project with a distinct philosophical discourse. This discourse was that of autonomous reason, which privileged the notion of the individual self as a supremely 'knowing subject', who, by means of the correct application of reason or 'mind', would have the capacity to discover the essential 'truth' of things by means of careful observation of phenomena in nature and social life. This development is of significance in our analysis of modernity. Although the human capacity for 'reflexivity' or self-consciousness did not begin with the Enlightenment, it received new impetus and attained a higher level of maturity through the efforts of Enlightenment thinkers to privilege the idea of the self as a rational, knowing subject and to promote this model as a norm of behaviour and outlook to which we should all aspire. Henceforth, in the post-Enlightenment era of modernity, the human self was encouraged to cultivate that acquisitiveness, that 'never-to-be-relaxed monitoring of behaviour and its contexts', as Anthony Giddens put it, that is characteristic of modern reflexivity.[7] The perils inherent in the acquisition of reflexivity for the subject, whereby reflexivity became the preferred norm and aspiration, and where even reflection itself could be reflected upon, were clear to see. The consequence was a perpetually unsettled, often deeply troubled, outlook on the world.

Just as significant was that this optimistic faith in the emancipatory potential of human reason to yield the truth of the world and thereby improve it mutated into the 'categorical fixity' of Enlightenment thought as David Harvey put it, whereby it was posited that there was only one possible, supposedly correct form of representation and it was taken as 'axiomatic that there was only one possible answer to any question'.[8] This urge to attain certainty of meaning, the obsession to make the truth of the world transparent through the application of reason, added to the anxieties vexing modern consciousness, as it meant that whatever did not conform to this ordered certainty of meaning became suspect, even threatening. It ensured that perpetual state of tension and conflict with the uncertain, the different, the 'other' or, what Zygmunt Bauman has conceptualised as 'ambivalence'. The 'other' of order, Bauman tells us,

> is the miasma of the indeterminate and unpredictable. The other is the uncertainty, that source and archetype of all fear. The tropes of "the other of order" are: undefinability, incoherence, incongruity, incompatibility, illogicality, irrationality, ambiguity, confusion, undecidability, ambivalence.[9]

The aim of modernity, for Bauman, a necessity in effect, was to ruthlessly eliminate ambivalence, these tropes of the 'other' which presented themselves to modern consciousness as inconveniences or problems to be mastered and brought under rational control, all of which acted to accentuate and perpetuate the restlessness and anxiety that afflicted modern consciousness.

There was another dimension to this compulsion to establish certainty of meaning and eliminate 'ambivalence' which has a bearing on this study. For in seeking to make the truth of the world transparent primarily through the application of mind or reason, rationalism served to marginalise the claims of traditional metaphysical or even long-established 'supernatural' truths. The nineteenth-century fetish for positivism compounded this undermining of tradition and the sacred, most notably that positivist obsession to found science as the supreme arbiter in the field of knowledge and delineate an even sharper division between the realms of fact and traditional speculation, whether metaphysical, religious, mystical or otherwise. Applying their tried and trusted principles of direct observation and experimentation, positivists sought to discover the causal relationships underlying individual phenomena in social life as well as nature, apparently ordered and consistent patterns of causality that were amenable to mathematical analysis and prediction. With the onward march of rationalism and positivism, the traditional realms of metaphysics and the sacred were to be pitilessly swept aside, which had the effect of expelling magic, mystery and 'gods' from the world.[10]

There was a further aspect to modernity that has salience for our understanding of modernity, and by implication modernism, in regard to British socialism. If modern consciousness was never still or at rest, as it reflexively sought to destroy ambivalence, then a similar state of restlessness characterised the wider project of modernity. Here we encounter a further important dimension to modernity – modernity as designating a quite specific category of time or experience of historical time. As Bauman informs us, modernity's universalising project of 'progress' was always restlessly dissatisfied with the present, which was always deemed to be deficient and intolerable.[11] Modernity was therefore always pointed towards the horizon, forever propelled on a forward march. This helps explain that irrepressible will to subdue and destroy the present in the name of some brave new future which characterised modernity's Faustian project of creative destruction. This restless urge to supersede, or 'break' with, the present in the name of a future deemed to be better than what had been, has Enlightenment origins. Although, as with reflexivity, consciousness of a past and new age preceded the Enlightenment, the idea that the new age or new time was *qualitatively superior* to that which preceded it began with the Enlightenment. As Reinhart Koselleck tells us, prior to the Enlightenment the relationship of a new time to a past age was merely chronological and sequential, with no suggestion that a 'qualitative transcendence' of that past had taken place. Within this pre-Enlightenment static experience of time and the world, although every day brought something new, 'the new is not fundamentally different from what has already happened before it', while it was generally supposed 'that nothing fundamentally new could occur until the end of the world'.[12] The crucial new ingredient which led to a displacement of the 'blank', neutral 'chronological' idea of time, by time as new time which qualitatively transcended that which had been there before, was that Enlightenment idea of an open future, the future as a site of potential where new developments could take place. Modernity, according to Peter Osborne, thus acquired a peculiar dialectical quality, designating both a chronologically defined period of time but more significantly time conceived in terms of 'a qualitatively new, self-transcending temporality'.[13]

There were two additional distinguishing temporal features in Koselleck's intriguing model of post-Enlightenment modernity that need to be mentioned here, in that they, too, have a bearing on our analysis of British socialism in relation to modernism. Firstly, one's own time was not just experienced as qualitatively different to that which went before but was simultaneously experienced as a period of *transition*. Again, this 'epochal consciousness', a perspective that one was living through a transitional time, began to cohere by the close of the eighteenth century and marked a significant new departure from earlier ways of experiencing time. Secondly, those experiencing the peculiar qualities of time under conditions of modernity experienced this time as constantly *accelerating* time.[14]

There is one final, important point to make in regard to the new sense of time introduced by the Enlightenment, which has relevance for our study of British socialism and its relationship to modernism. Although the future-orientated concept of time promoted by Enlightenment thinkers claimed to be 'progressive', marking a departure as it did from the static time of traditional societies and signifying unbounded optimism in the future as an arena of development and improvement, this notion of time operated within certain limits imposed on it by Cartesian principles. Always eager to attain categorical certainty of meaning, rationalism adopted a fixed-point perspective on the future, which assumed that there was one, supposedly truthful judgement on how tomorrow should be shaped. This led to the future being viewed in a deterministic way. Though open, the future was always knowable and amenable to rational ordering which tended to collapse it into a 'single temporal series', as Dorreen Massey put it.[15] In this characteristic conception of the Enlightenment and modernity, with temporality squeezed into a single pathway and the future almost pre-given, the future always constituted a limited realm of possibility.

The new, always unsettling temporal consciousness ushered in by the Enlightenment, particularly that sense of time experienced as constantly accelerating time, surely helps us to better comprehend that aspect of modernity mentioned above – the disconcerting sense of the transient, fleeting, ephemeral, contingent and fragmentary felt by those caught in the maelstrom of modern life. It should be noted here also, though, that this sense of time experienced as accelerating time should not be attributed solely to eighteenth-century Enlightenment assumptions. The material processes of modernisation which were gaining enormous momentum during the nineteenth century also impacted the modern experience of time. The late nineteenth and early twentieth centuries in particular, that is the period covered by the socialist revival, witnessed the beginnings of extraordinary technological advances, which added to the overwhelming impression of lives speeding up. The innovations which brought ever-faster transportation systems in road, rail and sea sped up the movement of people and goods; developments in wireless telegraphy, electricity, optics and printing technologies facilitated the faster movement of information, while the arrival of cinematography and a mass-circulation press transformed and widened the cultural landscape. As David Harvey informs us, these technologically induced shifts in the experience of time have links to the imperatives of capitalist modernisation, as the need for a rapid 'turnover time' of capital became crucial to the necessity to maintain and increase profit levels. As time became increasingly equated with money and vice versa, this not only saw goods, services and information being moved around at an ever-faster pace, but it also occasioned increased attempts to impose stricter regulations of temporal discipline on the work process through speed-up of production, efforts to elongate the working day and the imposition of strict time schedules measured by clock time.[16]

It should be said as well that time under conditions of modernity, driven by the Enlightenment idea of progress, the needs of industry and the urgencies of the market assumed an increasingly homogenising, universalising and totalising character as the nineteenth century unfolded, to such an extent that by the end of that century a situation of 'world-wide simultaneity' was coming into play. This situation, which Helga Nowotny describes as 'the perception of events and of processes which occur at the same time in different corners of the world', certainly became more of a reality for millions with the introduction of standard public time or Greenwich world-time in 1884.[17] The significance of this for our study of the 'moment' of the socialist revival is that by the mid-1880s and 1890s more and more people, in Britain and elsewhere, were being subjected to the tyranny of the homogenising and ever-accelerating time of modernity. Many, however, sought release from this 'profane' mode of time and found spiritual comfort in the socialist faith.

The character that time came to assume under conditions of modernity had spatial implications as well. Indeed it is important to stress that there was a spatial as well as a temporal dimension to modernity. Modernity's Faustian aspiration to secure dominion over and give form to 'formless' nature in the name of progress entailed the requisition and regulating of space, as space, like time, became integral to the acquisition of power and wealth and the successful flow and turnover of capital. The material processes of modernisation also had the effect of shrinking space. The dynamically innovative transportation and communication systems that were moving people, goods and information around at an ever-faster pace by the late nineteenth and early twentieth centuries made the world contract as once distant places were absorbed into the new global arrangement. For Anthony Giddens, modernity also brought a tearing away of time from space as the former acquired the characteristic of 'empty time' as clocks, calendars and eventually Greenwich world standard time began to express a uniform measurement of time that was purely abstract, in that it did not link time with place as in pre-modern societies.[18] The ever-wider diffusion of this abstract 'empty time' then acted to control or 'empty' space, a process which involved a severing of space from place, as the latter became increasingly subjected to a novel form of social coordination which was marked by 'distanciation' or control at a distance by 'absent others'. It was the development and diffusion of the new communication and transportation technologies mentioned above that enabled these 'absent others', whether anonymous corporate capitalists or regulatory state institutions, to exercise their influence over time and, ultimately, vast stretches of space and place.[19]

How then should we define and explain modernism? As mentioned above, modernism is organically related to modernisation and modernity, in that it emerged and developed in reaction to them both. This reaction was protean and complex, as we shall see. Nevertheless, we can identify certain intrinsic elements to modernism. To the extent that modernisation and modernity were global phenomena, increasingly so by the close of the nineteenth century, it follows that modernism as a reaction to these trends had an international reach, though its effects were felt more deeply in urban centres undergoing particularly rapid change or experiencing acute cultural ferment, such as Paris, Berlin, Prague, Vienna or London. Modernism's reach also extended beyond that realm usually cited in the scholarship – art, literature and the avant-garde – to embrace social and political phenomena and movements. As already mentioned therefore, this book identifies with a 'maximalist' concept of modernism. As for its relationship to modernisation and modernity, modernism was a phenomenon and form of consciousness which contained a highly anguished response to those forces. In this respect, modernism should be viewed as a reaction to the dramatic changes wrought by modernisation and modernity. In other words, modernism expressed and registered that sense of alarm, alienation and even rage felt in the face of the relentless disintegration of traditional frames of reference and established forms that included the 'emptying out' of time and space. The disorientation felt as the familiar waned or even withered away was compounded by the rapid proliferation of the new – forms which of themselves could be frustratingly fleeting and transient. As expressed through the particular medium of art and literature, modernism in this sense was a response 'to the scenario of our chaos', the artist not just set free by the new but functioning under acute 'historical strain' as with the introspective reflections of Yeats, Thomas Mann or Eliot or the uncompromising imagery of Dada or Surrealism.[20]

This troubled reaction to those forces that swept away the familiar and abruptly ushered in the new was often informed by aesthetic, ethical and spiritual considerations. For modernists, something vital was being lost in the modern age of materialism, rationalism, positivism, reflexive individualism and time conceived in terms of a 'self-transcending temporality'. By the mid-nineteenth century, increasingly so by the century's close, many felt that the contemporary age of modernity that they were living through was aesthetically, morally and spiritually regressing, even though there had been tangible material advances in the realms of science, technology, transportation, communications and industrial performance. Thus although modern civilisation was materially improving, it came, as Roger Griffin described it, 'at the cost of beauty, meaning and health, both spiritual and physical', which meant that it 'was rushing nowhere, ever faster'.[21] This mutation of progress into 'decadence' was evident in those striking material manifestations of modernisation, the cities and new towns that exploded into life across the nineteenth-century landscape in those parts of the globe undergoing acute modernisation. In the modernist imagination, this expanding urban milieu was cast as a forbidding place which generated a range of ailments and habits inimical to a healthy existence, including economic privation, psychological trauma and even 'biological degeneration'. The 'dysgenic living' that was thought to mar life in the cities encouraged modernism to develop a further strand to its profile, a social modernist concern for health and hygiene. We shall return to this theme in relation to the socialist revival in a subsequent chapter.[22]

With regard to the changing nature and perception of places like the modern city, modernism was acutely sensitive as well to the increasing control exercised by the abstract 'empty time' of modernity over space and ultimately place, and the aesthetic and spiritual implications of this. Anthony Giddens' take on this feature of modernity has been mentioned, while David Harvey has stressed that modernism saw the need to address the issue of time's 'annihilation of space', the reduction of space to a 'contingent category', as one of its most vital tasks.[23] Indeed, modernists were keenly interested in the issue of space, and it needs to be recognised that modernism was as much a spatial project as a temporal one. Modernists felt suffocated by mainstream spatial structures as much as by the temporal logic of modernisation–modernity, and sought to imagine and produce new spatial configurations beyond the mainstream. It should not surprise then to find that certain categories of 'socialist modernists' that we will be looking at in this book were highly critical of contemporary capitalist space and endeavoured to forge new arrangements of space to those they usually encountered in the spatial world of modern capitalism.[24]

Modernism also registered anxiety about another potent sign of material progress – the 'machine age', the veneration of mechanical power that so defined the Victorian age and its utilitarian materialist 'anti-culture'. Modernism claimed that this attitude towards the machine killed the aesthetic sensibility and reduced work to a soulless mechanised activity, devoid of beauty, creativity and pleasure. This modernist antipathy towards the modern city and the machine figured as an element in the discourse of the socialist revival, eloquently so in the reflections of Edward Carpenter and William Morris.

Post-Enlightenment rationalism also came in for modernist criticism, particularly the positivist claim that the truth of the world could be made transparent through reasoned reflexive enquiry. Modernism, on the other hand, explored the potential thought to be inherent in alternative sources of 'knowing', namely the irrational, the unconscious, the emotions, intuition, and even mysticism and the occult. In relation to the latter, it should not surprise us that notable modernists of the era of high modernism were deeply interested in Theosophy, including Piet Mondrian, Wassily Kandinsky, Walter Gropius, Edvard Munch, Pablo Picasso, Paul Klee, Henri Matisse and William Butler Yeats.[25] Modernism challenged Enlightenment rationalism in another sense. Many modernists were fascinated by the regenerative power of myths. For them, myth had the capacity to reveal new meaning in life, as well as make known a new, invigorating sense of time outside or beyond the alienating, linear time of modernity. Artistic modernists intrigued by myth included Picasso, James Joyce, T.S. Eliot, Ezra Pound, William Butler Yeats and Le Corbusier. This fascination with myth also flags up the strain of 'primitivism' within modernism, as in some of Picasso's work or in Stravinsky's controversial staging of *The Rite of Spring* in 1913. It is no surprise then that the socialist modernism we will be looking at in this book should contain a high dose of myth, which we will look at more closely in Chapter 3.

Modernism did not just register awareness of the problems thrown up by modernisation and modernity. Neither should we interpret modernism as essentially an outpouring of despair in the face of the storm. More than this, modernism explored ways to escape the contemporary turbulence. In one important respect, this meant seeking ways to escape the tempest of modern time and in so doing find shelter from the decadent fallout from progress. How then to bring about this new temporal state, which it was hoped would make the fragmented subject of modernity whole again? Roger Griffin, Frederic Jameson and Karl-Heinz Bohrer have written of those existential moments within modernism when the subject of modernity experienced a stepping out of the continuous time of progress and the continuum of history, a moment of exhilaration and insight whereby 'normal' time and thus modernity itself was transcended.[26] Jameson and Bohrer see this 'moment in time and in history, which is nonetheless grasped as a moment that finally separates itself from time and from history' in the words of the former, as primarily an aesthetic moment.[27] In doing so, they tend to confine these 'sudden' liberating moments of aesthetic perception, moments which are completely autonomous of history and any temporal influences for Bohrer and which are relatively autonomous for Jameson, to the avant-garde of artistic modernism, as with Joyce's 'epiphanies'. Roger Griffin, too, sees these invigorating moments outside of time and history as an important aspect of modernism, though he offers a more expansive conceptualisation of them. According to this understanding, such 'epiphanic' moments were more than aesthetic. They could be profoundly spiritual, fleeting though sublime episodes where the individual self finds 'spiritual union with something "higher" '.[28] Here the liberated self achieves cosmological awareness, a moment of profound insight where there is realisation of the interrelatedness of all things and all humankind. Such moments outside of 'Enlightenment' or normal time, which could be ecstatic as well as revelatory, were supreme moments of 'Being' that should not be viewed as the preserve of the avant-garde. They could be experienced by those active in the political field as well, including those active in socialist politics, as we shall see in Chapter 2.

There was another dimension to 'Being', which offered the prospect of release from time and history as defined by Enlightenment rationalism. This speaks to that modernist effort to connect to the universal and eternal in the midst of the storm of change. For the modernist artist, this meant identifying and extracting from the maelstrom of life those elements thought to possess or express timeless qualities and communicating these qualities through the art form. Another permutation of this desire to connect to the universal and eternal relates to the need for the subject to find anchorage against the temporal storm by drawing on energies thought to reside in 'permanent' metaphysical and spiritual values. This could be attained by securing a hold on the familiar or preserving the sacred, or at least those elements of the sacred that were deemed to transmit timeless or metaphysical values. Here, the individual self stridently asserted the primacy of metaphysical and spiritual 'Being' over that transitory, always restless state of 'Becoming' that apparently blighted the self during the turbulent era of progress. David Harvey contends that there is a spatial dimension to this aspect of 'Being'. He interprets modernism's favouring of 'Being' over 'Becoming' as a spatial project, in that it privileged 'the spatialisation of time (Being) over the annihilation of space by time (Becoming) ... '.[29]

It would be a mistake to see modernism solely in terms of a preoccupation with fleeing the storm, securing respite from the contemporary or the new, searching out a resting place or subduing the tyranny of modern profane time, though modernism could harbour all these inclinations, as we have seen. Rather, modernism exhibited these quite contradictory impulses, in that it also embraced the storm and sought to manipulate its energies, aggressively engaged with the new and even attempted to create a new sense of time within existing time. We touched on the latter above, for example, in identifying the attraction of myth for many modernists. If we do not take account of this dialectical or contradictory quality of modernism, if we do not observe that strand within it that was bracingly alive to the exciting possibilities thrown up by modern life, we will see it partially or one-dimensionally. As Marshall Berman has argued, to be 'modern' was to find oneself in an environment 'that promises us adventure, power, joy, growth, transformation of ourselves and the world – and, at the same time, that threatens to destroy everything we have, everything we know, everything we are'.[30] Or in the words of a contemporary to be modern implied, at once, 'flight from life' and 'the analysis of life'.[31] The urge to engage with the new in modernism could involve the production of new meanings and forms of representation which both spoke to the new circumstances and expressed a desire to break free from them. Innovation and novelty of form became the hallmark of this modernist urge to not just engage but reconfigure the new, often generating bizarre compounds of seemingly paradoxical elements. Modernism, Bradbury and McFarlane wrote, searches out 'new juxtapositions, new wholes', as in Strindberg's desperate 'attention to alchemy, that unique fusion of reason and unreason, science and magic', or Yeats's 'evolutionary cosmology, with its search for unity between time and the timeless, the dancer and the dance'. In a similar vein, the best modernist works 'balance on the sensibility of transition, often holding in suspension the forces that persist from the past and those that grow from the novel present. They turn on ambiguous images: the city as a new possibility and an unreal fragmentation; the machine, a novel vortex of energy, and a destructive element'.[32]

The urge to 'break out' and discover alternative sources of meaning and forms of representation which both responded to and transcended the new directs us to the radical, even revolutionary, streak within modernism. This radicalism, alongside that more conservative inclination to embrace the universal and eternal, represented another of those innovative and often strange fusions of quite disparate elements that made up the modernist sensibility. James McFarlane states that in the 1890s in particular, 'a new shrillness of tone began to manifest itself' in Europe alongside an iconoclastic, irreverent desire to re-evaluate and supplant, all of which was driven by a heightened expectation of radical change based on the assumption, often derived from an encounter with Nietzsche's thought, that history had arrived at the 'terminus of a long era of civilisation'.[33] It is here that we encounter another important aspect of modernism – the feeling that history was on the cusp of radical and dramatic change, brought there not just by onrushing modern progress but also by a concomitant collapse of values and culture. There is a definite temporal dimension to this 'programmatic' variant of modernism in which the desire to transcend modernity and the malaise of decadence, as Roger Griffin argues, 'expresses itself as a mission to change society, to inaugurate a new epoch, to start time anew'.[34] In setting their face against the narrow, deterministic Enlightenment vision of the future with its singular temporality and pre-given 'rational' future, programmatic modernists advocated alternative futures or rival temporalities. It is here that we come upon a utopian dimension to modernism, not least because through utopian imagining our thought can break free of the present and luxuriate over pleasurable pictures of alternative futures.

There is another feature of this utopian dimension to modernism that has relevance for our re-conceptualisation of the British socialist revival. An era perceived to be in a state of imminent dissolution and thus on the cusp of profound change abounds with utopian imagining. At this perceived 'terminus' of one era and imminent arrival of another deemed to be culturally, morally and spiritually superior, there is heightened awareness that the future constitutes an exciting realm of possibility, an outlook premised on the understanding of history not as unfolding in accordance with a single, homogenous trajectory but as an open, indeterminate process. Such 'moments' are pregnant with feelings of hope, dreams and all manner of utopian visions and schemes crafted in the genuine expectation that new worlds are possible.

Having engaged with the concept of modernism, as well as with the concepts of modernisation and modernity, we have now arrived at a point in our analysis where we can more readily identify an affinity between modernism and British socialism as manifested during the socialist revival. It is to this matter that the following chapters will now turn.

2
The Spiritual and Epiphanic Modernism of British Socialism

Late Victorian British socialists felt that their age was one of change and transition and that they were living on the threshold of a new, truly modern era. Though sharper during the 1880s and particularly the 1890s, this mood of heady expectancy had hardly lessened during the Edwardian years. The modern era that beckoned on the horizon promised much. It would bring social and economic justice but also an enlargement of the human self. The 'new' socialist man and woman that would emerge once freed from the exploitations and spiritual constraints of Victorianism would be persons of a new type equipped with enhanced capacities for human 'fellowship'. This desire to attain for the individual a higher state of spiritual 'Being' with greater capacities for human fellowship was an intrinsic feature of the socialist revival. Indeed, British socialism was one of the principal 'revitalisation' movements of the *fin de siècle* which addressed the deep crisis in spiritual and cultural values thought to be afflicting Victorian Britain as it edged towards the century's close. Many socialist activists believed that they were engaged in a mission to achieve a break with the decadent old world of Victorian materialism, positivism and possessive individualism. They hoped to usher in a new age that would be characterised not just by socio-economic justice but by a heightened sense of spiritual awareness which once attained would bring sublime insight into the organic unity of all and generate a corresponding love for one's fellows. These two aspirations, the desire for greater equality in social and economic matters and the urge to aspire to a higher realm of spiritual 'Being' based on an awareness of the unity of all, would fuse in contemporary socialism. It should be emphasised here that this fusing of the social with the spiritual was distinctly modern. It was characteristic of a more widespread modernist reaction in late Victorian and Edwardian Britain to some of the problems inherent in modern life under conditions of modernity. Socialism offered its adherents even more than a tantalising vision of a more harmonious future which beckoned on the horizon. With conversion to socialism and entry into the 'purity' of socialist consciousness would come an invigorating feeling of escape from the alienating, 'profane' time characteristic of modernity into a new transcendent consciousness. This passage into a new, higher consciousness would take the form of a mystical experience for many converts. This chapter will look at this spiritual dimension within the socialist revival, and the forms that it assumed. Before we do so, however, it is necessary to provide some context for this discussion by looking at the quite unique conjuncture of the Victorian *fin de siècle* itself.

The sense of the passing of the old and the impending arrival of a new age that gripped socialists and other late Victorians can partly be traced to the shifts in consciousness that the Enlightenment bequeathed to the European sensibility. We looked at some of these changes in consciousness in Chapter 1. There was that restless compulsion to break with the present and the past in the name of a future considered superior to that which had gone before. We also noted that post-Enlightenment modernity passed on epochal consciousness as well as temporal consciousness, the feeling that the time one was living through was a transitional time. This being said, these adjustments in consciousness brought by post-Enlightenment modernity do not provide a complete explanation of the restless, often fraught, late Victorian state of mind. This was because the late Victorians were gripped by something deeper and more fundamental than an awareness of change taking place as such. This stemmed from the particular circumstances of the late Victorian age itself. It was an age which had its own quite distinct dynamic, when change, as Frederic Jameson put it, was 'stirring convulsively within the present' and the world seemed 'poised on the edge of a thoroughgoing metamorphosis'.[1] The sense that something momentous was stirring in the present was most pronounced in the 1890s, and the stirrings were felt in Britain and extended far beyond the socialist camp. In his classic survey of the ideas and art of 1890s Britain, Holbrook Jackson, one-time Fabian socialist and co-editor with Alfred Orage of the *New Age* journal, has made reference to the heady mix of ideas, movements and expectations rousing in that decade. For Jackson, they were born of a determination to 'taste new sensation' for the sake of change and personal growth. As he put it, 'life tasting was the fashion, and the rising generation felt as though it were stepping out of the cages of convention and custom into a freedom full of tremendous possibilities'.[2]

How should we explain these convulsions, the heady sense that the times seemed poised on the edge of fundamental change? Perry Anderson contends that late nineteenth- and early twentieth-century Europe was an over-determined historical moment of a quite exceptional character composed of a 'force field' of several distinct currents or 'co-ordinates' which intersected to form the context within which the modernist sensibility emerged.[3] Two of the three principal co-ordinates that intersected to generate Anderson's force field, or over-determined historical configuration, have particular relevance to the modernist moment in late Victorian Britain, the perception that society was in the throes of fundamental change and poised on the verge of a new time.[4] The first of these was the key technologies of the so-called Second Industrial Revolution, a process that was in full swing in late Victorian Britain. Its principal inventions in wireless telegraphy, telephones, automobiles, cinematography and new printing technologies exploded with great force on society, bringing a dramatic broadening of social space, imaginative horizons and cultural experiences. Innovations in production techniques relating to, for instance, the use of steel, electric power and new chemical products hit with equal force, often bringing unwelcome and painful adjustments to working patterns and working environments for those at the sharp end of production. The second co-ordinate that Anderson cites, which has relevance to our study of the modernist moment in late Victorian Britain, is that of the 'haze of social revolution drifting across the horizon of this epoch', which 'gave it much of its apocalyptic light' and which portended the immense social and political upheavals to come.[5] A contemporary to these events, the socialist Edward Carpenter certainly felt the convulsions that issued from this powerful aspiration for radical social change. He likened this social movement which first burst the dam of 'smug commercialism and materialism of the mid-Victorian epoch' in 1881–2 to 'a great river, fed by currents and streams flowing into it from the most various directions and gathering a force which no man can now control and a volume too great to be confined'.[6]

Perry Anderson's model of a force field of distinct currents which intersected to give the late nineteenth century its unique complexion, thereby creating a space for the modernist sensibility to enter, is certainly compelling. This said, his force field of co-ordinates is too narrowly defined, at least as applied to late Victorian Britain. To Anderson's co-ordinates of the Second Industrial Revolution and the prospect of impending socio-political upheaval we should add that other late Victorian economic narrative, the so-called Great Depression or Long Depression that ran, albeit with a few temporary abatements, from c.1873 to c.1896. The upheaval, uncertainties and miseries wrought by this economic crisis were palpable, and propelled many into the new socialist camp. The crisis featured falling prices that persisted until the mid-1890s, a corresponding squeeze on profit margins, a successful German and American challenge to British capitalism's monopoly in world markets and a domestic growth rate that stubbornly hovered below 2 per cent per annum for much of the crisis period. We should add to this as well growing unemployment rates, which were especially high in 1879–80, 1885–7 and 1891–3. For many contemporary observers, including socialists, these trends were indicative of serious market failure and a systemic crisis of major significance. The economic model based on Manchester school free market economics that had held sway since the advent of the 'First Industrial Revolution' was malfunctioning and appeared to have arrived at the terminus of a long era of domination. Even as it neared its apparent end, the competitive model of wealth production continued to emit those stark extremes of affluence and poverty that were endemic to the system. Annie Besant commented in 1890 on the 'coexistence of wealth and penury, of idle prodigality and laborious stint; the terrible fact that "progress and poverty" seem to march hand-in-hand; the growing slums in large towns; the huge fortunes and the starving poor'.[7]

We should also throw into the mix that corresponding retreat of Victorianism in other fields. Old certainties associated with Victorian science, positivism and materialism seemed to be breaking apart, as in physics where hitherto well-established mechanical explanations and models no longer supplied answers.[8] There were other currents feeding into the force field of co-ordinates shaping the late Victorian era. One was an awareness of the approach of the *fin de siècle*. This was a particularly poignant *saecula*, in that there emerged an abundance of what Frank Kermode has called *fin de siècle* phenomena, which fuelled the impression that one was living at the dawn of an exceptionally new time. These phenomena included a heady atmosphere of excitement and expectation as the *fin de siècle* dawned, a heightened sense of endings and beginnings and an equally heightened feeling that the transitional time one was living through was an 'End-dominated age of transition' markedly different to other transitional moments.[9] The nineteenth-century *fin de siècle* also contained high apocalyptic content, the conviction that the age was awash with decadence but that out of all this odium would come regeneration or a new age.

Another of the currents bringing pressure to bear on this particular historical moment was spiritual in makeup. It is highly likely that the late Victorian period was an acute liminoid moment. Roger Griffin contends that from c.1850 Europe experienced a protracted phase of liminoidality as a result of the temporal and psychological pressures wrought by the maelstrom of modernisation and modernity, but particularly as a consequence of an awareness that progress was de-spiritualising the times.[10] In such a situation of acute liminoid stress, a need was felt to revitalise society and the self, to replenish that store of metaphysical energy or 'transcendence' that had run dry during the years of decadence and spiritual blight. This revitalisation was necessary in order to overcome the spiritual and cultural crisis and effect the passage to a new state. This new state was to be a higher realm, spiritually and culturally superior to that which had gone before. According to Griffin, the desire to bring about a liminoid passage to a higher state is more likely to occur during moments of economic and socio-political tension, a situation which certainly corresponds to the late Victorian era in Britain. British socialism emerged in the context of this liminoid climate. As mentioned in the introduction to this chapter, socialism was one of the principal revitalisation movements of the *fin de siècle* which spoke to the deep crisis in spiritual and cultural values believed to be afflicting Victorian Britain. Many of the socialist converts hoped to usher in a new age that would be more spiritual as well as more egalitarian, an age that had shed the allegedly decadent values of the old world of Victorian materialism, positivism and self-interestedness. But socialism could also bring a more immediate feeling of spiritual regeneration. For many, conversion to socialist faith brought an invigorating feeling of liberation from the alienating 'profane' time of modernity into a new temporality or transcendent consciousness which was interpreted as a mystical experience.

How then to revitalise the times, a prospect that seemed so tantalisingly possible given the proximity of the new century? How to go about replenishing the store of metaphysical energy or transcendence that had run dry during the years of Victorian decadence and spiritual blight so as to pass to that new and higher state? How also to bring about that corresponding enlargement of the human self, which offered the hope of an exhilarating feeling of escape from the ever-accelerating, oppressive profane time of modernity, the prospect of widened spatial horizons and the opportunity to enter into deeper communion with one's fellows? For many socialists during the revival period, this regeneration would not come about solely through economic or political means. It need hardly be said that socialists of all hues during the revival years were enraged by the grinding poverty and degradation that afflicted workers and their families during the era of modern progress. This sense of injustice was evident from the very start of the revival. In the early 1880s William Jupp felt the 'spirit of social and political reform' enter powerfully into his life. Jupp was in full-blooded revolt against a 'ruthlessly competitive system' that produced such 'degrading poverty' for the many amidst such 'demoralising superabundance'.[11] This revolt propelled Jupp, along with other like-minded idealists, into the socialist Fellowship of the New Life, which was formed in late 1881. Though deeply moved by the plight of the proletariat, Jupp and his comrades in the Fellowship believed that a change in the external conditions of life was not in itself the true path to socialism. While they did not rule out the need to work for economic and political reforms to improve workers' material conditions of life, they equated socialism not with a materialist doctrine, institutional adjustment or a revolutionising of society's economics, but with a vital spiritual life. According to Jupp, all who joined the Fellowship of the New Life felt the pull of something more vital, instinctive and intuitive than the desire to engage in mainstream reformist politics. As he explained it, they 'saw that an inward and spiritual reform was not less important than drastic changes in outward and material conditions' and that the first of all reforms was 'self-reform'.[12] The Fellowship's journal *Seed-Time* put this urge for a new and vital spiritual life down to the 'evils' of modern Victorian 'civilisation', where the individual 'cannot enjoy or fulfil his own best and deepest life' and where 'the sacredness of the human personality is ignored'.[13] That Jupp was himself searching for something more vital or metaphysical in life can be seen from a conversation that took place between him and Maurice Adams at the start of the 1880s. Adams later collaborated with Jupp in the Fellowship of the New Life. During their warm and intimate exchange, Adams made Jupp 'realise the worth of that spiritual experience which comes of the effort to reach beyond appearance to the reality of things, not only by the soul's direct vision, but also by reason and reflection, by sheer and strenuous wrestling with the deeper mysteries of life and the world'.[14]

It is important to realise that this longing to reach out for something more vital or spiritual beyond the phenomenal world of appearance and the narrow framework of Victorian civilisation was not an idiosyncrasy peculiar to the socialist thinking of William Jupp and his comrades in the Fellowship of the New Life. This was not a marginal or fringe aspect of the socialist revival, an aberrant phenomenon outside the mainstream of contemporary socialist agitation. The socialism of the revival period was never a wholly materialist doctrine at its core. While mindful of the need for those experiencing economic hardship to attain the material necessities of life, there was always this modernist reaching out for more fulfilled life beyond merely economic concerns. As to the nature of this vital spiritual life, it involved the individual, dismayed by Victorianism and desirous of spiritual release from its effects, entering into new relationships with things based on a new, more transcendental conception of life. This worked on a number of levels. It meant establishing new levels of intimacy with one's 'fellows' based on an understanding that each was part of a single whole and a belief that the true self could only be realised if one lived 'resolutely in the whole', that is, in a spirit of fellowship with others. As we 'work for the regeneration of society', proclaimed the Fellowship of the New Life, we maintain 'that the New Life must be the outcome of the New Spirit and that, to that spirit, the spirit of fellowship and service, we must yield ourselves … '.[15] For William Jupp, true fellowship meant 'a mystic communion of soul, deep and sacred as life itself', a most intimate 'fellowship of heart known only to those who are made one in affection and in a common yearning for all that is best and holiest in human experience'.[16]

This heavily spiritualised and mystical brand of socialism presupposed a more intimate relationship with nature. It was only through sublime awareness that they were bound together by an organic relationship to the totality of all things in nature that individuals ascended to the sublime consciousness of spiritual communion with their fellows. Thus, fellowship socialists saw no duality or conflict between the world of nature and the spirit or soul of 'man', the soul being an organic part of the totality through which it lived, grew and developed its 'personality'. Here we see the influence of Walt Whitman and American Romanticism on the socialist revival.

As well as Whitman's ideas, the immanentist theological beliefs of Ralph Waldo Emerson found their way into fellowship socialism, particularly the notion that a Divine 'over-soul' was present in and connected all living things in nature, and all Creation.[17] The Divine over-soul was imagined to be God's love, or God's directing 'hand', a vital force flowing through all nature, while the Divine was understood as an inner spiritual state which once attained brought a sublime insight into the oneness of all living things and generated a corresponding love for one's fellows. A portion of this Divine over-soul was thought to exist in each of us, though each individual had to be brought to awareness of it, which would come intuitively rather than through the application of reason or 'mind'. An awareness of the Divine within could also arrive through a profound revelatory 'epiphanic' experience, a mode of conversion to which we shall return below.

It should be stressed as well that this belief that a portion of something sublime was latent in all of us, and that conversion to socialism would bring realisation of this, was not confined to those socialists who drew inspiration from Emersonian transcendentalism. Caroline Martyn, for instance, an ILP and Fabian activist during the early 1890s, believed that her propaganda work for socialism aimed to bring the individual to an awareness of a sublime presence within, which she referred to as 'a particle of that universal spirit' latent within all of us.[18] Similarly, we should not assume that the experience of mystic communion with nature or the sense of experiencing oneness with the totality of things, those modernist moments of stillness and calm seemingly outside of the melee of normal time and history, was felt only by those who identified with Emersonianism or who were connected with the Fellowship of the New Life. In his autobiography, Fenner Brockway tells of that moment when he first entered into a form of 'universal consciousness' when a young ILP activist in the late Edwardian years. It was George Bernard Shaw's concept of the 'life force' which Brockway interpreted as the creative force in life which was making for good, and which provided the impetus for his initial epiphany. Speaking of this creative life force, Brockway recalled:

> Sometimes in great moments of beauty one can feel it, linking oneself with all that has been and is and will be, and then working within it and with it for a harmony in life which expresses it. This realisation of oneness with a universal life had come

to me in the deep silences of Nature.... The consciousness of
universal identity uplifted me sometimes for days and became my
religion.[19]

It needs mentioning, too, that for Brockway, as with many who
turned towards socialism during the revival years, 'the spiritual
experience came first'.[20]

Entry into the Divine, universal consciousness or universal spirit
of socialist fellowship seemed to bring an even greater feeling of liberation as it offered the prospect of opening out space and time into
realms even beyond the world of nature. At a date very close to the
fin de siècle, and at a time when he was still active in local branches
of the Fellowship, it appeared that William Jupp experienced a profound epiphanic moment whereby he entered a state of exhilarating
oneness with the universe. At that moment, Jupp felt kinship with
a vaster life, a sublime awareness of a universal order with whose
spirit and purpose the highest human ideals of good and beauty were
organically connected. Writing in the third person, Jupp recalled that
'the flow of light into his mind that evening was like a gift of joy
direct from the fresh sweet fountains of life itself. It brought that
sense of mental exhilaration, of pure exultant happiness, so naturally coincident with any fresh illumination of the soul.'[21] Again,
we should not assume that this entry into a wider universal consciousness, this 'sudden' liberating moment of awareness seemingly
outside of time and history which brought a feeling of oneness with
the universe, was the preserve of those attached to the Fellowship
of the New Life. Like many of those associated with the Fellowship,
the ILP activist and Ashington miner Chester Armstrong worshipped
at the shrine of Walt Whitman during the revival years. Whitman,
he remembered in his autobiography, 'had the effect of lifting me
to points of spiritual elation, hitherto inexperienced'.[22] These profound moments of spiritual elation included that invigorating feeling
of transcending the normal confines of space and time and passing into a state of universal consciousness of a type similar to that
experienced by other contemporary socialists. Whitman, Armstrong
effused, 'opened for me the doors of the cosmos, and henceforth
I was a denizen of the universe'.[23]

Another ILP activist, the Bolton socialist James William Wallace,
claimed that he was elevated into an ever higher state of consciousness during these years – that of 'cosmic consciousness'.
It seemed that this epiphany of cosmic consciousness was of a

more enduring nature than those exhilarating 'momentary' bursts of insight associated with universal consciousness. Wallace's illumination apparently occurred in January 1885 following the death of his mother, and was likely reinforced as he turned for consolation to the writings of Walt Whitman.[24] Wallace later likened this transcendent experience to a rebirth similar to a religious awakening, which left a lasting impression and revolutionised his 'Being'. Wallace felt an:

> opening of the spiritual senses, and consequent recognition of spiritual realities as of supreme and transcendent importance, and of one's unity with the race, which, when it happens to a man, so completely revolutionizes his whole outlook on life and all his desires and aims as to amount to a new birth. It is the appearance within himself of a new centre of consciousness dominating all the rest, and gradually bringing them into ever closer harmony with itself.[25]

Wallace was part of a small study group of Bolton socialists and Whitman enthusiasts who referred to themselves as 'The Eagle Street College'. From 1885 the group held weekly evening get-togethers at Wallace's terraced house in Eagle Street, Bolton, where they discussed socialism but also matters that were more spiritual and esoteric. The latter was in keeping with their love for Whitman and also that search to attain more fulfilled life which characterised much of the socialism of the revival years. In time, an almost mystical atmosphere of intimacy and fellowship would prevail amongst participants in the Eagle Street group. 'There were times,' Wallace later recalled of such discussions, 'when it led us, by imperceptible stages, to a deepened intimacy, in which the inmost quests and experiences of the soul were freely expressed, and each grew conscious of our essential unity, as of a larger self which included us all.'[26]

The fellowship socialist Edward Carpenter claimed to have ascended into the purity of cosmic consciousness as well. His epiphany occurred in the early part of 1881, at the point when the socialist revival was just starting up. We should be grateful to Carpenter for leaving us with some of the best testimony as to the nature and meaning of cosmic consciousness. For Carpenter, cosmic consciousness was a state of consciousness beyond and transcending 'self-consciousness' – that state of mind characteristic of the 'intellectual' or 'civilised' man. As with James William Wallace, Carpenter's experience of cosmic consciousness also seemed to transcend that more temporary state of universal consciousness, as it induced a quite lasting transformation in 'Being'. Carpenter thought self-consciousness a curse that bedevilled his Victorian contemporaries. In his essay on 'Civilisation: Its Cause and Cure' that he penned in 1889, he wrote of that 'strange sense of mental unrest' that afflicted the individual self in the era of modern civilisation.[27] He likened this mental unrest to a 'disease' that 'penetrates down even into the deepest regions of man's being', a condition of 'ill-health' at the very centre of modern life.[28] In his observations on this 'modern condition of everlasting strife and perplexity', Carpenter was advocating release from the modern condition of 'reflexivity' that we discussed in Chapter 1.[29] As we saw in that chapter, the acquisition of reflexivity or self-consciousness brought consequences for the hapless modern, not least an always restless and often deeply troubled perspective on things. Those of his Victorian contemporaries 'who live by fire and candlelight', Carpenter observed, 'are filled with phantoms; their thoughts are Will-o'-th'-wisp-like images of themselves, and they are tormented by a horrible self-consciousness'.[30] Similarly, in *From Adam's Peak to Elephanta* which appeared in 1892, he referred to self-consciousness or 'individual consciousness' as a form of thought which is 'fluid and mobile like quicksilver, perpetually in a state of change and unrest fraught with pain and effort'.[31]

Cosmic consciousness, on the other hand, was the consciousness of the coming fellowship man of the future, a condition that promised relief from the mental strife of self-consciousness. Though Carpenter's cosmic socialism was always orientated towards the future, the acquisition of cosmic consciousness entailed a conscious reconnection backwards to an earlier, primitive mode of consciousness, a consciousness not plagued by the 'whence and whither which now vex the modern mind'.[32] The 'naive insouciance' of the primitive impressed Carpenter.[33] The impulses of primitive 'man' were clearer and more unhesitating than those of the modern. There was an absence of 'self-knowledge' and inner strife, and a life lived more in harmony with unconscious instincts, the body and the natural world. Primitive man also had cosmological awareness. He instinctively felt his unity with 'the slow lapse of the constellations', and that he should contemplate himself as something separate from the vast expanse of the universe was beyond his awareness.[34] How then to reconnect backwards so as to access that inner peace characteristic of primitive consciousness? This could be done by accessing and participating in myths, legends and traditions that kept alive for us a consciousness of this earlier 'Paradise' of spiritual contentment. Here Carpenter posits a metaphysical and mystical notion of self and ancestry that transcended time and spatial boundaries, whereby each human soul carries within itself 'some kind of reminiscence of a more harmonious and perfect state of being' which was at one time experienced and which the myths, poetic legends and traditions kept alive.[35] An instinctive feeling of oneness with the cosmos and nature characteristic of an earlier Paradise would return to us as well if the modern body emerged from all those 'hiding places' which had shut it off from the light of the sun. These 'hiding places', the houses with curtains closed against the world of nature, the elaborate garments worn by the modern and the ugly polluted towns, were the accessories and accoutrements of civilisation. Instead of hiding away, the bodily organs should be given up to nature, particularly the sun which, being the visual image and embodiment of the soul and 'the allegory of the true self', should be adored and taken into oneself.[36] There was to be a move away from civilisation and its obsession with hiding places, material possessions and status rankings towards a de-materialised life close to nature in all areas of life. With a return to a 'common life' of plain habits and open-air work and leisure close to the sun would come insight into the true nature of 'Being', a rebirth of the spirit and a reconnection to the cosmological awareness that characterised life in an earlier, primitive age. For his part, Carpenter was to prove the model cosmological socialist, spurning all worldly pleasures and giving himself up to a simple life close to the elements on the utopian rural idyll he created at Millthorpe.[37]

This effort on the part of those socialists during the revival years to infuse their socialist project with something more vital or metaphysical beyond conventional economic issues exhibits an unmistakably modernist dynamic. There was that modernist innovation and novelty of form that we find in the synthesising of the spiritual and the political in the outlook of so many contemporary socialists. A similar novelty of form was apparent in the fusing of primitivism and progressivism that we find in Edward Carpenter's mystical cosmological socialism – that effort to reconnect backwards to call forth earlier modes of consciousness and spirituality to aid the plight of modern man. Modernist, too, was that attempt of the individual to enter into new organic relationships with the whole community of his fellows, nature and the great cosmos based on a new, more transcendental conception of life. Entering the higher life of intimate oneness with 'his' fellows, the natural world and the cosmos was to bring enlargement of the spiritual self and expanded consciousness. The ideal of spiritual self-enlargement was itself a quintessential feature of the *fin de siècle* modern attitude and response to the new, as was the aspiration to experience heightened consciousness. This goal of achieving self-enlargement and a new consciousness based on a new, more transcendental conception of life should not be confused with what Frederic Jameson calls the 'inward turn of the modern', the stereotypical image of the modern as outsider, marginal and rebel who retreats inward into ever-more extreme forms of subjectivity and introspection to escape the maelstrom of modernity.[38] Rather, the socialist self discussed above was longing for a fuller sense of self-hood beyond the narrow self-possessed, self-interested individual self which Victorianism aspired to, an expanded self which would be immersed in a world at the point of being thrillingly and radically reformed and 'worthy of ecstasy'.[39] At the root of this reaching out for more fulfilled selfhood and spiritual life, then, was always this desire to remain in touch with the social and the political and bring about wider material improvement alongside the goal of spiritual redemption. That the two, the socio-political and the transcendental, worked hand in hand at that unique moment of the *fin de siècle* did not escape the attention of Holbrook Jackson, that acute observer of life and culture in *fin de siècle* Britain. 'A wave of transcendentalism swept the country,' observed Jackson of the *fin de siècle*, 'but it was not remote, it was of the earth and of the common life and hour, seeking the immediate regeneration of society by the abolition of such social evils as poverty and overwork, and the meanness, ugliness, ill-health and commercial rapacity which characterised so much of modern life.'[40]

We can detect strains of modernism in other areas of the fellowship or transcendental socialism that we have been looking at. The change 'stirring convulsively' in late Victorian and Edwardian Britain was keenly felt and there was always a confident gaze towards an alternative radical future. William Jupp and his comrades in the Fellowship of the New Life felt that 'the age of fellowship had dawned', and looked to discover ways that their newly adopted ethical conduct could bring about the anticipated realisation of the 'new life'.[41] Holbrook Jackson commented that Emersonian ideas were rife amongst those seeking self-enlargement around the *fin de siècle*. As we have seen, fellowship socialism had absorbed the immanentist beliefs of Emerson, which would have contributed to this optimistic sense that a new, more progressive future was coming.[42] History, it seemed, was unfolding in accordance with a Divine will or purpose, a vital force representing God's love which would ensure the eventual passage to a harmonious social order based on the unity of all things, which fellowship socialists of an Emersonian persuasion interpreted as socialism.[43] Though not obviously a form of modernism, when fused with assertive political agendas aiming to socially and spiritually regenerate the future, Emersonian immanentism most definitely served as an agent of the modernist political project.

Even Edward Carpenter, whose socialism was so heavily infused with nostalgia for a vanished primitive past, always looked confidently to the arrival of a radical future. History and life, for Carpenter, was 'exfoliating' towards cosmic consciousness, that is, ascending towards a higher state of human fraternity or fellowship. Competitive capitalism was but a husk to Carpenter, within which the new life of cosmic consciousness or fellowship was forming inside. This 'upward growth and unfoldment of all organic life' he asserted, would bring the emergence of the 'perfect Man' of fellowship 'towards whose birth all creation groans and travails'.[44] It is worth adding at this point in relation to Edward Carpenter, by way of reinforcing the connection between the socialist revival and modernism, that Carpenter was himself a significant figure in the history of early modernism. Carpenter's notion of evolving and higher levels of cosmic consciousness and overall mystic philosophy is said to have influenced the thinking of a number of contemporary modernists in a variety of fields, including Wassily Kandinsky, D.H. Lawrence and the anarchist Ferrer Association's Modern School based in New York.[45]

There was also that characteristically modernist bursting out of the continuum of time and history, in this case into the pure, heady consciousness of cosmic consciousness. It should be said that, in its purest form, cosmic awareness arrived by way of a profound epiphanic modernist moment to which only a select 'enlightened' few of contemporary socialists were privy. As mentioned, Edward Carpenter was amongst that number and has left us with a telling description of that feeling of oneness with all things whereby, as he says:

> ... there seems to be a vision possible to man, as from some more universal standpoint, free from the obscurity and localism which specially connect themselves with the passing clouds of desire, fear, and all ordinary thought and emotion; in that sense another and separate faculty; and as vision always means a sense of light,

> so here is a sense of inward light, unconnected of course with the
> mortal eye, ... for the sense is a sense that one *is* those objects and
> things and persons that one perceives (and the whole universe) –
> a sense in which sight and touch and hearing are all fused in
> identity.[46]

It seems that in such 'visionary' moments, normal profane time with
its usual offering of emotions and fear is transcended, if only temporarily, and there is a projection into the reassuring 'cosmic time' of
the eternal now. Such feelings of elevation find an echo in that lost
paradise of the primitive cosmic world which so attracted Carpenter
where, as Mircea Eliade informs, there was a need to live in an eternal
present outside the duration of normal profane time and history.[47]

As well as time, with socialist cosmic consciousness there was
also that characteristically modernist bursting out of the confines
of the space of contemporary modernity or the particular space of
Victorianism. In their search for a more transcendental conception
of life and a fuller sense of self-hood, cosmic or fellowship socialists
reached out to spaces beyond the phenomenal world of appearance,
as in their efforts to access a hitherto hidden domain of spiritual
reality beyond the range of sense. There was an expansion of spatial
horizons, too, in that desire to achieve an almost mystical oneness in
fellowship with all things in social life and nature and, via these con-
nections, oneness with the Divine. A further enlargement of space
came as well, with that reaching out for kinship with a living universe, for those socialists privileged enough to attain cosmological
awareness in its purest form, as with Edward Carpenter.

Nowhere was this modernist urge to burst out of the confines of
the conventional space of modernity in an attempt to draw on new
sources of spiritual energy more apparent than in the efforts of some
socialists to blend socialism with Theosophy. Annie Besant's embrace
of Theosophy is well known. Less well known is George Lansbury's
interest in Theosophy. As with many of his socialist contemporaries,
Lansbury's socialism was made up of highly variegated elements,
in that it registered the influence of the SDF's Marxism, Christian
Socialism and Tolstoy.[48] To this mix we should add an attraction to
Theosophy, which eventually led him to join the Theosophical Society in 1914. Apparently it was the Theosophist aim to establish 'a
universal society based on Brotherhood' which particularly appealed
to Lansbury.[49] Socialists who found in Theosophy a spiritual supplement to their political views could be found in all areas of the revival.

Herbert Burrows, who tried to fuse Marxism with Theosophy, was an SDF activist, while Margaret McMillan, who also felt the pull of Theosophy, was a leading figure in the ILP.[50] Percy Redfern, who felt 'strongly attracted' to Theosophy during his early years as a socialist, was active in the Co-operative movement and the Labour Church.[51] Similarly, when Alfred Orage moved in a Theosophical direction, joining the Theosophical Society in 1896, he was a Fabian.[52] It was the desire to combat the de-sacralising tendencies of modern life and capitalism and develop a spiritualised form of socialism that led these socialists to embrace Theosophical ideas. Along with many non-socialists at the *fin de siècle*, they considered it entirely in keeping with the contemporary mood to go in search of hidden sources of spiritual reality beyond the immediate range of visual perception in order to regenerate the times. Theosophy promised redemption of the soul as well. Percy Redfern claims that socialists felt they could be 'born and reborn' by embracing Theosophical beliefs, a sublime journey of perpetual rebirth leading to the joy of personal redemption.[53] It is worth noting, too, that Redfern mentions in his autobiography that 'many socialists' during the revival years were attracted by the 'divine wisdom' of Theosophy.[54] These would have included some socialist feminists. We know that some socialist feminists joined the Theosophical Society, including Dora Montefiore, Annie Kenney, Clara Codd and Charlotte Despard.[55] As an addendum to the above, it should be mentioned that some *fin de siècle* occultists, most notably Alfred Orage, believed that Theosophical socialism was compatible with contemporary Nietzschean ideas concerning the need to create a new 'higher type' of heroic individual, or 'superman'. Orage's highly intelligent socialist 'superman' would be equipped with what he called 'superman consciousness', a heightened transcendental consciousness which had almost limitless potential to access realms far beyond the earthly and material world of appearance and the scope of what could be attained by 'normal' human consciousness.[56]

Other contemporary socialists who dabbled in the paranormal were the Fabians Frank Podmore and Edward Pease. Podmore and Pease were members of the Society for Psychical Research, an elite body founded in London in 1882 which examined psychic or paranormal phenomena.[57] The Society had a pluralistic membership, to say the least. Its President between 1892 and 1894 was the aspiring Prime Minister Arthur Balfour. Even Edward Carpenter wondered whether there was indeed a 'fourth dimension' of space of a kind not so dissimilar to his notion of cosmic consciousness. This fourth dimension, for Carpenter, might hold an unbounded spatial reality that had the potential to provide means of knowledge and perception which to the ordinary sense would seem 'miraculous'.[58] It should be noted as well that the idea of the fourth dimension was entirely consistent with the modernist impulse. Many avant-garde modernist artists were fascinated by the prospect of an expanded and potentially infinite fourth dimensional space, including Marcel Duchamp, Francis Picabia, František Kupka, Kazimir Malevich and Umberto Boccioni.[59]

Turning to another group within the late Victorian and Edwardian socialist movement, we should see the modernist impulse at work as well, even in that most curious of contemporary socialist bodies, the Labour Church. Formed in 1891, it was at its most influential during the 1890s in that decade when *fin de siècle* passions were at their height, and surely would have been touched by the ferment and heady feeling of expectancy and desire for the new that swirled around that decade. The founder of the Labour Church, John Trevor, was certainly touched by the mood of the times. 'These are stirring times in which we live,' he wrote in the Labour Church's newspaper in 1892. 'No brave, true-hearted man could wish for better. Never in any age, I believe, has a small amount of self-sacrifice yielded a larger reward, or a glad harvest followed the sowing so rapidly as now.'[60] Additionally, it seems that Trevor had a series of epiphanic experiences which progressively elevated him to new, ever higher levels of consciousness similar to those achieved by others who 'awakened' to socialism during this period. These exhilarating bursts of new consciousness involved that typically modernist stepping out of the continuum of normal time, and the equally typically modernist transcending of the boundaries of the conventional space of modernity. It was during the early 1880s while living in the countryside that Trevor first felt that a 'new and deeper life' was rising up within him. He seems to have had an epiphany in his garden, as toiling with spade and hoe quickened his 'spiritual nature', while working close to the crops, soil, weeds, birds, rain and sun produced within him the liberating awareness 'that all life was animated equally by a Divine Presence'.[61] This 'birth of a new sense' would give new powers of insight and the exhilarating 'conviction of oneness with all things' that seemed to accompany the ascent into those higher levels of 'cosmic' or 'fellowship' consciousness experienced by other socialists during the revival years.[62] As a former Unitarian minister and convinced believer in the Emersionian

Divine, it should not surprise us that Trevor referred to this evolving consciousness as 'God-consciousness'. With this initial awakening of 'Being' it was as if, 'like a sponge lying in water', Trevor later recalled, 'I seemed embossed in Nature, and to drink in God from my divine environment.'[63] The passage to God-consciousness was to entail a progressive ascent to the light. This involved an ever higher and wider sweep of consciousness from 'Self-consciousness' to 'Collective-consciousness' to 'Universal-consciousness'. From there, it moved upward to the sacred realm of 'God-consciousness', which brought that 'inner awaking to a higher order of life' and put the individual into a divine relationship of love and fellowship with all things.[64]

We can detect a strain of modernism in another area of the Labour Church project. The Labour Church was confidently orientated towards an alternative future, believing that history was on the cusp of change in a radical direction. John Trevor's thinking was infused with the Emersonian idea of history unfolding towards a higher state of unity and fellowship in line with God's divine purpose. This was felt to be towards a socialist future. Society was to be taken there by the coming class of the Labour movement, which was the living expression of God-consciousness and God's divine purpose of advancing humankind's upward development in the direction of an order based on a universal awareness of the kinship of all. For Trevor, it was the authentic, divinely inspired 'cry for brotherhood, for human relations with all men, which rises from the soul of the Labour Movement'.[65] This harmonious future of human fellowship Trevor saw clearly. He was to stand before the world as a prophet, 'announcing the dawn of the day that is to be', rather than as a 'preacher' of the established Church. The latter, kept down by custom, routine and association with the established order of things, lacks 'that wide sweep and far look which is demanded for reformation and progress'.[66] As 'Prophet of the new', it should come as little surprise that when the Labour Church launched its first news organ it was entitled *The Labour Prophet*. We should also mention other characteristically modernist elements that could be found everywhere in Labour Church thinking, namely the monist blending of the spiritual and the material, the fusing of the transcendental and the political, the rejection of the values of the materialist present and the conviction that the new age had to be spiritually superior to the present. With the Labour Church then, as with others seeking to realise a new self in the higher consciousness of a socialism based on fellowship with all things, the effort to arrive at a personal experience of transcendence based on the new, higher consciousness of 'God-consciousness' always implied engagement with the modern world and its ills. There was almost a longing, even a spiritual need, to immerse oneself in a world seemingly on the cusp of a radical transformation. It would be useful to conclude this chapter with John Trevor's eulogy to a philosophy of life which filled his days with meaning and purpose during the Labour Church years:

> My religion, when I really think of it now, takes away my breath. The height it places me on makes me giddy ... it is not an Oriental religion of repose. It is a religion of whirling activity, of straining effort, of expansion joyous to the verge of pain. And I know it is real. I know it represents what we are, and how divine we are to be .... It is a religion of creative insight and power, which will one day have this ball of Earth in its grip, making it sing a merrier song than now as it spins its way through space.[67]

3
Socialist Utopian Modernism: The Myths of the Kingdom and the Golden Age

As we saw in Chapter 2, the late Victorian and Edwardian era in Britain was an 'over-determined' historical moment of quite exceptional nature. It was a moment of tremendous convulsions and ferment, particularly so during the decade leading up to the *fin de siècle*. These convulsions, which marked the atmosphere, cultural life and politics of *fin de siècle* Britain, were brought on by a quite explosive mix of currents and circumstances. There was the temporal consciousness and epochal consciousness inherited from the Enlightenment; the shock of the new technologies and restructured processes of capitalist modernisation indicated by the Second Industrial Revolution; the stirring of powerful social forces clamouring for change; the disturbance wrought by the protracted economic downturn of c.1873–c.1896; and the undermining of mid-Victorian certainties, which included the breaking down of accepted paradigms of mid-Victorian knowledge. To this compound of co-ordinates we should add the glut of *fin de siècle* phenomena released by the proximity of the new century which fuelled a belief that a new age was at hand, one superior to that which had gone before. We should also add to the mix, the acute and protracted liminoid circumstances relating to modernity that prevailed in Britain and much of continental Europe at this time. These circumstances were a product of the temporal, psychological and cultural strains felt by those caught up in the maelstrom that was modernity and particularly that sense that onrushing progress was de-spiritualising life as it pitilessly swept aside the mysteries, gods and spirits that had traditionally been present in the world. There was a dialectic at work during these times, however, as these temporal, psychological and cultural strains brought forth their negation in an awakened spiritual sensibility and optimism about constructive change. The era was thus perceived by many living through it as an age of genuine transition which was tending towards an alternative future perceived to be positive, creative, self-fulfilling and more spiritually enlightened though which, as yet, had not taken definite shape. For their part, contemporary socialists were convinced that this new modern era beckoning on the horizon was taking a distinctly radical form and that a new age of fellowship was dawning. This new age would be marked not just by social justice but by a new, more spiritual or transcendental conception of life. This heightened sense of spiritual awareness once attained would bring insight into the organic unity of all things and generate an instinctive feeling of oneness with one's fellows, nature and the cosmos. This urge to forge more gracious relations with things based on an expanded spiritual consciousness and a more spiritual conception of life, 'entering into fellowship with the stars' as John Trevor put it, was reflected in the 'wave of transcendentalism' that Holbrook Jackson noticed had swept *fin de siècle* Britain and which also surged through the socialist camp.[1]

Transcendentalism was not the only force surging through the socialist camp during these decades, however. The spiritual or liminoid crisis engendered by modernity and the general turbulence of the times set in motion another impulse driven by that urge to go beyond the contemporary decadence and pass into a new age. As Holbrook Jackson noticed, 'there were visions about' during these years.[2] These visions were high in utopian content, and it is the contention of this chapter that the decades either side of the *fin de siècle*, broadly c.1880–c.1910, were witness to a genuine utopian moment in relation to socialism in Britain. British socialism was saturated with utopian thinking during these years. A variety of forms would overtly express, mediate, convey and evoke the utopian aspiration within contemporary socialism, ranging from the utopianism embedded in more conventional socialist writing and rhetoric to the utopian sentiment we can discern in some popular socialist myths of this period. We will look closely at two of the more prominent socialist myths during the course of this chapter: the eschatological myth of the Kingdom and the myth of the Golden Age. It needs to be emphasised, too, that this utopian aspiration within the socialist revival, as with those socialist efforts to attain spiritual or cosmic consciousness, would reveal an unmistakably modernist component. It will be one of the tasks of this chapter to bring this modernist component to the fore.

As mentioned, the utopian impulse pervaded the socialism of the revival years. Some of the more explicit literary expressions of socialist utopias are well known, most notably William Morris's utopian novels, *A Dream of John Ball* (1888) and *News from Nowhere* (1891). There were other utopian socialist novels that appeared in these years, including *The Sorcery Shop* (1909) written by the Clarion socialist Robert Blatchford, H.G. Wells's *A Modern Utopia* (1905), C. R. Ashbee's *The Building of Thelema* (1910) and the imported utopia *Looking Backward, 2000–1987* (1888), written by the American socialist Edward Bellamy. The one-time Guild Socialist G.K. Chesterton also wrote a utopian novel, *The Napoleon of Notting Hill* (1904), in this period, though the socialist message is often elusive here. Though not wholly utopian in intention, other contemporary socialist literature contained sizeable and explicit utopian passages, such as Blatchford's *Merrie England* (1893). There were also utopian daydream and sleeping dream versions of escape to pleasurable worlds without masters and excessive toil, of the type that featured in socialist newspapers of the day.[3]

Utopian visions of a harmonious future socialism could be mediated through less overt or obvious means as well, such as seductive metaphoric evocations of the socialist future and literary embellishment. Indeed, as Ernst Bloch tells us, in the 'wishful landscape' of literature there is always utopian function operating.[4] Fellowship socialists would frequently draw on the primordial metaphoric association of spring with regeneration to convey socialist hope and the sense of a new beginning. For the Clarion activist Alex M. Thompson writing in 1895, the arrival of spring, symbolised by the newly established annual socialist ritual of May Day, meant the awakening of new, fresh life:

Then shall hatred change to love as winter turns before you now to spring; the barren branches of oppression shall fructify and be made fair with the leaves of mutual aid; the prickly bushes of strife and rivalry shall blossom into bowers of sweetest roses.[5]

For Keir Hardie, too, spring and the May Day ritual signified new life and a new beginning:

And so the May Day of the socialist movement is thus more significant than at first appears. It is the return to one of the oldest festivals of which history, traditional or mythical, gives us a glimpse. It is as if we were at the beginning of things again, and were painfully starting afresh to build up a new philosophy of life.[6]

The metaphor of the sun, particularly the dawning sun, could serve as an equally dazzling image to impart that sense of the coming of a new, more beautiful time beyond the 'winter' or darkness of capitalism. Thus we have the Edwardian socialist Robert Noonan's metaphoric flight of fancy in *The Ragged Trousered Philanthropists*, as Frank Owen, the working-class socialist hero of the novel, contemplated the 'inevitable' demise of the 'atrocious system' of capitalism:

> Mankind, awaking from the long night of bondage and mourning and arising from the dust wherein they had lain prone so long, were at last looking upward to the light that was riving asunder and dissolving the dark clouds which had so long concealed from them the face of heaven. The light that will shine upon the world wide Fatherland and illumine the gilded domes and glittering pinnacles of the beautiful cities of the future, where shall dwell together in true brotherhood and goodwill and joy. The Golden Light that will be diffused throughout all the happy world from the rays of the risen sun of Socialism.[7]

In a similar vein, one of the McMillan sisters, Rachel McMillan, wrote of socialism opening up 'a sunlight track one can joyfully look along'.[8]

The utopian aspiration can also be discerned in myth. These myths were often, though not always, immersed in traditional Christian mythology, imagery and idioms. We will be looking at the most prominent of these myths in some detail later in this chapter. The mode of expression could be as varied as the form. As well as the more structured utopian speculation which appeared in socialist writing, there was the unstructured utopian reverie of the type that emanated from socialist open-air platform venues during the revival years. Here, socialist orators afire with the new evangelism would proceed to present their audiences with enticing 'aesthetic' visions of the socialist world to come, as we will see below.

How should we account for the ubiquitous presence of this utopian impulse within the socialist revival? Utopianism certainly flourished in the liminoid climate of the times, acting as a comforting spiritual antidote to modernity. Utopian dreaming provided respite from the maelstrom unleashed by modernity, a sanctuary within which the self could rest or even replenish the store of spiritual energy that had waned during the years of Victorian 'progress'. Here utopian imagining has been viewed as a spatial construct, an imaginary enclave above or outside the rush of modern life. As Frederic Jameson put it, utopian space is a 'pocket of stasis within the ferment and rushing forces of social change', a 'pause' or 'a-historical enclave' beyond the bustle of the social.[9] The notion of the utopian space as a 'pause' points up the temporal dimension to the utopian function. As well as acting as a space beyond the melee of the social, utopian imagining provided a temporal enclave outside the rush of normal historical time. In this conception, utopian thought is a suspended moment of time outside of normal time. In the context of this study of modernism and socialism, utopian thought needs to be conceptualised as a moment of constructive contemplation ripped out of the narrative of Enlightenment-modernist or historical time. According to this understanding, the utopian mental space represents a triumph of 'Being' over that restless state of 'Becoming' characteristic of the modern condition. Here, the connection between the utopian aspiration and modernism is affirmed for, as David Harvey tells us, modernism was itself a spatial project which always sought to privilege 'the spatialisation of time (Being) over the annihilation of space by time (Becoming)'.[10]

This being said, even if utopian imagining was a 'pocket of stasis', a 'pause' or a moment of contemplative 'Being' above the rush of modern life and time, much of its power to attract those seeking release from the strains of Victorian and Edwardian modernity came from its intrinsic futural thrust and capacity to present an alternative vision of the future. Moreover, this vision of the future overflowed with optimism. Socialist hope concerning alternative, other futures would run free in comforting utopian imaginative spaces. The strong futuristic thrust of the utopian vision and the pleasurable pictures of the future that could be painted in these visions rendered utopian imagining particularly relevant to the liminoid circumstances of the times. This was even more so given the 'over-determined' historical moment that was the late Victorian and Edwardian era, with its combustible mix of circumstances which so unsettled the times. The utopian impulse clearly flourished in such an atmosphere of volatility, change and expectation.

This contention that the decades either side of the *fin de siècle* were particularly conducive to an outpouring of utopian sentiment is informed by Ernst Bloch's thinking. As Bloch tells us, times perceived

to be at the point of changing in a radical new direction are particularly productive of utopian imagining.[11] A reworked version of the
Freudian unconscious was articulated to explain this. In each of us,
claims Bloch, in the realm of the unconscious, resides the capacity for
utopian imagining or creative forward-thinking, a condition referred
to as the 'Not-Yet-Conscious'. In contrast to the Freudian conception of the unconscious as the 'No-Longer-Conscious', a 'place' where
'forgotten', 'discarded' or 'repressed' material is stored, the Not-Yet-
Conscious represents 'something coming up', that is 'newly dawning
consciousness with new content'. The Not-Yet-Conscious, for Bloch,
is the source of the utopian impulse. It is the unconscious of the
creative 'other side', of 'forward dawning' or 'morning air' in contrast to the regressive 'musty cellar' of the Freudian unconscious.
It should also be emphasised that Bloch believed that the utopian
impulse is always towards something creative within us, a reaching out for the 'fulfilled moment' – the desire for life that is more
abundant, meaningful and spiritual. As mentioned, the potential for
the proliferation of the Not-Yet-Conscious, those creative 'thoughts
in the stage of incubation' that venture beyond, is greater at times
of perceived radical change. All times of change in a radical direction 'are filled with Not-Yet-Conscious', that is utopian content, even
'over-filled'. At such a moment, there is awareness that the future
constitutes a realm of genuine possibility, a perspective premised on
seeing history as an open, indeterminate process. Such 'moments'
are pregnant with feelings of hope, or, put another way, the historical moment abounds with utopian imagining. In such periods, Bloch
tells us 'man distinctly feels that he is not an established being, but
one which, together with his environment, constitutes a task and
an enormous receptacle full of future'.[12] Hope quickens as awareness
sets in that the world is full of propensity towards something positive
which, as yet, had not taken definite form but is latent with the possibility of more 'fulfilled life'. Thus, where possibility reigns, so does
hope. As already noted, the heady aspiration for change at the *fin
de siècle* was palpable. It issued from every pore of the social body,
was particularly acute during the 1890s and spilled over into the
Edwardian years. British socialism emerged and flourished in this vortex of change and heady atmosphere for the new, and socialists were
convinced that the new meant a radical new world of justice and
equality. It was this vortex and atmosphere which stimulated, quickened and sharpened the utopian impulse as contemporary socialists
sought to anticipate, foretell and dream the new. Drawing on Bloch's

conception then, the late Victorian and Edwardian era needs to be viewed as a utopian-modernist 'moment', whereby the future was perceived by many socialists as an exciting realm of possibility pregnant with hope and latent with the prospect of more creative life and humane relationships beyond liberal-capitalist modernity and its decadent 'Victorian values'.

In such a moment of volatility, change and expectation, utopian fantasies helped awaken latent political energies. Pleasurable fantasy and that characteristic imaginative playfulness in the crafting of the utopian vision in particular could arouse dormant political energies in any as yet unconverted believers. It is a characteristic of utopian imagining to portray not just a better world but a more beautiful world. This tendency of utopianism to aestheticise the new world to come, to present an 'aesthetically-heightened', even poetic image of the socialist future, was guaranteed to arouse the emotions in times of volatility and change. Percy Redfern, a *fin de siècle* Nottingham socialist, has left us with a recollection of the appeal of utopian rhetoric. Redfern recalled attending socialist open-air meetings during the 1893 coalminers strike. Whereas some socialist speakers tried to draw on basic Marxist economics or 'Fabian diagrams' to help explain capitalist exploitation and convert the assembled miners to socialism, it 'was not this caricature, with its kernel of bitter half-truth' that convinced. Rather, it was the poetic utopian dream of the socialist future presented by Margaret McMillan that made an impression. 'She came with a vision of health, joy and beauty in working lives', remembered Redfern, 'to be demanded and created by the people themselves, ...We listened with respect, touched by something vaguely, unattainably fine; and then we went back on strike.'[13]

It should not surprise us as well that the atmosphere of anxiety, volatility, change and expectation that pervaded the late Victorian and Edwardian era unleashed utopian millenarian fantasies within contemporary socialism. These millenarian fantasies were usually expressed through the utopian language of the Kingdom, which has its origins in Christian eschatological belief. There are frequent references in socialist writing equating the socialist future with Christ's coming Kingdom. A few examples should suffice to demonstrate this. Keir Hardie, socialism's spiritual leader for much of the revival years, wrote that 'all who pray for the coming of Christ's Kingdom on Earth' should declare themselves socialist.[14] The very act of engaging in the socialist fight against capitalist tyranny, declared the then Fabian socialist Stewart Headlam in 1899, means that we are 'by degrees' working 'to establish the Kingdom of Heaven upon earth'.[15] In his autobiography, George Lansbury saw his long years of socialist agitation which began in the early 1890s as an effort in 'establishing the Kingdom of Love'.[16] In a similar vein, he equated the socialist project to that 'age-long task of bringing Christ's Kingdom of Joy and Peace into the lives of men and women here and now'.[17]

It seems entirely appropriate that the utopian message of the Kingdom resonated with the time of the socialist revival. The Christian utopia of the Kingdom of God on earth as expressed in biblical prophecy is one of the most long-standing, enduring and compelling of the social utopias. The utopia of the Kingdom has inspired millenarians throughout the Middle Ages and beyond, and its chiliastic message of a future aeon of justice and equality became more strident, more widely disseminated and more likely to be heard during times of unrest and change.[18] It also seems appropriate that the language of the Kingdom should have found its way into that utopian strand within the socialist revival. The Christian utopia of the Kingdom has always contained within it a devastating critique of the existing order of things. It has been taken by many furthermore to be a future-orientated utopia of this world. This was the promise of a 'fresh leap on to new earth', rather than a leap 'into inwardness and the other world' as in St Augustine's transcendental rendering of the City of God or St Paul's purely 'other worldly' utopia of the City of God.[19] This is certainly the case with probably the most influential vision of the Christian-utopian Kingdom, which was formulated by the Calabrian abbot Joachim of Fiore in c.1200. Joachim divided history into three successive stages based on the Blessed Trinity, 'Father', 'Son' and 'Holy Ghost'. Each of these stages represented a genuine progression which was bringing humankind ever closer to the glory and illumination of the Kingdom. The first stage – that of the 'Father' – was that of the Old Testament based on the law, power, fear and servitude. The second stage – that of the 'Son' – was the age of the New Testament based on grace, wisdom and the Church. The third stage – the age of the 'Holy Ghost' – which would succeed the previous two and was yet to come, was the most significant. This was the age of the Kingdom of the 'Holy Spirit', a final age which was to bring not only spiritual illumination but the long awaited aeon of social justice. In 'immanentising the eschaton' as Eric Voegelin put it, in immanentising the end or anticipated final age of the Kingdom, Joachim's conception brought the Kingdom into the domain of consciousness and possible experience in the earthly realm.[20] The

Joachite eschatology of the Kingdom was therefore to be experienced not in terms of a purely Augustine transcendence but as a paradise appearing within history. In speaking of a coming mystical classless democracy freed of corruption, masters and opulence moreover, Joachim's message of the Kingdom unambiguously reached out to the poor. The Christian social utopia of the Kingdom has therefore, particularly in its Joachite conception, shown an enduring capacity to instil radiant hopes of a better dispensation in the hearts of the dispossessed.

The capacity to instil hope and heighten expectation is intrinsic to Christian millennialist eschatology in another respect. As we have seen in this book, many socialists during the revival years were of the conviction that the era they were living through was one of genuine transition and that an alternative, radiant future was imminent. The sense that the time one was living through was a transitional or 'in between' time is also evident in Christian millennialist eschatology, where there was a sense of living in between two momentous events – the birth of Christ and the second coming of Christ or *parousia* at the eschaton or end of time. In Christian eschatology this 'in between' time or transitional time was a time of anticipation. It could induce utopian feelings of radiant hope, where it was felt that there was something coming and that the *parousia* was close. As stated in Mark, Chapter 13: 35 of the *New Testament*: 'Watch ye therefore: for ye know not when the master of the house cometh, at even, or at midnight, or at the cockcrowing, or in the morning.' Not surprisingly, references to a 'second coming' can be found in contemporary socialist writing. When Ramsay MacDonald recalled his earlier conversion to the socialist faith, he remembered that 'we had all the enthusiasm of the early Christians in those days. We were few and the gospel was new. The second coming was at hand.'[21] At the *parousia* or eschaton there was to be both atonement and salvation, for not only would justice be administered on all according to the righteousness or otherwise of their earthly lives, but there would be established that glorious Kingdom of God on earth. The eschatological expectation of a glorious new dispensation or 'second coming' that socialists felt and that sense of living in an 'in between' time would have been heightened still further by the proximity of the era of the socialist revival to the new century. As Frank Kermode pointed out, this moment brought forth quite acute *fin de siècle* phenomena. This was an awareness of being in a time that was neither the end nor the beginning, and a heightened sense that the transitional moment that one was living through was a time of genuine crisis and change and the prelude to a new world reborn into perfection.[22]

This prophetic belief underpinning apocalyptic eschatological thinking that a new dispensation would arise from the crisis of the old world, an age of rebirth and new life, was entirely consistent with the modernist imagination. Many of the 'fictions' of the leading literary modernists, notably Ezra Pound, William Butler Yeats, T.S. Eliot and James Joyce, contained apocalyptic eschatological content of the type mentioned above. Frank Kermode has identified apocalyptic thinking in early modernism, as has Mircea Eliade.[23] Entirely consistent with the modernist sensibility as well is the temporal future-orientated dimension within the utopia of the Kingdom. This refers to the capacity of this powerful myth to generate a sense of a new time beyond the continuum of present time. The utopia of the Kingdom spoke to that desire within modernism to go beyond present circumstances in a further, spatial sense. The myth of the future eschatological Kingdom contained within it the wishful aspiration for 'depth and infinity' intrinsic to all religious feeling, what Bloch has called the longing to feel at home 'in the mystery of existence'.[24]

As to the inauguration of the Kingdom itself, there was no consensus as to how this would come about. In some interpretations, the apocalyptic element was dark and strident. George Bernard Shaw, himself no lover of socialist 'religious illusions', wrote of that strain within the socialist revival, heavily influenced by Marxism, which held that socialism would consummate itself in a great day of judgement and wrath 'called "The Revolution" ', where all the lusts of capitalism and competition would be 'cast out, leaving the earth free for the kingdom of heaven on earth'.[25] Tom Barclay, one of the pioneers of the 1880s socialist revival, though a freethinker and member of the Leicester Secular Society as well as the Marxist SDF, evidently harboured just such a cataclysmic apocalyptic interpretation of the socialist future. Barclay wrote of the 'last great battle of the world' which would bring a 'paradise of purity, of concord, of love'.[26] The socialism of Rowland Kenney of the ILP struck a similarly stark, cataclysmic note. Kenney 'desired the millennium, even if it had to be brought in through the chaos of red revolution'.[27]

The socialism of John Trevor of the Labour Church also contained eschatological content. Trevor made frequent references to 'that Kingdom of God on Earth for which we are working'.[28] But this was no cataclysmic apocalyptic eschatology of the type advanced by some of his socialist contemporaries like Barclay and Kenney. Trevor's socialist eschatology grew out of an immanentist faith which posited the notion that God's living and eternal presence could be found in all things in the world and that history represented the working out of His divine will.[29] This was a conception of God 'pressing upon the opportunities he has himself prepared, and manifesting himself in constantly ascending spheres throughout the world's history...'.[30] Trevor and other immanentist socialists thus saw this historical unfolding of God's divine purpose as progressive, believing that it was moving inexorably towards the fulfilment of a world of universal fellowship, which they interpreted to be socialism or the 'Kingdom of God on Earth'. But here there was no talk of socialism consummating itself in the day of Judgement in the final, possibly violent confrontation of the Revolution. There was to be an eschatological fulfilment in the Kingdom of God or socialist fellowship through gradual evolution and peaceful conversion. In this understanding, socialist evangels were to go forth to awaken the masses to an awareness of the divine within them from which, once felt, would come entry to that higher order of a life of universal love and fellowship. This said, Trevor and his fellow Labour Church socialists certainly 'immanentised the eschaton', thereby rendering the end 'this worldly' and closer, at least in consciousness, heightening their chiliastic expectations of the impending arrival of the Kingdom of God or the new dispensation of socialist fellowship.

Despite this lack of consensus as to how the Kingdom would come about, there was general unanimity amongst contemporary socialists of a Christian-utopian persuasion that the future socialist Kingdom would represent an ascent to a higher plane of spirituality. This higher plane was envisaged in terms of an arrangement founded on ideals of love and spiritual fellowship. Again, it is not difficult to identify some continuity of theme here between these socialist utopias of spiritual fellowship and the Christian eschatological utopias of the Kingdom, with the latter also promising a future universal order of love and spiritual brotherhood. This continuity of theme is most apparent in relation to the socialist utopias of spiritual fellowship and that conception of God's Kingdom on earth articulated by Joachim of Fiore, the twelfth-century Calabrian abbot whom we met above. As we saw, Joachim posited a notion of history based on the three successive stages of the 'Father', 'Son' and 'Holy Ghost', each of which brought the light and illumination of the Kingdom represented by the age of the 'Holy Ghost' ever closer. As mentioned, this final age was to bring social justice and spiritual illumination. This latter stage was to be a state of expanded grace, genuine spiritual insight and perfect freedom, as had existed during the original paradise. According to Joachim, in this progressive ascent to the light of the Kingdom we go 'from illumination to illumination, from the first heaven to the second, and from the second to the third, from the place of darkness into the light of the moon, that at last we may come out of the moonlight into the glory of the full son'.[31]

There is a similar notion of a threefold ascent to the light of pure spiritual illumination within the socialist revival, which was touched on to some extent in Chapter 2. This was the notion, very explicit in Edward Carpenter's writings, of a three-stage progression from 'simple' consciousness, to 'civilised' or modern self-consciousness, to 'cosmic' consciousness. The first stage of 'simple' consciousness was that associated with 'primitive' man.[32] As we saw in Chapter 2, Carpenter admired aspects of primitive consciousness. Though representing an early stage in the evolution of consciousness, it was a consciousness in harmony with the natural world and the 'slow lapse of the constellations'. Human consciousness then evolved to a second stage according to Carpenter. This was the purely individual self-consciousness associated with 'man' in the era of modern 'civilisation' or, from the point of view of this chapter, the individual in the era of modern liberal-capitalism. Within this stage, man would be characteristically self-interested or alienated depending on his place within the power structure. Although on the face of it, he appeared more 'intellectual' and 'advanced' than the 'primitive', he was most certainly plagued by the mental unrest and angst associated with the modern condition of 'reflexivity'. The third stage of cosmic consciousness, as with Joachim's conception of the 'Holy Ghost', represented the most significant and sublime stage. It was the consciousness of the coming socialist man of the future, a condition that promised not only relief from the mental stress of self-consciousness or reflexivity but a life lived more completely in the fullness of spiritual fellowship. This life of inner peace and perfect freedom, one lived instinctively in harmony with one's fellows and the vast expanse of the cosmos, had, as yet, only been glimpsed by a few socialist 'prophets' of this future bliss but would be the privilege of all come the arrival of the socialist 'Kingdom'.

There was also more than a hint of the Joachite notion concerning the passage to the illumination of the Holy Ghost in the immanentist eschatology of John Trevor of the Labour Church, with its notion of a progressive, upward sweep of consciousness to the sacred realm of 'God-consciousness'. Although Trevor occasionally spoke of this ever-wider sweep of consciousness in terms of four stages, arriving at God-consciousness having passed through 'Self-consciousness', 'Collective-consciousness' and 'Universal-consciousness', other times he made reference to a threefold development in consciousness more in keeping with the Joachite model. Thus, he also spoke of this 'working out' of consciousness in terms of 'Self, Universe, God', at other times in terms of 'Human Consciousness, World Consciousness, God Consciousness'.[33] One thing seemed certain, though. For Trevor and other immanentist socialists, human life was aspiring to the final utopia of the Kingdom of God-consciousness where there would be a divine state of spiritual fellowship and love between all. As he explained it: 'It seems to me that no life is real until it becomes God-conscious, that all unfoldings [*sic*] of consciousness have this as their final cause, and that no form of consciousness becomes complete until the height of God-consciousness is reached.'[34]

As already established in Chapter 2, such explorations of consciousness on the part of contemporary socialists, the aspiration to experience heightened consciousness, were typically modernist endeavours. This applied to both Edward Carpenter's striving after 'cosmic consciousness' and John Trevor's efforts to enter the higher realm of 'God-consciousness'. We can identify another current of modernism running through socialist attempts to attain the utopia of the Kingdom. To identify this current, we need to turn our attention to the question of myth, both as a more general concept and in relation to the socialist aspiration to bring about the Kingdom. It has also been mentioned in previous sections of this book that in its efforts to regenerate the times and the self, to fashion a more transcendental conception of life to overcome the decadence of modern 'civilisation', modernism would strive to access alternative sources of spiritual energy beyond the immediate range of visual perception and the constraints of normal historical or modernist time. These alternative sources of renewal could extend to the unconscious, the irrational, intuition and even mysticism and Theosophy. Modernism was also not averse to drawing on more archaic or mythological sources of renewal in its efforts to reinvigorate the times and the self.[35] Many leading modernists invested their art with myth, including James Joyce, T.S. Eliot, Le Corbusier and Picasso.[36] As James McFarlane tells us, myth appealed to artistic modernism because of its capacity to impose order and meaning of a symbolic and even aesthetic kind on the chaotic, transient, fleeting, contingent and fragmentary nature of reality under modern conditions.[37] There is a temporal aspect to myth as well, which has particular significance for our discussion in this chapter of the utopia of the Kingdom, and indeed other strains of utopian modernism within the socialist revival. Time assumes a quite specific character within myth. Myths have particular potency within cultures not just because they convey a narrative, story or history of sacred worth to the community, sacred 'truths' which moreover harbour exemplary rules for the guidance of moral behaviour within the community, but because they also tell of and amplify the time of the origins of things. This is significant for our analysis of socialist utopian modernism because of the tendency of myths to ennoble the time of origins, to proclaim that this earliest time was a time of strength and purity. As Mircea Eliade tells us, myths claim that the time of origins of something, a community, an institution, a form of human activity, an event, is the most significant time because it was the moment of 'creation' of these things.[38] Because it was the moment of creation the time of origin or birth is deemed to be the 'prodigious', exemplary time, when something new and significant first erupted into the world. Within this framework of the myth of prodigious origins the time of origins is sacralised, while time itself assumes a sacred character within the myth in a more general sense. To immerse the self, art or political movement in the myth then, was to partake of the mythical time of origins, that original time of supposed strength, fertility and purity, become contemporary with it and thereby draw on its creative energy and sacred power. What takes place here is that immersion in the myth enables an almost magical 'return to origins', that is, enables a community or culture to return to the original source of its power, to rediscover its 'roots', its original strength and virtue as it were. The origin myth thus acts as a source of renewal, a font of regeneration, or as Eliade explains it, 'the return to origins gives the hope of a rebirth'.[39]

There is a further function of the origin myth that is noteworthy. The nostalgia for origins or that initial moment of creation also indicates a thirst for 'Being' over the contemporary state of 'Becoming', a desire to co-exist with a sacred moment of time and thereby obtain some ontological release from the depressing chronology of normal historical time.[40] When immersed in the mythical time of origin, the self 'emerges from profane duration to recover an unmoving time, eternity'.[41] To inhabit the 'sacred' time of myth, then, was to enter an alternative time and thereby cast aside, if only temporarily, the burdens imposed by the alienating time of modernity.

We can see the origin myth at work in the socialist eschatological utopia of the Kingdom, which contained within it the myth that the earliest time – the time of the origins of the world – was a time of plenitude and perfection. This is the myth of the original or lost earthly 'paradise', which was deemed to be a primordial state of innocence, bliss, spiritual contentment and genuine equality. Before we continue, it is important to emphasise at this point that the myth of the return to blissful and virtuous origins evident within the utopia of the Kingdom, and indeed other socialist utopias spoken of during the revival years, in no way implied a backward-looking, anti-modern orientation. On the contrary, these socialist myths were aggressively future-orientated in that they optimistically proclaimed that there was to be a glorious return to the blissful and virtuous conditions that prevailed at the time of origins at some future point in time. These futural myths were part of that category of 'origin myths' which take the idea of the 'perfection of the beginnings' and projects it into the future. According to Mircea Eliade, this variation of the origin myth is very evident in the Christian apocalyptic and millenarian mythologies, and we can certainly see it at work in the apocalyptic and millenarian utopias of the socialist revival.[42] Thus the eschatological mythology of the socialist Kingdom to come implied the future restoration of contentment, virtue and spiritual plenitude that had attained during the original earthly paradise. We can see the myth at work, with its characteristic blending of beginning and end, or past and future, in contemporary socialist references to that glorious return to Eden that was to come with the arrival of the socialist future. Thus, the then spiritually inclined socialist, and later first Labour Chancellor of the Exchequer, Philip Snowden wrote (c.1907) that 'socialism comes as the angel of light, bearing to mankind this message of truth' and of the need for all 'to follow the beckoning angel who is waiting to lead us back through the gates of paradise into an Eden of intellectual joy'.[43] We can also see the myth at work in the Joachite-influenced notion of the upward passage to the socialist Kingdom, where this final age of the Kingdom or 'Holy Ghost' was to recover the condition of perfect freedom and spiritual illumination that had characterised the original paradise. It should be emphasised that as well as apocalypse, myth and the thirst for 'Being' over 'Becoming', the creative compounding of future and past or 'forwards and backwards' as in the promise of a return to the bliss that was there at the 'beginning' was another quintessential feature of the modernist sensibility.

Quintessentially modernist, too, was the component within the origin myths, again evident in the socialist utopias of the Kingdom and the return to Eden, which maintains that a phase of extreme decadence or degeneration always precedes the establishment, or restoration, of the new and better dispensation. This association between decadence and renewal, between degeneration and regeneration, was fundamental to these myths, for it seems that a 'fall', whether a cosmic cataclysm, crisis or just a progressive devaluation of the times, was the necessary pre-condition which permitted renewal or 'rebirth'. This 'fall', which precedes and permits regeneration, is often understood to be at its most extreme during the 'moment' of transition. This was that interlude or 'in between' time that seemed to announce both the end and the beginning. Socialist eschatologists were convinced that their own contemporary 'moment' was marred by extreme decadence. Take the following comment by Keir Hardie, who likened the 'decadent' mid-Edwardian age he was living through to that of the Rome that was struck down by the northern tribes:

> ... Ill-gotten wealth and debauchery had corrupted the early patriotism of the Roman Patrician, and idle dependence upon the largess of the rich had destroyed vigour of the Plebians, so that when the barbarians thundered at the gates of the Eternal City there was no force of manhood within to deny them entrance.... We are reproducing in faithful detail every cause which led to the downfall of the civilisations of other days – Imperialism, taking tribute from foreign races, the accumulation of great fortunes, the development of a population which owns no property, and is always in poverty....[44]

It needs to be stressed at this point that this situation of decadence also contained the seeds of hope for it was a characteristic of origin myths, as in Christian apocalyptic eschatology, that the contemporary malaise was but a sign of the regeneration and paradise to come. As Mircea Eliade explained in *The Myth of the Eternal Return*, the moment of decadence 'should not be regarded as a sign of pessimism. On the contrary, it reveals an excess of optimism, for, in the deterioration of the contemporary situation, at least a portion of mankind saw signs foretelling the regeneration that must necessarily follow.'[45]

Keir Hardie was certainly one such prophet of the purer dispensation to come. In the same text where he wrote of the contemporary deca- dence, he declared in another passage that 'capitalism is the creed of the dying present; Socialism throbs with the life of the days that are to be'.[46]

All the aforementioned elements, which it should be re- emphasised are typically modernist – the strong sense that the present age was decadent, an urge for a new beginning, the yearning for 'Being' over 'Becoming', the search for archaic sources of regener- ation as in the recourse to myth, the creative fusion of 'forwards and backwards' as in the origin myth and that heady expectation of an imminent return to an earlier state of bliss – were there in another of the prominent socialist utopian myths of the revival period. This was the 'Golden Age' myth. As with the eschatological utopia of the Kingdom, Golden Age references were plentiful in socialist discourse. Writing in 1886, Annie Besant saw socialism as 'that Golden Age which poets have chanted, which dreamers have visioned [*sic*], which martyrs have died for . . . '.[47] Other contemporary socialists referred to it, too, like Rachel McMillan.[48] Edward Carpenter was very familiar with the Golden Age myth, too, as was William Morris.[49] The myth was very well known to the prominent Scottish ILP activist John Bruce Glasier as well.[50] It seems that the Golden Age myth was also widely disseminated during the revival years. Under the lecture titled 'Dreams of the Earthly Paradise', the myth was a favourite theme of Glasier's during the 20 plus years that he lectured from socialist platforms during the revival period.[51] For his part, Glasier inclined to the view that a Golden Age had indeed existed in the remote past. The existence of this idyllic early state was apparently vindi- cated by the widespread survival of the myth itself for Glasier, and that this further confirmed the truth of the socialist vision of man's innate goodness.[52]

Glasier was also well aware of the Golden Age myth's long ances- try, which can be traced back to the Ancient world. The Greek poet Hesiod in c.700 BCE, in *Works and Days*, was the first to elaborate on the myth, to be followed by other Classical writers, notably the Roman poets Vergil and Ovid. Many of the principal qualities of the Golden Age which would become generic to the myth originate with these early writers. As with the glories of the coming Kingdom, it is not difficult to see why these qualities would appeal to socialists like Glasier. For the Graeco-Roman writers, the Golden Age was the first or original age, a terrestrial paradise free of care, grief, coercion, laws, toil and war. This original Golden Age was also abundant. The earth and trees gave of their fruits spontaneously, without the scars and sweat of cultivation. As Book 1 of Ovid's *Metamorphoses* described this sumptuous paradise: 'it was a season of everlasting spring... [and] there flowed rivers of milk and rivers of nectar, and golden honey dripped from the green holm-oak'.[53] These blissful conditions spontaneously nurtured that state of primal goodness that radiated from this original Golden Age. There was an innocence or fresh-ness that came with living on more intimate terms with the earth, the cosmos and the gods. This carefree life of ease and plenty also meant that individuals enjoyed long and healthy lives. This early aeon was also egalitarian, communistic even, one without stations and private property. As Ernst Bloch and Norman Cohn have pointed out, the egalitarian aspect of this original time of innocence received even greater emphasis in contemporary and later reflections on the Golden Age myth. This can be seen with Iamboulos' Island of the Sun, a 'land of wine without mine and thine', and the second-century satirist Lucian's lament on that earlier time when people 'were of gold'.[54] All who lauded the earlier Golden Age also believed that subsequent ages were inferior to the first age of gold. There had been regression in these later ages, a fall into decadence and worse, which they indicated by metaphorically associating these succeed-ing aeons with inferior, baser or meaner metals, usually silver, brass and iron.

Another aspect of the Golden Age myth which would have appealed to socialists during the revival years was that version of the myth which held that the Golden Age was recoverable or retrievable in the present. Even here the myth branched off into different forms. One popular version would cast the Golden Age as a 'wished-for' mode of life on a faraway earthly or even island paradise discoverable by means of a conscious and determined exodus from 'civilisation' and its ills. Such paradises at a distance were usually green, fertile and natural, as in a garden. This spatial version of the Golden Age as recoverable co-existed with a temporal account of the restora-tion myth. This was the conviction that the age of gold would come again in the future, what Bloch calls the 'Golden Age of tomorrow'. Norman Cohn contends that this future-orientated account of the myth first appeared in the Middle Ages against the backdrop of con-temporary social upheavals, such as the English Peasants' Revolt of 1381.[55] It seems, though, that this variant originated in the Ancient world with Vergil's fourth *Ecologue*, where he prophesises the return

of a new Golden Age complete with the rebirth of a new generation of 'golden men' in the wake of the falling away of the 'iron
race'.[56] With Vergil, and certainly with later medieval interpreters of
the myth, there is no longer a Hesiodic lament for an age of gold
deemed to be irretrievably lost. Instead, as the Golden Age is propelled into the future, there is that creative confluence of 'forwards
and backwards' that we saw in the millenarian and eschatological mythologies of the Kingdom. It is this tradition within Golden
Age thinking, which brings anticipation of a restoration of the joys
of an earlier age, which found its way into the socialism of the
revival years.

There was an additional basic tension, or difference of emphasis, within the Golden Age tradition which has some bearing on
how the myth was interpreted within the socialist revival. This was
the contrast between that notion of the Golden Age as a time of
simplicity based on few needs and frugal contentment, and that
which casts it as a time of lavish pleasure, 'the merry life which
goes short of nothing' in the words of Ernst Bloch.[57] The latter could
even extend to unabashed sexual pleasure, the idea of the original
Golden Age as an amorous and sensual paradise where love was freely
available.

There is a further variation on the Golden Age myth that one finds
in contemporary socialism that needs mentioning. This is the 'Merrie
England' myth that featured in the thinking of some prominent
socialists, including William Morris and Robert Blatchford. Broadly,
this aspect of the myth held that there had been a golden age of
labour during the Middle Ages. For our purpose, in relation to this
chapter, the salient point concerns that strand within the 'Merrie
England' myth which idealised this earlier golden age of labour,
spoke of its passing with the arrival of commercial capitalism and
wage labour, and anticipated its return with the coming of socialism
at some point in the future. As with the more typical Golden Age origin myths, there was the assumption that there had been an earlier
perfection, that there had been a fall in succeeding ages but that the
earlier perfection would return.

It should be emphasised that there was no universal, single version
of what the past Golden Age looked like, in the same way that there
was no universally agreed interpretation of how the age of gold to
come would look. This was as true for late Victorian and Edwardian
socialists as it was for others in earlier times who had sought to imagine the nature of the golden time that was to be. The same broadly

held for those who embraced the Kingdom myth and sought to picture the future socialist Kingdom. Thus, though certain fundamentals of these myths were accepted, namely that there had been an earlier perfection, that there had been regression in subsequent ages and that the earlier perfection was recoverable, beyond this basic framework the imagination was free to ponder on the look of the future perfection. In other words, the imagination was free to indulge in those creative 'thoughts in the stage of incubation' which we know as the 'Not-Yet-Conscious', the well spring of the utopian impulse. And in the heady atmosphere for change that suffused the late Victorian and Edwardian decades, socialists would dream creatively of the new and craft a variety of pictures of the perfect world to come. In keeping with the times and the new modernist politics that emerged at the *fin de siècle* of which fellowship socialism was a part, their dreaming could be wonderfully erratic. These utopias could knit together fragments from a variety of sources and influences and fuse seemingly contradictory elements to create novel forms which mischievously deviated from the pattern of development charted by the advocates of modernisation and progress. Many of the familiar signs associated with modern life and modernisation under capitalist conditions would magically disappear in these utopias. Of the principal home-grown socialist utopias, only the Fabian H.G. Wells's utopia, a modern technocratic vision extolling the virtues of 300 mph trains, deviated from this pattern.[58]

William Morris's *Nowhere* is the best-known socialist utopia of these years. A creative fusion of forwards and backwards, modern and medieval, polemic and poetry, socialism and anarchism, it offered transcendence to a wonderfully eccentric, mythical neo-Gothic utopia stripped of many of the usual signs of late Victorian modern life. *Nowhere* was a utopia without capitalists, money, machines, wage labour, alienating work, hierarchies, extravagant needs, ugly utilitarian buildings, sprawling commercialised urban spaces and bourgeois parliaments.[59] There are less well-known socialist utopias, though they too displayed delightfully eccentric features and had erased many of the recognisable features of modern life under capitalism. In his utopian novel *The Sorcery Shop*, published in 1909, Robert Blatchford offered his readership a regenerated 'new England' without politicians, banknotes, thieves, prisons, beggars or guns for war. Even locks on the doors of houses would disappear in Blatchford's 'new England'.[60] This was no pastoral utopia, it should be said. The modern city did figure here but it had been aestheticised. Manchester, for example, was reconfigured as a beautiful garden. A 'marvellous dream city', Blatchford's Manchester sparkled with marble palaces and roofs, towers and gables which protruded 'like red and white islands out of a broad sea of blossom', all of which was set in an orchard plain of flowering trees.[61] The new Manchester moreover indicated that a magical return to an earlier state of perfection had been attained. As the 'wizard', one of the novel's main characters, explained it: 'This city of health and beauty, of happy homes, and noble palaces, of trees and flowers, this Paradise regained.'[62]

Many of the familiar signs of modern life under capitalism had also disappeared from the utopia of J.C. Kenworthy of the Fellowship of the New Life.[63] In Kenworthy's socialist 'Kingdom of Heaven on earth' to come, there were no prisons, police, lawyers, magistrates, armies, states or private ownership of houses and land, while even the railways and cities had been ripped up and gold and silver had been used to make cooking vessels and ornaments. Although time spent at work would only be a few hours a day and the worker could work 'at pretty well what he likes best', Kenworthy envisioned a future life in socialism of plenty and abundance. The utopia sketched out by John Bruce Wallace's *Brotherhood* magazine was equally enticing. In this vision, the landlord and the 'usurer' had been cast out of the social body, and healthy, happy homes and lives, and freedom from care and want, would be within the reach of all, 'obtainable by two or three hours work each day'.[64] The 'Future Golden Age' of Wallace's *Brotherhood* moreover would be 'the age of poetry, of art, of beauty'.[65]

The standard indicators of modern life virtually disappeared altogether in Edward Carpenter's utopia.[66] Like the other socialist utopias just mentioned, Carpenter's utopia envisaged the return of an earlier state of perfection. This new dispensation would not be characterised by plenty and abundance, however. Rather, it was to be attained through people throwing off the trapping of 'civilisation' and cultivating lives of studied simplicity, frugal contentment and scaled-down needs. The socialist man of the future would not be housed in large towns and cities, for example, and habitation, along with clothing, would conform to a simple design. Diet, too, was to be elementary, comprising mostly fruit and grains.[67] This return to nature and communal life 'is the way back to the lost Eden, or rather forward to the new Eden' said Carpenter, exhibiting that typical modernist melding of forwards and backwards.[68] There would be no laws, government, 'private accumulations' or wage labour to tarnish this new Eden either. From all this would spring a person of a new type, infused with a spontaneous and instinctive sympathy and instinct of helpfulness towards others.

We will encounter the wonderfully unconventional imaginary socialist utopias of Carpenter and his socialist contemporaries again later in this book when we turn our attention to the issue of space in relation to the socialist revival in Chapter 5.

4
Experiments in Social Modernism: The Communities of Hope

As mentioned in previous chapters, a heady and compulsive aspiration for change surged through the decades on either side of the *fin de siècle*. This mood for change and hopeful expectancy of the new did not take place in a historical vacuum. It arose in a period marked by tremendous volatility. This volatility was a product of a quite explosive collision of technological, social, economic, epistemological, temporal and liminoid circumstances and trends which together generated that 'over-determined' historical moment of the late Victorian and Edwardian era. Some of these circumstances and currents were home-grown, still others emanated from sources wider afield. All these circumstances and currents were aspects of the maelstrom that was modernity. As we have seen, the British socialist awakening of these years emerged in the context of all this volatility and flux, while the socialist project itself has to be seen as one of the main 'revitalisation' movements of the *fin de siècle* which offered its followers a way out of the maelstrom. Again, as previously discussed, this awakening brought forth a host of socialist groups and socialist converts. The former ranged from more formal political bodies such as the Socialist League, the Fabian Society and the Independent Labour Party, to less conventional groupings such as the Labour Church and the Clarion movement. There were many others, of course.[1] There was a further glut of socialist formations which sprang up in this period, though of a different type to those discussed in this book up to now. These were the various experiments at building small-scale socialist communities beyond the mainstream of capitalist life. As with the various manifestations of socialism considered hitherto it should not surprise us, given the nature of the times, that these applied socialist utopias proliferated during the late

Victorian and Edwardian era. Although different in many ways to the previously discussed socialist formations, these community experiments did share some characteristics with these more formal groups. Like the latter, they did not conform to a standard uniform profile in terms of their ideological makeup. In many of these community schemes, socialists would live and work with communitarian types of very different ideological persuasions and aspirations. This mix of elements should come as no great surprise to us. As with other manifestations of *fin de siècle* socialism we have considered up to now, these radical community experiments were delightfully eclectic modernist montages. In other words, they were wonderfully extravagant expressions of 'politics in a new key' that perfectly reflected and caught the anxieties and hopes of these turbulent times. This was not the only strain of modernism running through these community schemes, however. At another level, they need to be read as experiments in social modernism. It is the task of this chapter to bring to the fore these various strains of modernism at work in these efforts of utopia-building. It would help in the fulfilment of this task if we began by identifying the various radical community schemes which sprang to life in this period.

These community experiments came in various shapes and sizes. Whereas the majority involved a group of adventurers in pursuit of the perfect arrangement, others could involve a sole enthusiast earnestly searching for this ideal in the spirit of solitary isolation, as with Henry Thoreau at Walden Pond. Some experiments were short-lived, while still others endured beyond the time frame of this study. Some have left ample testimony as to their activities, while others have left few written traces. While all bear the marks of these turbulent decades, some experiments drew on traditions that fell outside this period.

The first inkling that the budding socialist movement would display this communitarian side to its character came when a small group of Sheffield socialist working men participated in the experiment in co-operative living at Totley farm during the early 1880s. The Totley Colony experiment was initially inspired by John Ruskin who purchased the 13-acre farm just outside Sheffield in 1876. For Ruskin, the Sheffield proletarians who engaged in 'useful labour' on the farm were to be the 'Life Guards of a New Life'.[2] The intention was to run Totley farm as a model vegetable and botanic garden offering co-operative work to Sheffield workers and their families. Although it had some success supplying vegetable produce to the Sheffield markets, the co-operative venture was floundering by the mid-1880s. The next outburst of communitarian activity took place further south when members of the Fellowship of the New Life embarked on an experiment in communal living in Bloomsbury, London, during the 1880s. These mainly lower-middle-class pioneers of the new life encouraged others to establish 'colonies' on similar lines through the columns of the Fellowship's news organ *Seed-Time*. Clearly registering the influence of the American utopian tradition, particularly the writings on life-style and self-sufficiency by Thoreau, as well as Tolstoy, Fellowship socialists sought to realise their aim of bringing about an ethical transformation in their personal lives by giving themselves up to live a life based on co-operative principles in domestic economy and work and 'simplicity in all the relations of life'.[3]

The communitarian impulse was felt just north and south of Bloomsbury, in north London, and in Croydon, Surrey. The north London experiment was launched c.1891 by a Congregational pastor from Ulster, John Bruce Wallace, a socialist and avid exponent of co-operative working. Inspired by the tireless Reverend Wallace, who also published a magazine entitled *Brotherhood* to spread his ideas on co-operation, the communitarians of the 'Brotherhood Church', as the experiment became known, operated from a once-derelict church at Southgate Road, Hackney.[4] From there the Brotherhood community branched out to establish a food co-operative in nearby Downham Road. Converts to socialism seeking a more spiritual dimension to their newly acquired belief were inspired by such experiments. The then Croydon-based socialist convert Nellie Shaw, feeling 'the need of something warmer, more vital, more appealing to the idealistic side of our natures than mere economics', with others went on to found 'The Croydon Brotherhood Church' in 1894 based on the 'splendid example set us by Bruce Wallace'.[5] A mainstay of the Croydon group was J.C. Kenworthy, one-time Congregational Minister, Fellowship of the New Life member and avowed Tolstoyan. Kenworthy had previously collaborated with Bruce Wallace in the Southgate Road Brotherhood Church. Before long, the experiment had fanned out to establish a range of Brotherhood schemes. These included the Croydon Brotherhood Store, the Croydon Brotherhood Dressmakers, the Croydon Brotherhood Publishing Society, which printed the group's journal *The Croydon Brotherhood Intelligencer*, and Brotherhood House, a home run 'on very free lines' for young men interested in embarking on co-operative living.[6] Many of the Croydon activists, particularly Kenworthy as mentioned, were fired by Tolstoyan New Testament ideals as well as socialist principles. Tolstoy had stressed the need to found a more moral conception of life based on equality, tolerance, Christian love, frugality, community of property and possessions, and physical labour close to the land. Tolstoyans also turned their back on violence and many of the laws and conventions of the capitalist state even, for the more devoted followers of the prophet, legal marriage and money.

Seeking a closer approximation to the Tolstoyan ideal of 'mutual aid' and the need to live and labour close to the land, a small band of disciples left Croydon in Autumn 1896 to found a land colony on 23 acres of land in Purleigh in Essex.[7] Though joined by Kenworthy and boosted by an influx of Tolstoyan Russian émigrés, the Purleigh Colony only survived until 1900, at which point local health authorities officially closed it following an outbreak of smallpox brought to the community by some 'tramp guests'.[8] Additional community experiments sprouted up in rural Essex around the same time, one at Mayland in 1895, Ashingdon in 1897 and Wickford in 1898.[9] The smallholding colonies at Ashingdon and Wickford displayed the usual blend of Tolstoyan anarchism and socialism. A similar blend of radical anarchism and socialism was evident in the Mayland endeavour, though here the anarchist link was to Peter Kropotkin rather than Tolstoy. Though strongly socialist in its initial aspirations, having been started up by a Manchester printer named Thomas Smith who came to socialism and communitarianism through reading Robert Blatchford, the Mayland Colony soon attracted Kropotkin's interest.[10] Kropotkin apparently found the innovative small-scale horticultural methods practised on the Colony's 11 acres to his liking, even visiting Mayland at one stage. The Mayland effort excited the interest of socialist luminaries as well. Keir Hardie visited the Colony, as did George Lansbury and Beatrice and Sydney Webb.[11]

Tolstoy was the clear inspiration, though, behind a further attempt to found the perfect community which took place further west, when a breakaway group from the Purleigh experiment set up the Whiteway Colony in August 1898. The site chosen for the Whiteway experiment comprised 41 acres of hilly ground in the Cotswolds in Gloucestershire, near the villages of Sheepscombe and Miserden.[12] The Whiteway experiment exhibited a characteristic mix of Tolstoyan Christian brotherly co-operation, primitive communism and socialism. All this joined with 'a simple childlike belief in the inherent goodness of human nature' in the words of the Whiteway stalwart Nellie Shaw.[13] The Cotswolds colonists sought to 'live a happy, idyllic life, free from carking care and the responsibility of property'.[14] For Shaw, a 'spirit of love' was 'a living force amongst us' during Whiteway's early halcyon days, 'making the joy or sorrow of one the joy or sorrow of all'.[15] There was some outbreaks of disharmony in paradise later on, however, which led to communal living and cultivation being abandoned in 1901 for a more pragmatic arrangement based on independent small-holdings.

Radical community experiments involving socialists sprang up further north as well. In the midlands, a Brotherhood Circle of Derby was established c. late 1890s under the guidance of a local notable William Loftus Hare. Influenced by Tolstoy once again, the Circle published a journal, *The Candlestick*, to spread the Tolstoyan message.[16] Not surprisingly, the north of England, parts of which had felt the full impact of the juggernaut of capitalist modernisation, hosted a number of community experiments. A few enthusiasts of the simple life founded a land colony just outside Sheffield in 1896. Norton Colony, as it was called, was inspired by the 'back-to-the land' socialist Edward Carpenter, as well as anarchism, and engaged primarily in horticultural work utilising five green-houses and a large garden.[17] Norton Colony was a short-lived commune. It wound up its affairs in 1900 when the lease on the land ran out. There was also the Brotherhood Workshop in Leeds and the Blackburn Brotherhood Colony, established in 1897 and 1899 respectively. Both of these experiments exhibited that recognisable blend of Sermon on the Mount Tolystoyan anarchism and communitarian socialism.[18] Leeds later became home to another Tolstoyan-influenced utopian community when a group established a stockings manufacturing co-operative in the Beeston district in 1904.[19] There was also the Daisy Hill Colony, founded by a group of Bolton working-class socialists in Blackpool c.1902, which was more self-consciously socialist.[20] So, too, was the Mirfield Community in Yorkshire, though here the prevailing influence was Christian socialism. Mirfield was a monastic community of socially conscious monks which grew out of Charles Gore's Oxford-based Society of the Resurrection. Moving to Yorkshire in 1887, this socialist-leaning spiritual community was once visited by Keir Hardie and hosted socialist meetings on its grounds.[21]

Further north still, we find the Starnthwaite Mills Colony in Cumbria and the Clousden Hill Free Communist and Co-operative Colony near Newcastle upon Tyne. The Starnthwaite Mills Colony was started in 1892 by the Reverend Herbert V. Mills, a Unitarian minister. Socialists came from far afield to participate in this experiment in communal living and industrial co-operation at the Starnthwaite mill and neighbouring 127-acre Browhead Farm. These included the Bristol socialists Katherine St John Conway, Dan Irving and Enid Stacy.[22] This being said, as with some of the other *fin de siècle* community experiments, socialist harmony did not always reign in the Starnthwaite Mills commonwealth. Its brief history was marred by internal disquiet when socialist colonists discovered the less-than-socialist methods and aims of the Reverend Mills. Apparently the Reverend Mills seemed intent to confine the scheme to being a substitute for the Poor Law in the form of providing self-supporting, dignified work for the unemployed, rather than engaging in an experiment to establish a full-blown socialist utopia.[23] Expulsions of dissenting socialists would be the outcome of this misunderstanding, including the Bristol socialists. The Starnthwaite Mills scheme eventually wound up in 1901. The Clousden Hill Colony, a land colony and market garden covering 20 acres on the outskirts of Newcastle leased at a rent of £60 a year, had a similar brief life-span and chequered history. More Kropotkinite anarchist than socialist, it nevertheless attracted comradely interest and support from the local ILP after its foundation in 1895. Kropotkin also visited the Colony during its early phase and was reported to be 'delighted with the immense amount of good work that the energy and determination of the colonists had accomplished'.[24] Later hit by internal dissension, the experiment floundered in 1898. Though lingering on for a further few years as the Clousden Hill Co-operative Nurseries, the Colony ceased trading in 1902.[25]

There were efforts to experience this different mode of life on a smaller scale. These efforts were usually modelled on Henry Thoreau's exercise in self-sufficiency at Walden Pond.[26] The most well known is Millthorpe, Edward Carpenter's seven-acre small-holding at Bradway just south of Sheffield. Millthorpe was quite idyllic. It was set in a secluded rural idyll composed of a cottage and three fields descending gently down to a brook and a wooded valley below. Carpenter began his experiment at 'simple living' close to the land and the elements at Millthorpe in 1883.[27] In the years that followed, Millthorpe would become a place of pilgrimage for disciples of the simple life. The socialist and one-time member of the Fellowship of the New Life, Henry Salt sought to simplify his life in accordance with Thoreau's example at Walden Pond as well. Salt retired from modernity to a cottage amidst the Surrey hills. There he found 'more than a change of residence: it was an emigration, a romance, a strange new life in some remote antipodes, where the emblems of the old servitude, such as cap and gown, found new and better uses'.[28] In Salt's secluded homestead, the former would provide shade for a young vegetable-marrow, while the latter was cut into strips so as to fasten creepers to the wall. As with Millthorpe, Salt's cottage at Tilford became a site of pilgrimage for simple life disciples.[29] Thoreau influenced the Scottish socialist Dugald Semple also. In 1909 Semple felt he had had enough of 'the close, unhealthy confinement of town life' and decided to go and live in a bell tent and dilapidated omnibus on Linwood Moss, near Paisley, a secluded spot surrounded by peat bogs and a pine wood.[30]

Mention should be made, too, of the arts and crafts colonies that appeared during the decades on either side of the *fin de siècle*. These experiments would look to William Morris for inspiration, rather than Tolstoy or Kropotkin. One such experiment was the colony of craftsmen established in the idyllic Cotswold market town of Chipping Campden in 1902 by the socialist fellow-traveller Charles Ashbee.[31] The Chipping Campden Colony survived for five years. During this time it sought, in the spirit of Morris and John Ruskin, to preserve traditional customs and ways of working, as well as beauty in workmanship. Similar efforts to uphold the spirit of craft production were started up at nearby Broad Campden shortly after the demise of the Chipping Campden Colony, with some of these networks surviving into the Great War years.[32]

How then should we interpret or understand the various radical community experiments which sprang up during the late Victorian and Edwardian era? Existing interpretations have attempted to make sense of them by reference to earlier traditions, usually utopian or English Romantic, or by reference to certain contemporary movements and influences, usually English pastoral, Ruskinian, but also anarchist.[33] The presence of these earlier traditions and influences cannot be discounted in any attempt to make sense of these community experiments. This being said, this chapter offers an alternative perspective to those currently available in the existing scholarship. It views these small-scale utopias as expressions of the new modernist politics and social life that flowered with such wonderful colour and brightness during the decades on either side of the *fin de siècle*. With their display of extraordinary richness and diversity, these radical communities are conceptualised here as 'modernist collages', wonderfully extravagant examples of that effort, so typical of modernism, to break out of conventional frameworks and reconfigure the new in novel and exciting ways. As well as being fresh and innovative, the new meanings and forms of modernism could be quite eccentric in terms of their composition. Indeed, the production of compounds of seemingly contradictory ingredients was a quintessentially modernist exercise, a by-product of modernism's attempt to imagine and knit together new modes of representation, life and politics beyond the mainstream of modernity. We have seen this mix of seemingly contradictory elements at work in other areas of socialist life and politics during the revival years, and they are also evident in the political and ideological makeup of the small-scale community experiments. Socialists rubbed shoulders with Tolstoyan religious anarchists, other 'Sermon on the Mount' Christians, atheists, anarchist followers of Kropotkin, primitive communists, more orthodox Marxists, libertarian individualists, co-operators, Theosophists, Suffragettes, disciples of Emerson, Whitman and Thoreau, vegetarians, anti-vivisectionists, anti-vaccinationists, followers of Carlyle and Ruskin, and arts and crafts enthusiasts influenced by William Morris. Take the example of some early members of the Croydon Brotherhood Church. Here could be found the former Fellowship of the New Life member, spiritual socialist and Tolstoyan anarchist J.C. Kenworthy, whom we have already met, fellow Tolstoyan Arthur St. John, G.D. Blogg 'a sturdy Social Democrat', Mary Grover a 'Theosophist, Fabian and strong Suffragist', the Scotsman David Frazer and his wife who were 'both spiritualists', the socialists Fred Muggeridge and Nellie Shaw, an ex-Salvation Army member Arthur Baker, William Swainson, a follower of the American Christian mystic and communitarian Thomas Lake Harris, and a band of émigré Russian Doukhobors, former members of a dissident sect of primitive Christian peasants banished from Russia by the Czar.[34] More generally, those who gathered in brotherly co-operation at the Croydon Brotherhood Church were said to be 'Atheists, Spiritualists, Individualists, Communists, Anarchists, ordinary politicians, Vegetarians, Anti-vivisectionists, Anti-vaccinationists – in fact, every kind of "anti-"'.[35] At these gatherings, where 'a feeling of good fellowship prevailed', the eclectic group sang hymns or 'social songs', listened to readings from the Bible, Carlyle or Emerson, joined Kenworthy in prayer or listened to the latter giving anti-capitalist political sermon from the pulpit.[36]

These radical community experiments were modernist in another sense. An important aspect of their mission was to foster a healthy alternative to the 'dysgenic living' associated with modernity. As such, these community schemes should be read as experiments in social modernism. As some astute scholars of modernism have pointed out, amongst other concerns, the modernist project was driven by the imperative to counter the debilitating effects of modernity on health and the body. Modernism saw part of its mission as finding an antidote to the disease, dirt, pollution, squalor and physical fatigue that blighted existence for so many in the modern age.[37] In so doing, modernism became preoccupied with health, cleanliness, hygiene, proper diet and the culture of the body in a more general sense. As one account of post-1918 modernism has stated, it became a goal of modernism to 'clean up, to sterilise, to reorder, to eliminate chaos and dirt'.[38] This was a regenerative project to create 'a new Eden, a clean, white world blanched of the stains of the past'.[39] This imperative, to reverse the degenerative effects of modernity on health and the body, drove early modernism as well. Increasingly by the later decades of the nineteenth century, it was felt by many that the modern age was proving unfavourable to a genuinely healthy existence. This was particularly so in regard to a seemingly ever-expanding urban environment characterised by cramped and mean slums, foul odours, an absence of light and air, and dust and fumes from factory chimneys. Wherever one ventured in 'Shantytown', a label which matched any one of a number of Britain's towns or cities during the late Victorian and Edwardian years, said the socialist activist Robert Blatchford in 1892, one was met with 'filth':

.... We see, squatted on the unclean steps, lounging against the greasy door posts, gossiping at the entrances to narrow courts, our brothers and sisters of Shantytown, unwashed, unkempt, untaught, unloved; degraded, and not ashamed. It is the City of Dreadful Day. The air is thick and greasy; the kennels and the roadway are littered and unclean; and the smell – Pah![40]

In short, the urban spaces of modernity were havens for dirt, disease and pollution, spawning a deadly and devitalised atmosphere and an impoverished mass of physically stunted proletarians with a low disease threshold who were susceptible to a variety of ailments and debilitating illnesses. For many *fin de siècle* socialists, of course, economic or material deprivation was the handmaiden of spiritual deprivation.

The experimental communes that sprang into life either side of the *fin de siècle* need to be seen then as expressions of this modernist health agenda or, more accurately, as experiments in social modernism. This would be a wide-ranging agenda for a healthier lifestyle that focused on environment, dress, diet, issues concerning sexual freedom and body culture more generally. As Roger Griffin explained it: 'The call for a vegetarian life-style, for a new relationship with the body, for sexual emancipation, for "natural remedies", for enhancing the life spirit, was deeply bound up with less philosophically reflexive, more physical longings to get "back to nature" and find an escape from the degenerative aspects of modernity epitomised in the squalor of polluted, overcrowded, dysgenic cities.'[41] All these elements were present in some form or other and to some degree in the radical colonies that we have been looking at up to now. In their choice of 'back-to-the-land' locations and stress on co-operative working close to the land, many of these communities consciously sought to 'drop out' of urban life with its ever-attendant filth and squalor. This was certainly true of the colonies at Totley, Purleigh, Mayland, Ashingdon, Wickford, Whiteway, Norton, Starnthwaite Mills and Clousden Hill, as well as smaller affairs such as Millthorpe. Even those community experiments that did not set themselves up in a rural wilderness strove to forge some connection with wholesome nature. Thus the Fellowship of the New Life 'colony' in Bloomsbury organised regular 'rustic gatherings' for its members and discoursed on the virtues of 'more wholesome, simple and honourable modes of life in closer contact with the healthy forces of nature'.[42] A belief in the health-giving properties of nature lay deep in the DNA of *fin de siècle* socialists. 'Our new religion' of socialism, proclaimed Robert Blatchford, 'claims man back to freedom from commercial and industrial vassalage; tells him that he is as much a piece of Nature as the birds of the air or the lilies of the field; that he, no more than they, can be healthy or fair, nor in anywise complete without fresh air and pure water and sunshine ... '.[43] When, in June 1892, Blatchford returned from a visit to the Starnthwaite Mills Colony in Cumbria, he enthused about the delights of 'these few acres of free England', particularly their scenic beauty and capacity to restore devitalised urban bodies to good health. Blatchford was struck, for instance, by the change in physical appearance of two young socialist colonists who had languished in the ranks of the London unemployed prior to joining the colony:

The place agrees with the two men. Moore, who was ill and weak when he left London, now looks fit and fresh. His cough has left him, and he has put on eight pounds in weight. Binfield looks every inch a countryman. He has acquired a good bronzy colour and is the picture of health.[44]

Such were the health benefits of an open-air lifestyle thought Edward Carpenter – that modern man should abandon clothes as well as the city. Each gain in the direction of discarding the garments of modern overdress for Carpenter represented 'a gain in true life – whether it be the head that goes uncovered to the air of heaven, or the feet that press bare the magnetic earth or the elementary raiment that allows through its meshes the light itself to reach the vital organs'.[45] *Fin de siècle* colonists delighted in discarding or simplifying clothing, not just to flout Victorian and Edwardian convention but also to allow health and energy to stream into the body. At Whiteway, for example, men often bared their heads, legs and feet as they went about their work. In a similar spirit of liberation, some of the women colonists at Whiteway defiantly threw off the layers of uncomfortable, unhygienic clothing, footwear and headwear demanded by bourgeois propriety and wore skirts cut short, sandals and no hats, even during visits to town.[46] For his part, Edward Carpenter went about his open-air work at Millthorpe blissfully free of the usual constraints of Victorian dress and footwear. Sandals, in particular, would become an indispensible feature of Carpenter's mode of dress. In time, and following Carpenter's pioneering example, sandal wearing became an almost standard feature of the communitarian dress code. At Norton Colony, for instance, the colonists both wore and made sandals for sale locally at three shillings per pair. Apparently, the former habit aroused much local astonishment, with some locals convinced that the sandal-wearing strangers striding through their village were 'Egyptians'.[47] According to the biographer of the sandal-wearing Henry Salt, 'the sandal was the symbol of liberation'.[48]

The body was to be liberated from unwholesome food as well as suffocating Victorian garments and footwear. Eager to embrace naturalness in its widest sense, socialist simple lifers set about reforming their diet, which for many meant the adoption of a strict vegetarian lifestyle. Vegetarianism found many eager converts among *fin de siècle* socialists seeking radical alternatives to conventional 'wisdom', including high-profile figures like Annie Besant, George

Bernard Shaw, H.G. Wells, Beatrice Webb, Katherine St John Conway, Edward Carpenter and Tom Mann for a time.[49] Robert Blatchford, too, in his best-selling *Merrie England*, endorsed the vegetarian diet.[50] The inspirations behind Letchworth Garden City, Ebenezer Howard and Raymond Unwin, both of whom moved in socialist circles, took up vegetarianism as well.[51] Letchworth itself, the abode of many a progressive socialist during these years, abounded with vegetarians, some of whom even opened a 'Simple Life Hotel' complete with a 'food reform' restaurant. Among the ranks of less well-known socialists could be found many other vegetarians, including William Jupp, Herbert Burrows, Percy Redfern, Frank Podmore, Jim Joynes, Dugald Semple and John Bruce Wallace. Another was Henry Salt, whom we met above. The simple-lifer Salt was extremely vocal in advocating a vegetarian lifestyle. This included launching and editing a periodical entitled *Humanity* in 1895, which promoted the merits of a changed diet. For Salt, and indeed other socialist vegetarians, advocating a vegetarian diet was but a short step to championing the rights of animals. In any advance towards a genuine civilisation, he argued, following Tolstoy, the ending of the butchery of animals must be the 'first step'.[52] Salt gave forceful expression to these beliefs in his book *Animals' Rights*, which was published in 1892.[53] The benefits of a vegetarian diet were many, according to its socialist advocates, embracing both the body and character. John Bruce Wallace of the communitarian Brotherhood Church thought a vegetarian diet to be 'more favourable to calmness of mind, mildness of character, and purity of morals'.[54] Long-standing vegetarians were also, for Wallace, more resistant to rheumatism, fevers and wounds 'of every sort', and 'better fit both for bodily and mental effort' than 'flesh-eaters'.[55] A vegetarian diet was also more economical than a meat-eating diet and, most tellingly, 'it was the diet of un-fallen man in Eden'.[56]

It should not surprise us given their predilection for a healthy way of life that those abiding in the wider colony network favoured a reformed diet. Nellie Shaw has left us with a detailed description of the type of food consumed by the Whiteway colonists:

> With respect to our food, most of us are vegetarians – some from principle, all from necessity. We live simply and economically. Bread and a little butter, porridge and tea or cocoa for breakfast; beans, lentils, or some other pulse, cooked with onions and potatoes are the chief dishes at dinner time, varied occasionally with rice, rhubarb, or wholemeal pudding, or bread and cheese.[57]

As well as choosing a clean diet, colonists sought self-sufficiency in food and sold vegetable produce to local markets and other interested parties. The Clousden Hill colonists, for instance, sold produce to the Sunderland and Newcastle Co-operatives.[58] We have a description of the efforts of the Clousden Hill colonists to pursue healthy ways. The socialist Henry Nevinson recalled a visit he made to the Colony when he compiled a list of the produce growing on the farm. Included on Nevinson's list were 'leeks, cabbages, rhubarb, celery, strawberries, roses, pansies, and mushrooms'.[59] Also in livestock, noted Nevinson, 'about 100 chickens, 20 ducks, 3 cows, 6 goats, 2 horses, [and] some rabbits, a dog, one woman, and three children'.[60] Right living also meant insulating the body from the pollutants of cigarette smoke and alcohol. Colonists tended to consciously abstain from both practices. Alcohol was particularly abhorred, both within the colonies and the wider socialist movement. John Bruce Wallace's Brotherhood movement, for instance, campaigned to prevent the working classes from 'brutalising themselves with alcohol', while one ILP member thought that 'drunkenness keeps back socialism'.[61]

These small-scale utopian efforts at alternative living were deeply modernist in other ways. With the adoption of a more natural way of life came the improvement in the health of the body but also something deeper and more fundamental, namely the prospect of a genuine rebirth of the spirit that would come from reconnecting to sources of well-being which distinguished life in an earlier, pre-modern age. Through exposure to a more natural way of life, it was believed that the body, soul, nature and the great cosmos would achieve a more intimate balance, enabling the individual to experience a degree of contentment unknown to those mired in the decadence of the modern age. Attaining this higher life of intimate balance between body, spirit, the natural world and the cosmos would thus bring a fundamental re-ordering of life based on a greater degree of insight into the true nature of 'Being'. There would be a reconnection to those lost sources of physical and spiritual health that characterised 'Being' in the age before modernity when, as Roger Griffin put it, 'the firmament was still solid, where the cosmic order was intact, where Gods were near, where harmony, rootedness, and physical health reigned, where human beings lived in a harmonious state of being, rather than in the permanent exile of existence'.[62] The simple life advocate and cosmological socialist Edward Carpenter urged others to reach out for this more transcendental conception of life:

> The life of the open air, familiarity with the wind, and waves,
> clean and pure food, the companionship of the animals – the
> very wrestling with the great Mother for his food – all these things
> will tend to restore that relationship which man has so long dis-
> owned; and the constant in-streaming of energy into his system
> will carry him to perfections of health and radiance of being at
> present unsuspected.[63]

The mental and physical 'system' of Joseph Burtt was certainly
infused with an inner radiance during his spell at Whiteway Colony
between 1898 and 1899. We colonists said Burtt, 'felt we were gods.
After a few months at Whiteway my mind and body seemed to
be created anew.'[64] These feelings of rebirth into new, higher states
of 'Being' were not uncommon. The socialist simple-lifer Dugald
Semple, reflecting on his decision to abandon the towns and reach
out for new, more meaningful life in touch with the elements and
the cosmos, stated that 'I envy no man his wealth for I have been
granted a vision of the soul.'[65]

There was a further element of modernism at work in the outbreak of community-building that took place during the decades on
either side of the *fin de siècle*. Those who went in search of new life in
these years were fleeing from more than just the dirt, pollution and
dysgenic living they identified with the cities and towns of the modern age. They were also seeking to escape from the confinements of
mainstream spatial structures and the particular spatial experiences
associated with life under conditions of modernisation–modernity.
In so doing, they sought to imagine alternative conceptions of space
and forge new arrangements of space beyond the dominant spatial
framework of capitalist modernity. We should note as well that socialist communitarians were not alone in this endeavour. As we shall see
in Chapter 5, the impulse to break free of mainstream space could be
observed in other areas of the socialist revival. It surfaced as well in
the articulations of rival socialist space which featured in some of the
utopian socialist writing of this period. It is to this issue, the urge to
go beyond mainstream space and forge and imagine an alternative
socialist space, that we shall now turn.

5
Contesting Abstract Space

This book has sought to demonstrate an affinity between modernism and the socialist revival. Up to now, however, this relationship has been considered mainly in terms of time. But, as touched on in previous chapters, the experience of modernisation–modernity concerned space as well as time. This was a quite specific experience of space, as we shall see. Modernism, too, was keenly interested in the question of space. As David Harvey tells us, 'modernism takes as one of its missions the production of new meanings for space and time in a world of ephemerality and fragmentation'.[1] This modernist impulse to break out of mainstream spatial structures and explore new meanings for space beyond the maelstrom unleashed by the dynamic of capitalist modernisation was evident in a number of areas of the socialist revival, not least in the radical community schemes we looked at in Chapter 4. In seeking to realise their utopian desire to craft a better life, *fin de siècle* socialists made the bold decision to step out of the confinements of capitalist space and forge a new type of space, one which would have a very different profile and atmosphere to the mode of space they had experienced in mainstream modern life. We can also obtain some further sense of the nature of socialist space by considering those articulations of alternative socialist space which emerged from the utopian imagination of *fin de siècle* socialists. Before we turn to look at the spatial arrangements within the socialist community experiments, as well as those speculations on space which sprang from socialist utopian thinking, we need to consider the nature of the spatial environment which contemporary socialists were turning their backs on. This was the space produced by the processes of modernisation and modernity and the restless vigour of the dominant capitalist mode of production. This space tended to dominate life in the mainstream and had its own quite unique dynamic and profile.

The material processes of modernisation had generated enormous momentum by the *fin de siècle*. This extraordinary dynamism had much to do with the Enlightenment conception of progress, modernity's Faustian urgency to 'creatively' destroy the present in the name of a supposedly better future and the momentum generated by industrialisation, new technologies and the expansion of the bureaucratic nation-state. Add to this, the restless vitality of the capitalist mode of production during the eighteenth and nineteenth centuries which ensured that the modernisation process was propelled along at a frenetic pace. These developments and cumulative pressures would have tremendous implications for space, not least because they would involve new attitudes towards space and the production of new meanings and forms of space. Before we consider the new modern space, it is important to stress that this chapter rejects the notion of 'absolute space', namely those interpretations which view space as a neutral background, even an empty void, somehow outside of human behaviour and against which human action is played out. Rather, space is 'socially produced', the outcome of certain quite complex processes and interactions in the social and human realm. Put another way, in this 'relational' notion of space, the 'articulation of inter-relations brings space into being'.[2] Or, in a similar vein, as Durkheim stressed in *The Elementary Forms of Religious Life* (1915), space needs to be seen as a social construct.[3]

As for the new space of modernisation–modernity, it comprised a quite distinct system of space and spatiality. Zygmunt Bauman contends that 'modernity was born under the stars of acceleration and land conquest'.[4] In other words, the space of modernisation–modernity was aggressively imperialistic. In the era of 'heavy modernity', as Bauman puts it, the era of eighteenth-, nineteenth- and early twentieth-century modernity, the acquisition of territory was 'among the most compulsive of modern urges'.[5] This involved a mindset where empty space became 'a challenge to action and a reproach to idlers'.[6] As well as moving to 'fill the void' in the globe's many uncharted 'blank spots', the space of modernisation–modernity sought dominion over the previously existing spaces of pre-modern 'modes of production'. In this parallel expansionist agenda, modern space set out to appropriate the vast tracts of what had hitherto been the 'natural space' of the pre-modern world focused on nature, the village and the town. Indeed, the success and effectiveness of the emerging capitalist civilisation which was driving the modernisation process necessitated the requisition and regulating of vast expanses of 'natural space' in the interests of consolidating the new economic and institutional arrangements. Highly efficient spatial mapping and organisation would be crucial to the exercise of control over these large areas of appropriated space, as well as to the maintenance of the power of new elites, capitalist wealth and the successful reproduction of the new system.[7] This spatial project had an extensive reach. Within national borders, a process which unfolded in Britain during the eighteenth and nineteenth centuries, regions and locales that comprised of stretches of natural space of varying size became increasingly integrated into national networks of economic, technological, bureaucratic and political organisation.[8] Even more significantly, by the closing decades of the nineteenth century the space of modernisation–modernity acquired an increasingly transnational, if not yet global, character. A key driver here was the increasingly feverish capitalist urge for accumulation. Stimulated by the need to maintain the fast turnover of capital, profit levels and an edge in competitive markets, and facilitated by the development of new information, transportation and scientific technologies, the new transnational system would preside over a seemingly ever-increasing flow of resources, goods, money, information, ideas and people across national spatial borders, which left few geographical regions and locales of the world untouched.

There was another important consequence to note. As it proceeded to swallow up vast expanses of 'backward' global space and pre-modern natural space, a project of spatial stretching across and within national boundaries, modern space contrived to erase spatial difference, to render space homogenous. This process was portended in that tendency within the Enlightenment conception and treatment of space to convert the confused, 'free flow of human experience and practice' into rationalised totalising spatial configurations.[9] As the juggernaut of modernisation–modernity picked up pace during the nineteenth century, the erasure of spatial difference became more pronounced. The 'abstract space' of capitalism in the words of Henri Lefebvre, that all-encompassing space driven by the urge for accumulation, integrated markets and infinite growth, worked to either completely dissolve or break up hitherto established 'natural space' focused on nature, the village and the town, or press it into the service of the new way to things.[10] Or, to put it more starkly, abstract space, 'which is the tool of domination, asphyxiates whatever is con- ceived within it'.[11] In any case, as it set about becoming a world-wide system, modern capitalist space tended towards the elimination or 'flattening out' of previously existing spaces, spatial practices and codes of spatial representation, those supposedly primitive, irrational or 'backward' spatial forms that defined and gave meaning to the pre-modern world before the new 'gods' of reason and science estab- lished their domination. In this sense, modern space was a secular or de-spiritualising space which, as it proceeded to commodify space as private property or lots, worked to ruthlessly expunge the traditional gods and spirits associated with *place* from its space.[12]

In a similar vein, Doreen Massey has spoken of the dominant 'grand narrative' of modernity that was reluctant to acknowledge spa- tial multiplicity, that is, acknowledge the co-existing spatial hetero- geneity which characterised the real nature of space in the world.[13] There was a temporal dimension to the totalising spatial project of modernity for Massey. Spatial difference collapsed into a single pathway, such as in the narrative of 'progress' or the narrative of 'modernisation', whereby different spaces were interpreted as differ- ent stages in 'a single temporal development'. The consequence of this discursive manoeuvre was to view co-existing spatial difference in terms of a 'historical queue', with the dominant space of Western capitalist modernity defined as 'advanced', other spaces or 'places' being seen as lagging behind or even 'backward'.[14] Groups of people, as with those who favoured a nomadic way of life, could also fall victim to this discursive manoeuvre, as Zygmunt Bauman informs us. The 'chronopolitics' of modernity placed nomadic peoples 'not just as inferior and primitive beings, "underdeveloped", but also as backward and "behind time" ...'.[15] The space of modernity, then, was never innocent of power relations. As a container of power, the new space harboured within it hierarchical relations of domi- nation and subordination and worked to reproduce these unequal relations through its various spatial practices and codes, often in quite subtle ways.

Power relations were evident as well in a further trait of the space of modernisation–modernity. The ever-more sophisticated commu- nications and transportation networks that were propelling the raw materials, goods, information, knowledge, people and money across national borders at an ever faster pace by the *fin de siècle* seemed to make the world shrink, as once far-distant locations became inte- grated into what was fast becoming a single world system. With the local, along with the individuals who inhabited these local 'places', becoming more and more entwined in these intricate transnational highways of trade, finance, knowledge, information and culture, they became subjected to distant influences and forms of control which were often oppressive. Moreover, these 'distanciated' networks of control at a distance by 'absent others' as Anthony Giddens put it, usually faceless capitalist elites or the anonymous institutions of the modern bureaucratic state, brought new developments in our sense of space and time, not least in the experience and perception of 'here and now'.[16] As explained by some scholars of modernity and space, with modernity's arrival 'our experience of here and now has increasingly lost its immediate spatiotemporal referents and has become tied to and contingent on actors and actions at a distance. The experiential here and now of modernity is thus in a real sense nowhere yet everywhere.'[17] We could extend this observation on modernity by saying that with its arrival power was in a real sense nowhere yet everywhere.

This notion of the space of modernity as a container of not just power but decentred power, power as being everywhere yet nowhere, is most evident in the insights provided by Michel Foucault on the nature of space and power under conditions of modernity. With Foucault, we are made aware of the way modernity generates new spaces, spatial mechanisms and spatial representations or 'discursive' spaces, which together act to 'discipline' and control human bodies. Foucault's thinking on discipline certainly has relevance in terms of those seeking to flee from the oppressive spaces of capitalism in *fin de siècle* Britain. Moving from the military, the asylums and prisons, these spatial frameworks and their associated disciplinary techniques became embedded in the architectural design of the workshops and factories of capitalism and proletarian housing estates, as well as the schools which functioned to reproduce the habits, behaviours and mental outlooks required by the wider system. What was being formed for Foucault 'was a policy of coercions that act upon the body, a calculated manipulation of its elements, its gestures, its behaviour. The human body was entering a machinery of power that explores it, breaks it down and rearranges it. A "political anatomy", which was also a "mechanics of power", was being born.'[18] Foucault contends that modern disciplinary power did not have an obvious centre or locus, such as a centralised state apparatus. In other words, it should not be viewed as a secondary emanation from a single, primary source or cause. Rather, modern disciplinary power operated through a plurality of physical spaces, spatial arrangements and discursive spaces which, nevertheless, still served the aim of the modern state to control the population in order to maximise productivity. In this manner, detached from any primary point, modern power was implicit or 'immanent' in the constitution and operation of a range of disciplinary machineries and discourses which diffused through the entire social and institutional structure established by modernisation–modernity. Disciplinary power was indeed everywhere and nowhere under conditions of modernity. It was exercised almost automatically, via a coercion that was impersonal and often imperceptible, resulting in a spatialised mode of social control of 'docile' subjects that was both subtle and highly sophisticated. In other words, it was achieved through the positioning of the individual in physical space, a hierarchical distribution of the subject within an arrangement of unequal spatial relations, a meticulous regulation of bodily movements even down to movement and gesture, and the operation of a plurality of techniques of control lodged in the various institutional sites, fields of 'official knowledge' and discursive practices of the modern state.

The modern era also had its own characteristic spatial profile. According to Henri Lefebvre, every emerging civilisation or 'mode of production' is obliged to produce a space, 'its own space'. This entails the production of a set of spatial practices and codes of spatial representation appropriate to the new way of things or 'system'. Lefebvre constructs a threefold conceptual framework to explain the process whereby a civilisation or mode of production works to produce these spatial practices and codes. At one level are the 'representations of space', which refer to the dominant space in society, the mode of space which is most closely connected to the centres of power in society. It is the space most expressive of the mode and relations of production and 'the "order" which those relations impose'.[19] It is therefore hegemonic and subsumes the dominant forms of knowledge and ideology in its assumptions, signs, codes and practices. This is the 'conceived' space of professionals, planners and others tied to the dominant order, which includes cartographers, geographers, engineers, architects, developers and other agents of the system. Then we have the 'spatial practices', which emit or 'secrete' the dominant civilisation's space. This is the popular or commonsensical 'perceived' space of everyday social life. Finally, there are the 'representational spaces'.[20] These are the 'lived' spaces of the imagination, which are often consumed by official 'conceived' space and taken-for-granted 'perceived' space, but nevertheless do have the potential to creatively transcend 'conceived' space and 'perceived' space and even reconfigure these spaces in different ways. Needless to say, this third space in Lefebvre's threefold conceptual framework has the potential to be the most radical of spaces and thus has particular relevance for our study of space and spatial conflicts during the socialist revival years.

It needs to be stressed as well that each aspect in Lefebvre's conceptual triad is in a dialectical relationship with the other two. Thus the Middle Ages, for example, in producing its own quite distinct space would feature all the three aspects of space in a dialectical embrace. There were the medieval representations of space, dominated by the conception of 'a fixed sphere within a finite space' comprised of the Earth, the 'fires of hell' below that and the luminous Cosmos inhabited by God, Heaven, the angels, the fixed stars and the 'radiant Glory of the Trinity' occupying the upper half of the sphere. Then we had the 'representational spaces' of the Middle Ages, which tended to be creative interpretations of cosmological representations, as with the major pilgrimage road to Santiago de Compostela which equated to the Milky Way 'that led from Cancer to Capricorn on the vault of heaven'.[21] Spatial practice in the Middle Ages, for its part, included these great pilgrims' ways, as well as crusaders' roads and the networks of local lanes close to manors, monasteries, cathedrals, castles and peasant communities.

As for the spatial practices associated with the modern era, or more specifically the modern era as it had developed up to the decades either side of the *fin de siècle*, they were appropriate to the dominant social order and generally conformed to the conceptions of space, or 'representations of space', associated with the various professional planners, architects and social engineers working on behalf of the system. These 'perceived' spatial practices included the growing complex of financial institutions, commercial centres, industrial plants, office and workshop complexes, and an evolving education system, all of which were supported by an extensive physical infrastructure and communication network which included railways, roads, sea lanes and telegraph systems. Add to this, of course, that quite distinctive spatial arrangement spawned by the advance of modernisation and modernity and the needs and purposes of capitalist political economy, the city. With its increasingly spatially segregated enclaves of homogenous zones, functions and activities, serving to differentiate private from public, rich from poor, residential area from 'shantytown', inner commercial from outer suburb, the modern city could be the very antithesis of community and a healthy existence for many. In other words, the city could be the locus of anonymity, detachment, loneliness, withdrawal, disconnections, isolation, seclusion, fear and even mental illness.[22]

How then to develop a socialist spatial response to a rapidly changing world increasingly dominated by the oppressive 'abstract' space associated with capitalism and the dynamic of modernisation–modernity? Indeed, what were the prospects of articulating an authentic socialist spatial response in the face of the aggressively homogenising tendencies of modern space, a space that seemed intent on 'papering over all differences' and refusing to embrace or even acknowledge spatial heterogeneity? Additionally, even if circumstances permitted the production and co-presence of socialist space, what would this space look like? Also, what would be the relationship of this space to modernism? We will now turn to consider such questions.

It is important at this stage in our analysis to emphasise that modern space, despite its best efforts to appropriate 'other' spaces and fashion them according to its agenda, was open to contestation by rival conceptions and arrangements of space. As Henri Lefebvre points out, abstract modern space was never free of spatial 'contradictions'. These contradictions, moreover, had the potential to expose cracks in the fabric of the dominant space, openings which could then be filled by alternative conceptions of space and even rival counter-spaces of a quite radical nature. The co-presence of these contradictions in abstract space could be accounted for by the need of the system, with its 'flows' of capital, resources, commodities and information, to *ground itself* in specific locations of production and consumption if it was to successfully maintain and reproduce itself. In other words, the system of modern capitalism was never wholly or simply a 'flow' somehow detached from social interactions and determinations and, indeed, everyday life. There is then this paradigmatic opposition 'between exchange and use, between global networks and the determinate locations of production and consumption', which render modern capitalist space, paradoxically or dialectically, 'both *abstract* and *concrete* in character'.[23] It is a space which is 'abstract inasmuch as it has no existence save by virtue of the exchange-ability of all its component parts, and concrete inasmuch as it is socially real and as such localised. This is a space, therefore, that is *homogenous yet at the same time broken up into fragments*.'[24]

A number of observations relevant to our analysis follow from the above. Firstly, that the dominant mode of modern space was contradictory and thus vulnerable to contestation by those promoting rival conceptions and arrangements of space. Secondly, we should recognise the important role played by *places* in this friction. 'This conflict,' according to one scholar, 'arises from the inextricable tension between the usage and appropriation of place for social purposes and the domination of place (and space) as a productive and commercial force through private ownership.'[25] Thirdly, if we accept the proposition that modern spatiality could never wholly free itself from place-bound contradictions which were intrinsic to the system's need to maintain and reproduce itself, then it is reasonable to assume that these points of tension or contradictions could become even more acute during phases of rapid and marked social and structural change. As David Harvey points out, 'during *phases of maximal change*, the *spatial* and temporal bases for reproduction of the social order are subject to the *severest disruptions* [my emphases] ... and it is exactly at such moments that major shifts in systems of representations, cultural forms, and philosophical sentiment occur'.[26] To this, we should add that at such moments the dominant system of space is subjected to more intense scrutiny and challenge and there is increased scope for the emergence of other, possible, more radical conceptions and renderings of space. Stephen Kern recognised as much when he stated that the 'moment' of 1880–1918 was one of profound change caused by sweeping transformations in technology which shattered older forms of perception and understanding of time and space. In relation to the latter, new ideas about the nature of space challenged the traditional view that there was but one single space that was continuous and homogenous with properties which conformed to the axioms and postulates of Euclidean geometry.[27] Instead, the taken-for-granted assumptions of Euclidean space were challenged by those who viewed and depicted space as heterogeneous. These dissenters included artists, as with Cézanne, who helped to break up the uniform perspectival space that had dominated painting since the Renaissance when he painted objects as seen from several perspectives, and the Cubists who 'painted objects in a multiplicity of spaces from multiple perspectives'.[28]

In terms of our concerns in this chapter, another such phase of dramatic change, which overlaps to a significant degree with Stephen Kern's turbulent decades of 1880–1918, was the 'over-determined' moment of the late Victorian and Edwardian era. We have referred to this conjuncture in previous chapters but, briefly, it comprised a set of circumstances which included the social distress and shock to Victorian self-confidence arising from the protracted economic slump of c.1873–c.1896; the challenge to dominant paradigms of Victorian knowledge coming from innovations in fields like psychology and science; the major technological and economic restructuring entailed by the so-called Second Industrial Revolution; the stirring of powerful movements clamouring for social justice and political change; and the dawning of the *fin de siècle* which seemed to engender an almost apocalyptic conviction that the old 'corrupt' world of Victorian 'progress' had reached an impasse and was about to give way to a new, more egalitarian, less materialistic future. The injection of these supplementary 'conjunctural' elements, which hit almost simultaneously, into the mix of developments coming from more transnational and 'distanciated' networks of capitalist modernisation would expose the dominant spatial framework in late Victorian and Edwardian Britain to increased pressures and open up new possibilities for the production of rival conceptions and orderings of space. Britain's socialists would be at the forefront of these challenges to the dominant spatial order during these turbulent decades. Moreover, as well as recognising this spatial element within the socialist revival, we need to acknowledge the presence of a modernist component within the socialist spatial project. It is to these matters that we will now turn.

The most obvious expression of a rival socialist space to that of the dominant capitalist spatial framework during the revival years were those radical community experiments that we looked at in some detail in Chapter 4. As we saw in that chapter, the turbulent decades of the late Victorian and Edwardian era brought forth a glut of community schemes of varying shapes, sizes and duration. We identified the modernist component in these experiments, not least in the extraordinary eclecticism they exhibited in terms of their ideological makeup and the range of influences they drew upon. The attempt by these communities to break out of the narrow, conventional lifestyle frameworks of the Victorian age and craft a new mode of life beyond the mainstream of modernity was read as an expression of modernism as well. This was particularly the case in their social modernist attempt to forge an alternative, healthier way of life to the 'dysgenic living' associated with modernity. These community settlements need to be interpreted as expressions of modernism in another sense, in that they represented an effort to break free of the spatial framework of modernisation–modernity and reconfigure new modes of space beyond the mainstream. In their efforts to burst out of the confines of abstract homogenous modern space, socialist communitarians would champion the cause of spatial heterogeneity and proclaim the virtue of 'differential space'. The setting up of these differential counter-spaces represented an effort to liberate patches of space from the dense national and transnational networks of modern mainstream space and the disciplinary frameworks embedded in modern capitalist spatial practices. As such, these socialist efforts to re-appropriate segments of space exposed spatial contradictions within contemporary modernity and highlighted the presence of radically different conceptions of space in late Victorian and Edwardian society.

These alternative counter-spaces which appeared on the fringes of the prevailing homogenised spatial realm were modernist in a further sense. They were *place-bound* arrangements, which were firmly rooted in localised circumstances. With modernism, particularly social and political variants of modernism, place was to gain a new standing, giving rise to a more place-bound politics in a world being dramatically reshaped and homogenised by the abstract spatial flows of modern capitalism and the juggernaut of modernisation–modernity. As David Harvey informs us, in a development which had become quite marked by the late nineteenth century in many European countries experiencing modernisation, 'the identity of place was reaffirmed in the midst of the growing abstractions of space'.[29] Against this background of rapidly accelerating change, modernism would seek to explore 'the dialectic of place versus space' in numerous ways.[30]

As for the makeup of this differential socialist place–space, it had a number of identifiable characteristics. The allocation and arrangement of space in these community schemes aimed to be non-hierachical and egalitarian. Dwellings and living and working conditions for members of the communes tended to be uniform and equal. With the majority of these settlements, property was held in common. Thus, within the Totley Colony near Sheffield there was no private property, 'except in wives'.[31] The repudiation of the private ownership of space was sometimes affirmed through symbolism and ritual. On acquiring the Whiteway smallholding in the Cotswolds, the new collective owners proclaimed in a solemn evening ritual that the newly acquired land would never again be privately owned before proceeding to burn the legal deeds to the property because, as one of the pioneer colonists explained it, they wished the new acquisition 'to be at the service of anyone who desired to use it productively'.[32] In a similar egalitarian spirit, the layout of the alternative communities was spatially arranged to encourage community and social interaction. In terms of the physical layout and boundaries of the communes, they aimed at the creation of an open, accessible and collective space. In some colonies, as at Wickford Colony, there were no partitions or fences, and passage between dwellings and other areas within the commune was generally open and free.[33] The non-hierachical egalitarian spaces of the alternative communities also, of course, facilitated equality and co-operation in the realm of work and production.

These egalitarian spaces also helped facilitate the emergence of new freedoms relating to the body. As we saw above, and taking our cue from Foucault, the logic of modernity generated new spaces, spatial mechanisms and 'discursive' spaces, which together acted to 'discipline' human bodies. Subtle disciplinary procedures, which helped to regulate bodies in accordance with the requirements of the 'system', were lodged in the very arteries of modern capitalist space. This was as true for the built environment, as well as in the various discursive practices or fields of 'official truth' issuing from the modern state. Within the alternative egalitarian space of the radical community, however, the body moved relatively freely in an environment almost completely devoid of formal authority and rules. This was certainly the case at the colonies at Purleigh, Wickford, Clousden Hill, Norton, and Whiteway in its early 'communist' phase, and the Brotherhood Workshop in Leeds. As a Purleigh colonist stated: 'We have no rules. Each one is left to do as he or she likes, held in check only by one's good sense and the general opinion of comrades.'[34] With some communitarians, there was also a cheerful irreverence towards formal rules relating to personal relationships between the sexes. At Whiteway, for example, particularly in its earlier days, some colonists would adopt a quite bohemian attitude towards sexual relationships, with some couples deliberately flouting the 'bourgeois' marriage convention by entering a 'free union' arrangement.[35] Within their utopian space, colonists also tried to free the body from the normal conventions associated with capitalist time and establish new relationships to time. At Clousden Hill Colony, for instance, there was no specified number of hours for a working day, and nor were there any wages to regulate hours and labour.[36] Clousden Hill Colony was not alone in seeking to dispense with money, the arch embodiment of distanciated networks of capitalist control. Colonists at Whiteway, the Leeds Brotherhood Workshop and the Blackburn Brotherhood also abandoned money in their pursuit of a life free of commodity production, exchange and all commercial fetters.

These alternative settlements were also spatially constructed and arranged to encourage greater interaction with nature. The majority were deliberately set up in rural surroundings, such as those at Purleigh, Mayland, Ashingdon, Wickford, Whiteway, Norton, Millthorpe, Starnthwaite Mills and Clousden Hill. Furthermore, within the settlement itself, the emphasis on becoming self-sufficient in food ensured that the physical separation between home and work close to the land was negligible and this served to enhance the emotional bond between members of the colony and the natural surroundings. This attempt to bond with nature and the great cosmos was often reflected in the particular spatial architecture of settlement dwellings. Dwellings were usually of modest, wooden construction with work doors and windows deliberately open to the elements. Light, air and sun would stream into these living spaces, blurring the distinction between the inside and the outside, or between interior space and exterior space. In a similar modernist spirit of breaking down the distinction between inside space and outside space, colonists would usually take meals and wash clothes and bodies out of doors. There was always a collective spirit to these outdoor activities. Meals were usually taken communally, while some colonists even favoured communal or 'mixed bathing' in the outdoors.[37] There was a similar blurring of the inside and the outside with sleeping arrangements. Some dwelling places in the communes would have wide verandas often used for open-air sleeping, while Nellie Shaw informs us that at Whiteway some male colonists had taken to sleeping out of doors.[38]

If there was a spatial architecture expressive of that simple, open-air life favoured by colonists, there was also a spatial architecture of the simple life in a more general sense. We can see this in the interior of the settlement dwellings. As Julia Twigg has pointed out, simple-life socialists and others fleeing the pressures of modernity would promote a rival aesthetic of interior space to that of the High Victorian interior favoured by the Victorian and Edwardian middle- and upper middle class.[39] In the privatised space of the latter, one would find an over-abundance of heavy furniture, decoration and furnishings, and private accumulations of luxury or mass-produced objects or ornaments. Heavy draped curtains added to the sombre atmosphere of

the Victorian and Edwardian bourgeois interior space, enabling, in
contrast to simple-life interior space, the inside to be isolated from
the outside.[40] The alternative aesthetic of interior space promoted by
simple-life socialists, on the other hand, eschewed the excessive furnishings, ornamentation and 'knick-knack' clutter of the bourgeois
villa. Instead, there was no such over-crowding in their homesteads,
while such furniture that did feature tended to reflect the principles
of William Morris and other Arts and Crafts enthusiasts. In its later
phase, for instance, when its philosophical outlook had passed from
'communism' to a form of 'mild socialism', Whiteway Colony was
blessed by the presence of the wood craftsman Fred Foster. Foster was
described as a 'true successor to the school of William Morris' and
supported the Colony by making 'beautifully finished' simple-life furniture for colonists' dwellings.[41] There was a further aspect to the
spatial architecture of settlement dwellings. The naming of homes
would reinforce simple-life principles and enable colonists to invest
meaning in the portion of space they had emancipated from the
domain of 'abstract' modern space and the networks of capitalist spatialisation. As Tim Cresswell informs us, 'naming is one of the ways
space can be given meaning and become place'.[42] Thus, two of the
homes at Ashingdon Colony in Essex were named 'Brotherhood Cottage' and 'Walden', the latter, of course, named after Henry Thoreau's
pioneering experiment in simple living at Walden Pond.[43] Again, we
can discern the modernist component in these various efforts on the
part of colonists to invest their portion of space in meaning. Naming
activities of the type just described, and other such attempts to make
home and surroundings more meaningful by associating them with
simple-life values, helped to ground personal and communal identity
in a world rapidly being transformed by the abstract spatial and temporal flows of capitalist modernisation. This search to find anchorage
and value through a sense of emotional belonging to a meaningful
place, rather than be cast adrift in the perpetual turbulence of a world
undergoing momentous change, was one of the aims of modernism
according to David Harvey.[44]

The radical community experiments were not the only expressions of socialist space during the late Victorian and Edwardian
decades of course, though they were, arguably, the most important. Restrictions on words mean that we are unable to explore
all aspects of the spatial politics of the socialist movement during
the revival years in this chapter. We should conclude this chapter,
though, by looking at another articulation of socialist space during

this period. These were those representations of 'alternative' social-ist space which were expressed through the utopian imagination of *fin de siècle* socialists. The socialism of the revival years, as we have seen in a previous chapter, was saturated with utopian thinking.[45] Utopianism tends to thrive at moments of volatility, when there is heightened expectancy that the times are poised on the brink of radical change. Late Victorian and Edwardian Britain, with its com-bustible mix of economic, technological and social developments, as mentioned above, was certainly one such moment. These decades provided a context highly productive of utopian visions of a social-ist future that was more egalitarian and spiritually fulfilling. These visions invariably contained some reference to the way that space would be configured in a future socialist environment and thus tell us a little more about the makeup of socialist space. Before we look at these renderings of socialist space that appeared in the imagination, it is important to mention the relationship between these imaginary articulations of space and modernism. The impulse to dream, to fan-tasise about experiences and worlds beyond the maelstrom unleashed by modernisation, was intrinsic to the modernist project. As well as providing a resting place or sanctuary seemingly outside the rush of modern life and time, the space of the utopian imagination could also offer up pleasurable visions of more fulfilled life beyond that offered by the dominant grand narrative of modernity or 'progress'. Henri Lefebvre, for his part, recognised the vital role played by 'con-ceptions of space that tend to form in dreams, in imaginings, in utopias', as well as in fantasy, literature and strands of artistic mod-ernism as with Dada and Surrealism, in challenging the hegemony of abstract modern space.[46]

These conceptions of socialist space forged in the imagination, or socialist 'representational spaces' in the language of Lefebvre, shared some characteristics with those arrangements of socialist space which materialised in the colony schemes. Simple-life and nature themes were again in evidence. As he speculated on the architecture of the higher life of the future, Edward Carpenter saw a vision of dwelling places 'so simple and elemental in character that they will fit in the nooks of the hills or along the banks of the streams or by the edges of the woods without disturbing the harmony of the land-scape or the songs of the birds'.[47] As with the counter-spaces of the community experiments, these imaginary socialist spaces would be egalitarian and accessible. Thus Carpenter's dwellings would sit in a truly collective and open space, a space so accessible to all that even the gardens would be welcome to the 'sacred and unharmed animals'.[48]

There is a strong aesthetic dimension to these conceptions of socialist space forged in the utopian imagination. Carpenter's space would be graced by beautiful Temples and 'Common Halls' and meeting places for dances, games and feasts attached to every settlement.[49] The aesthetic component was even stronger in the socialist spaces of the future imagined by Carpenter's socialist contemporary Robert Blatchford. In *Dismal England*, which was published in 1899, he wrote of 'the endless vistas of shadowy architectural ugliness' in the proletarian spaces of London's East End, with 'the hideous piles of model dwellings springing up from the sloppy pavements like goblin cliffs – their upper storeys swallowed in the towering cloud of smoke and fog'.[50] A similar lack of beauty characterised the spaces inhabited by proletarians in the industrial districts of the west Midlands. On visiting Cradley Heath and neighbouring districts, for example, Blatchford was met with a spatial environment which contained:

> no newsroom nor free library, nor even a concert-hall or gymnasium. There is no cricket-ground, no assembly room, no public bath, nor public park, nor public garden. Throughout all that sordid, dolorous region I saw not so much as one tree, or flower-bed, or fountain. Nothing bright or fair on which to rest the eye.[51]

A few years earlier and in a similar vein, in his best-selling socialist tract *Merrie England*, Blatchford wrote of the mean look and allocation of space in proletarian districts and abodes in Manchester. As with the East End and Cradley Heath, the houses in these districts were 'very ugly and mean', the streets were 'too narrow' and there were no gardens or trees to beautify the depressing scene.[52] Even the home of the more fortunate artisan in Manchester was 'badly arranged and badly fitted'. These artisan dwellings had rooms that were 'much too small' and windows 'that were not big enough', all of which resulted in 'a painful dearth of light and air'.[53] Proletarian homes in Manchester were further impoverished by a shortage of bedrooms and a lack of suitable spaces to maintain decent standards of hygiene. No surprise then that when Blatchford indulged in utopian fantasies about space in a future socialist environment he made sure that Britain's proletarians moved in a more spacious, gracious and beautiful world.

In his utopian vision of the 'Merrie England' of the future, Blatchford's socialist towns would be blessed with wide streets, fountains, avenues of trees, public theatres, public baths, gymnasiums, cricket fields, public halls and gardens for recreation, music and refreshment.[54] The houses in 'Merrie England' would be graced with a new spatial architecture as well. They would be liberated from the spatial constraints and conventions imposed on workers' homes by Victorian capitalism. Blatchford's Merrie England homes would not only be much 'loftier and larger' than the standard proletarian Victorian dwelling but their interior design would reflect a simple-life aesthetic. The interiors would therefore be cleared of 'all useless furniture' and conform to a more modest design modelled on Henry Thoreau's simple-life dwelling at Walden Pond and the simplified, though refined elegance of the Japanese home.[55] In a later utopian vision he offered up in his utopian novel *The Sorcery Shop* in 1909, Blatchford injected even more beauty into the socialist spaces of the future. In this vision, the 'new England' of the socialist future would be graced with 'spacious towns' surrounded by a 'noble panorama of blossoming woods, flowery meadows, green grass-lands, clean rivers, picturesque villages, and well-kept, winding roads'.[56] Along with the towns, the cities of new England would be pleasing on the eye and the senses. Gone were the miles of monotonous streets of suburban houses, the 'brick boxes with slate lids' that John Ruskin decried, 'all ugly' and 'all alike'.[57] Instead, Manchester was transformed into a 'marvellous dream city' set in a 'sea of flowers'. As for Chester Road, which ran through Manchester, it was now decorated by an 'avenue' of 'very handsome' homes and fruit trees passing along its entire length.[58] In his vision, London, too, was full of delights. Its revitalised socialist urban spaces, resplendent with spacious squares, graceful bridges, gardens, fountains and the red roofs of innumerable proletarian houses, spread 'as far as the eye could reach', a scene at once 'rosy, glittering, and beautiful'.[59]

Socialist spaces were nearly always beautiful in these utopian visions. The one-time Fellowship of the New Life socialist William Jupp had a vision of beautiful cities 'in the light of dawn and sunset, their streets wide and clean and smokeless, glorious with works of art, with gardens and open spaces and bits of wild nature creeping in among the houses and public buildings – centres and shrines of gladsome life'.[60] Similarly, the visions of future socialism that John Bruce Glasier offered his audience from platform lectures were full of 'beautiful' buildings, streets and gardens.[61] The ugly utilitarian buildings and hideously busy streets packed with fraught pedestrians and 'omnibuses crowded with spectators' which characterised the civic and public spaces of Victorian Britain simply disappeared in William Morris's *News from Nowhere*. So, too, did the entire 'brick and mortar desert' of Victorian London and the foul manufacturing districts of northern England.[62] Morris's socialist spaces were de-industrialised, ecologically sensitive and always 'aesthetically-heightened'. Morris favoured a medievalist aesthetic for much of the architectural style and decorative design on display in homes and buildings in *Nowhere*. As the wise socialist educator 'Hammond' explained it to William Guest: 'Like the medievals, we like everything trim and clean, and orderly and bright; as people always do when they have any sense of architectural power.'[63] We should not make the mistake here of interpreting Morris's favouring of a medieval architectural aesthetic in *News from Nowhere* as indicative of his desire to return 'England' to some mythic past. On the contrary, Morris's promoting of the medieval aesthetic should be read as an effort to combat the destructive pace of time unleashed by the processes of modernisation and capitalist development by anchoring his socialist utopia in a source of 'permanence', in this case the mythic heritage of an idealised medievalist past. As W.H.G. Armytage recognised in relation to Morris's attitude towards the destructive force of modern time, his work 'was irradiated by the passion of catching something from its [modern time] ever-rolling stream'.[64] Morris's love of a medieval architectural aesthetic should be read in a modernist key in another sense. This was that typically modernist melding of backwards and forwards that we find in his utopian vision of a future socialism imbued with the styles and atmosphere of a past age, in this case the mythic 'golden age' of architecture in the Middle Ages. We should recognise the strong futural thrust in this vision as well. In this latter regard, it would be appropriate to remind ourselves of the discussion in an earlier chapter regarding an assumption underpinning socialist Golden Age myths.[65] This concerned the conviction that there had been perfection in an earlier age, that there had been a fall in succeeding ages, but that the earlier perfection would return in the future aeon to come. In other words, and in relation to our focus on space in this chapter, the message of the myth was that the spatial environment had been more pleasurable and gracious in an earlier age, there had been a descent into vulgarity in the modern age of Victorian materialism and commercial capitalism, but that the beauty and grace of the earlier time would return to inform and shape the spatial milieu of the socialist Golden Age to come.

Finally, it should be mentioned that socialist space as imagined during the utopian years of the socialist revival often acquired a sacred or mystical aura. When contemporary socialists like Edward Carpenter, for instance, spoke of a return to communal life and nature as 'the way back to the lost Eden, or rather forward to the new Eden', they had a mystical vision of a more sacred space beyond the profane space of modern capitalist abstract space, a space which all could inhabit in a spirit of universal love and fellowship with all things.[66] This other dimension of space was often conceived as boundless or 'cosmological', sometimes conceptualised as a 'fourth dimension' of space beyond conventional Euclidean space, as socialists like Carpenter sought to enter a space even beyond the earthly realm as they aspired to live a life close to and on more intimate terms with the vast reaches of the 'great cosmos'.

6
The Return to Origins: Modernism, Socialism and Childhood

As mentioned in previous chapters, *fin de siècle* modernists were convinced that their age, the modern age of progress and 'civilisation', was undergoing a crisis of such profound magnitude that it was in urgent need of far-reaching cultural and spiritual regeneration. For this regeneration to come about, however, there needed to be a new beginning, a new start which would set in motion an alternative temporality to that of the homogenising, ever-accelerating profane time of modernity and progress. This belief that the age was in urgent need of a new beginning or rebirth was a fundamental aspect of modernism, including political modernism. We should remind ourselves of the circumstances prevailing at this time which convinced modernists of all shades and opinions, artistic, political or otherwise, that a new start was needed. Roger Griffin has referred to the acute liminoid conditions afflicting much of Europe from c.1850 onward, caused by the impact of modernisation–modernity and its accompanying temporal, psychological and cultural pressures.[1] The situation had certainly not abated by the *fin de siècle* and, if anything, had become even more critical. The human fall-out from this acute liminal situation, where it was felt that onrushing secularisation and progress were ruthlessly destroying the certainties and 'truths' associated with a pre-modern world populated by reassuring spirits and Gods, were desperate feelings of alienation, anomy, dislocation and uncertainty and of living in a time of perpetual crisis and transition without respite or closure. We should remind ourselves as well that liminoid conditions become most acute during moments of marked historical change, when there is heightened expectancy that the age is indeed about to experience a new beginning. The sense that history had arrived at a crucial turning point and was poised on the cusp of a new type of age was certainly felt by many during the late Victorian and Edwardian years in Britain. In such 'moments' the desire to usher in the new day that was dawning tantalisingly on the horizon takes on added urgency.

This chapter will look at one of the most potent representations of the new beginning for many modernists, that of childhood or the figure of the child. For many modernists, the figure of the child aptly represented the new beginning, the hope rising from the pain and decadence of the modern world. Childhood functioned as metaphor for the new beginning, while at other times there was a more direct focus on and appreciation of the particular experience of early childhood. In this latter orientation towards childhood, the child's alternative experience is held up as a sort of corrective to the adult world of modernity. This chapter will begin by exploring this relationship between childhood and modernism before moving on to consider the question of childhood and the socialist revival. In keeping with the mission of this book, this latter analysis will seek to identify and bring to the fore the undercurrent of modernism running through the socialist interest in childhood during the late Victorian and Edwardian decades. As we will see in the following sections, the socialist interest in childhood during these years was quite significant, to the extent that it took an organisational as well as a discursive form.

One does not need to look far to find the metaphor of the child as new beginning in the key texts of modernism. It is prominent in Friedrich Nietzsche's three-stage metamorphosis of the spirit set out in *Thus Spoke Zarathustra*.[2] In the ascent to spiritual awareness, the prophet of a new time, Zarathustra, has the camel and the lion occupying the first two stages of development respectively. At the first stage, the camel in the lonely desert represents the good, though compliant citizen weighed down with the burden of contemporary custom and values. Then, in the desert, a second metamorphosis occurs whereby the camel suddenly changes into the lion. The stage of the lion represents a rebellion against the cramping conformity of convention. The third and final metamorphosis of the spirit is the stage of the child, which pushes the rebellion of the lion further so that a genuinely new beginning becomes possible. This new beginning, this effort to go beyond the paralysis of prevailing convention and values, can only be achieved by the innocent child-like being. Nietzsche's child is indicated not just by innocence it should be said, but by active forgetting, that is, the active forgetting of the past. It is important to note that Nietzsche's past should be read as the past dominated by the profane time of modernity. In other words, it is only by interrupting or disrupting the flow of the homogenous, linear time of modernity through this act of desired forgetfulness that the burden of what is past can be lifted and a new beginning commence:

> The child is innocence and forgetting, a new beginning, a game, a wheel rolling out of itself, a first movement, a sacred yes-saying. Yes, for the game of creation my brothers a sacred yes-saying is required. The spirit wants *its* will, the one lost to the world now wins *its own* world.[3]

Nietzsche's child of innocence and forgetfulness, released from the dead weight of the past and convention, thus emerges as the truly creative being, one who stridently affirms and is assured in the new attitudes. In Nietzsche's hands, 'childhood' functions as a quintessentially modernist concept and metaphor and one most emblematic of that new beginning beyond the contemporary decadence that modernism sought to bring about.

The child did not just serve as a convenient metaphor for the new beginning for modernism. Many modernists believed that childhood was a more agreeable age to that of adulthood, that the child inhabited a realm of experience superior to that of the adult burdened by the strains of modernity. More than this, the child was held up as a figure of redemption with the potential to 'save' the adult world. What the adult world needed to do therefore was to reacquaint with this earlier mode of vital experience, to somehow re-connect backwards to this earlier time. The belief that the mature world of modernity could be redeemed through a return to an earlier age pervaded modernist thinking. It had its basis in the strange paradox within modernism that in order to achieve the transition to a new stage beyond the malaise of the present moment, there needed to be a movement backwards, a return to the earliest time as it were. Though always orientated towards the future, modernism felt that if the age was to begin anew, undergo redemption, then there should be a reconnection backwards to summon forth earlier forms of metaphysical energy or modes of experience. The same held true for the individual adult self. Redemption would come through a process of going back in time in order to go forward. There are a number of important ingredients to this aspect of modernism which need to be stressed for purposes of setting out the framework for this chapter.

There was, as mentioned, that paradoxical fusion of forwards and backwards, or future and past or, put another way, that creative compounding of the modern with the primitive, archaic or some other such 'moment' of the past. A second important ingredient was the stress on the primacy of origins. One does not have to look far to see modernism's keen interest in origins. T.S. Eliot was obsessed by origins to give just one example, believing that to understand modern 'man' required a reconnection backwards to the 'source', namely primitive man. Indeed Eliot's *The Waste Land* has been interpreted as 'a probe sent in search of a lost unity'.[4] This desire to become reacquainted with 'primitive' sources of human energy in order to alleviate the stresses of the modern condition was not just confined to the high priests of intellectual modernism. As Roger Griffin described it, the modern world felt this necessity 'to restore human contact with the primal, revitalising constituents of life ... '.[5] There was a further strand to this origin myth, for modernism not only stressed the primacy of primordial origins but ennobled, even sacralised, the earliest time. This 'beginning' of time was cast as a time of harmony and spiritual plenitude, a veritable 'Eden' of perfection and contentment. We observed this modernist sacralisation of the earliest of times in a previous chapter when we looked at two of the most prominent myths of the socialist revival: the eschatological myth of the Kingdom and the myth of the Golden Age. In both myths, this original time was cast as an earthly paradise overflowing with abundance and virtue. Blissful equality reigned then, too, a life enjoyed without stations, masters, private property and want. It was also carefree, gay and joyous, aspects of life that were particularly in evidence during the original Golden Age according to the myth. Such perfect social arrangements brought forth their human equivalents. Humankind back then was more gracious. Individuals simply radiated primal goodness. A third ingredient of the forwards–backwards paradox within modernism was the conviction that since this earlier time of innocence there had been regression, a lapse into decadence, a 'fall' from the original grace or paradise. A fourth important ingredient was the belief that the bliss of the beginning was recoverable. The fall into decadence was but a temporary state which would eventually give way to a glorious return to the perfection that prevailed at the time of origins. This utopian vision of a new dispensation, bathed in the harmony and goodness that was there during the earliest time, ensured that these modernist origin myths were always orientated towards the future. A fifth and final ingredient is the idea that to return to, or re-enter, the time and purity of origin provided an opportunity for regenerating the life of the individual, community or age.[6] We saw this in relation to the origin myths of the Kingdom and the Golden Age, those powerful and enduring myths which kept alive the apparent glory of the earlier paradise. To participate in such myths enabled the individual or community to magically inhabit the sacred moment of origin, to co-exist with that original time of strength and purity and draw on its power.

   Many of the elements of the origin myth discussed above would be present in modernist reflections on childhood. As mentioned, childhood would be celebrated as a superior age to that of later stages within the human life-cycle. As in other modernist origin myths of the earliest time, childhood was held up as a 'Golden Age' of innocence and perfection. Modernists thus tended to see the subsequent stage beyond childhood as regression, a 'fall' from the original state of innocence and grace. Hope sprang eternal in modernism, however, in that the perfection of the beginning was deemed to be recoverable. In other words, it was possible for the adult to 'return' to this earlier time of purity and creativity. Re-entering this earlier time, by reconnecting to this lost state of primal innocence, offered the opportunity to step out of the continuum of the historical time of modernity and reconnect to those vital experiences and creative energies stored in childhood. Therein lay the hope of regeneration. These sentiments were widely shared. Many of the leading figures in modern art, for example, represented the earliest time of childhood as the most vital time, a time with which the world of adulthood should seek to reacquaint itself. For them, the child had unique capacities. They believed that the childhood experience presented a window into a superior world overflowing with spontaneous creativity and honesty of emotion which was the wellspring of true art. Thus Picasso was convinced that in the ingenuity and creativity present in childhood lay the basis of genuine art. Indeed, Jonathan Fineberg has shown that artistic modernism was not just fascinated by the subject of childhood creativity but deeply indebted to children's art.[7] Many of the great masters and innovators of artistic modernism were directly influenced by the drawings and artwork of children, including Klee, Kandinsky, Matisse, Larionov and Miró, as well as Picasso. The child-artist's playfulness, primitive geometry and imaginative use of colour and imagery fascinated these modern artists, as did the child's inventiveness. The radical departure from convention that these modernist attitudes to art and childhood represented was clear. To achieve genuine creativity in art, the adult artist must 'unlearn' what he had learned through engaging with the artistic heritage of the past. To be genuinely creative, indeed to be truly modern, the artist should turn his back on the accumulated knowledge of the artistic heritage of the past. In other words, the true artist must proceed in the opposite direction to conventional artistic wisdom, and go back to childhood origins as it were.

The tendency to represent the earliest time of childhood as the most vital time, a time which harboured the potential to renew or redeem the fallen world of the adult, is evident as well in Nietzsche's writing. In the 94th aphorism in *Beyond Good and Evil*, he states that 'mature manhood' comes when one has 'rediscovered the seriousness one had as a child at play'.[8] The tendency to turn conventional wisdom on its head, turn the world 'upside down' as it were, by hailing childhood as a more superior time to that of adulthood is even more pronounced in the writings of another leading modernist thinker, Walter Benjamin. Benjamin's reflections on childhood, particularly his tendency to see revolutionary potential in the child's world and equate childhood with the socialist future, have particular relevance for our discussion later in the chapter on the issue of childhood and the socialist revival.

The theme of childhood was never far from Benjamin's thinking on modern life. It permeates many of his meditations on modernity and the modern world. In Benjamin's writings, the notion of childhood as a superior, prelapsarian age is very marked. For Benjamin, childhood was a unique age which exhibited the best of human attributes, qualities which the modern bourgeois adult had forgotten or even forsaken. To him, the figure of the child seemed to perfectly encapsulate the dialectical interplay between past and future. In his reflections on childhood, particularly in his Berlin memoirs, we find a genuine yearning or nostalgia for that time of lost innocence, the prelapsarian age of grace and contentment which preceded the later regression into bourgeois adulthood.[9] But the child, for Benjamin, was also a figure of hope for the future. In the unique, differentiated experience of the child could be found the potential to awaken dormant capacities in the adult, which included the dormant energies of creativity and joy. But, with Benjamin, the child was more than a figure of emancipation for the individual. As Carlo Salzini has shown, Benjamin also saw genuine revolutionary potential in the prelapsarian experience of childhood which could help redeem the modern adult world.[10] The child was therefore both a figure of redemption, who could save the individual, and a figure of revolution, with the potential to save the modern age.

For Benjamin, the child lived in and experienced a world that was pre-bourgeois and pre-modern. The child's mode of receiving the world was unmediated and unquestioning, and thus purer than that of the bourgeois adult. Unlike modern bourgeois man, who had a detached, superior and often condescending relationship to things in the world, the child's mode of reception involved a tender, even sensuous relationship with things which, to Benjamin, represented a superior way of engaging with the world. Here the lessons of nature are absorbed intuitively, via a sort of 'secret password' to authentic knowledge which the modern bourgeois adult, hampered by reflexivity and 'false consciousness', had forgotten. This superior mode of reception had much to do with the child's innate capacity to establish a mimetic relationship to nature and things in the world. This mimetic faculty, the capacity to creatively copy, imitate, express and represent as in drawing, dance or music, had been very familiar to ancient peoples. This mimetic gift, however, the capacity for producing 'magical correspondences and analogies' which rendered the world more immediate to 'primitive' man, had been almost lost to the modern adult. Instead, this gift had now become the prerogative of the child.[11] The child's mimetic powers enabled him or her through play and other forms of creative representation to not only imitate but become the 'Other', thereby annulling that artificial distance between the subject and the objective world that so defined the adult world's relationship to the surrounding environment. Mimesis thus implies a tactile, unquestioning relationship to the world, a relationship not grounded in Cartesian distinctions between subject and object or an attitude of detached superiority or mastery towards nature and the environment. This claim, that these gifts, including the gift of cosmic awareness, had become the preserve of the child, has relevance for the way British socialists of a 'cosmological' persuasion approached the subject of the child during the revival years.

Child's play, in particular, intrigued Benjamin. The mimetic faculty was alive and well in play:

> Children's play is everywhere permeated by mimetic modes of behaviour, and its realm is by no means limited to what one person can imitate in another. The child plays at being not only a shopkeeper or teacher but also a windmill and a train.[12]

The inquisitive, creative child in mimetic play magically re-enchants the world. Through play, the child creates enchanted spaces outside the disenchanted spaces of the bourgeois world, as in the magical oasis of the children's play room in the bourgeois apartment. There is a temporal dimension to this as well, for the child in play occupies an enchanted realm outside the continuum of history. The contemplative child at play 'like the Benjaminian "Angel of History", looks downward, backward, rather than up ahead (upward, forward) [*sic*], s/he looks at what falls down, gets left behind, is trampled underfoot, forgotten and forsaken'.[13] The child has the mimetic capacity to magically re-enchant even the most disenchanted features of the bourgeois world, as when bringing to life the discarded, forgotten objects of history.

> His life is like a dream: he knows nothing lasting; everything happens to him by chance. His nomad-years are hours in the forest of dream. To it he drags home his booty, to purify it, secure it, cast out its spell. His drawers must become arsenal and zoo, crime museum and crypt. 'To tidy up' would be to demolish an edifice full of prickly chestnuts that are spiky clubs, tinfoil that is hoarded silver, bricks that are coffins, cacti that are totem-poles and copper pennies that are shields.[14]

How then to realise the revolutionary potential in the child's world? For Benjamin, this involved a politics of memory and awakening. In order to move towards a state of genuine maturity, regenerate the life of the adult world as it were, the adult needed to unlock the mysteries to the child's world, re-enter its magical domain and become re-acquainted with its ways of seeing and engaging with the world. In other words, if the modern adult world was to be awakened from the spell of capitalist progress, an effort needed to be made to forge a meaningful re-connection to the childhood experience. This meant re-discovering those 'lost' capacities for creativity, delight and sensuous pleasure which the bourgeois world of 'progress', 'improvement' and 'education' had so ruthlessly purged from the adult condition. This 'return to origins' did not mean seeking refuge in the childhood experience. This was not a retreat into a lost world of infancy in order to dwell there and thus escape from the world. This was an effort rather to get in touch with these forgotten sources of 'Being' within the childhood experience in the hope of arousing the adult world to action. In other words, it sought to identify the untapped creative potential that lay in the earlier time of childhood and harness this energy to a revolutionary socialist political project aimed at bringing into being a world of a new type. Implicit in this as well was Benjamin's tendency, as previously mentioned, to equate the particular experience of childhood with the socialist future.

This re-orientation backward in order to go forward certainly required a stimulation and reawakening of the mimetic faculty. This was particularly crucial in relation to modern man's relationship to nature which, driven by the juggernaut and will to dominate, implicit in the Enlightenment vision of progress, had become horribly distorted. As Carlo Salzini points out, Benjamin saw bourgeois modernity as a 'fallen' condition where 'nature is approached without respect and exploited rapaciously'.[15] This effort to dominate rather than embrace the cosmic powers in meaningful intercourse meant that bourgeois modernity could not be trusted with the care of Mother Earth. Only the child, in his or her prelapsarian, non-hierachical, mimetic embrace of nature, sought harmony rather than domination of nature.[16] The message to the adult world was clear. It needed to rekindle a 'child-like' attitude towards nature if Mother Earth was to be spared further bouts of Faustian 'creative destruction'. That is, it should try to rediscover that mimetic approach to nature and the cosmos that was so familiar to ancient peoples and which was so gloriously preserved in the behaviour of the child.

The example of children's mimetic play could even help the adult to transcend the alienation of modern work under capitalism. Here Benjamin imagines a time when human labour will proceed along the lines of children's play, where work and play would be in harmony. It was a model of work influenced by the utopian socialist Charles Fourier, most notably the example of the 'passionate labour' engaged in by the dwellers in the *phalansteries*. As Benjamin stated in *The Arcades Project*, to 'have instituted play as the canon of a labour no longer rooted in exploitation is one of the greatest merits of Fourier'.[17] Work in such an arrangement, as with play, is creative, respectful, freely entered into and aesthetic. It was a model of work that was also free of the laws that governed labour under conditions of capitalist production and of that tendency of 'man' to exploit nature: 'Such work inspired by play aims not at the propagation of values but at the amelioration of nature.'[18]

We should now turn to consider the question of childhood and the socialist revival. In so doing, we will see that many of the modernist themes we identified above in relation to philosophical, artistic and literary modernism and childhood were present in socialist approaches to childhood during the revival years. As with those modernists in the fields of philosophy, art and literature, for many British socialists childhood provided a potent representation of the new beginning beyond the malaise of the modern bourgeois age. For them, childhood seemed to represent, even more than the labouring classes, the real hope of a socialist future. We see, too, in this socialist thinking on childhood that dialectical play of past and future and the stress on the 'return to origins', the contention that a return to the perfection of childhood origins offered the hope of redemption for the world of bourgeois adulthood. These themes are evident in one of the principal socialist texts of the revival years, William Morris's utopian socialist romance *News from Nowhere*. At one stage in the book, when in conversation with the novel's narrator William Guest, the character of 'old Hammond', the wise educator on the virtues of the new life, spoke of the idyllic post-capitalist, pastoral paradise of *Nowhere* in terms of a return to the purity of childhood origins:

> He [Hammond] sighed, and then smiled and said: 'At least let us rejoice that we have got back our childhood again. I drink to the days that are!' 'Second childhood', said I in a low voice, and then blushed at my double rudeness, and hoped that he hadn't heard. But he had, and turned to me smiling, and said: 'Yes why not? And for my part, I hope it may last long; and that the world's next period of wise and unhappy manhood, if that should happen, will speedily lead us to a third childhood: if indeed this age be not our third. Meantime, my friend, you must know that we are too happy, both individually and collectively, to trouble ourselves about what is to come hereafter.'[19]

There were other references in the novel to the qualities to be found in childhood. During the exchange of words between Hammond and Guest cited above, the former proclaimed that 'it is the child-like part of us that produces works of imagination'.[20] As with the great masters of modern art, Morris saw childhood as a time of genuine creativity and believed that artistic productivity in the adult flowed when the inner childhood spirit was nourished. References to the bliss and contentment of childhood are frequent in the novel, sometimes expressed in terms of nostalgia at its passing, as when Guest reminds himself of a time when he 'was a happy child on a sunny holiday, and had everything that [he] could think of'.[21] The children featured in *Nowhere* are also boundlessly happy. They reside in a prelapsarian world of contentment and uninhibited freedom, a world free of the blight of child labour and the restrictions of formal schooling.[22] Even the end of the dream, when Guest is plunged back into the alienation and misery of non-utopian reality in shabby Hammersmith, can be interpreted as a 'fall' into an adulthood marred by disenchantment and bourgeois philistinism. Moving beyond *News from Nowhere*, it should be noted as well that Morris, as with Walter Benjamin at a later date, found much to admire in Charles Fourier's efforts to make work more pleasurable by using children's mimetic play as a template.[23] It could be argued as well that the vitality of much of Morris's work came from his having rediscovered the 'lost' instincts and creativity of childhood. His friend William Butler Yeats thought so at least, saying that all Morris wrote seemed 'like the make believe of a child, who is remaking the world, not always in the same way, but always after his own heart . . . [and] out of unending pictures of happiness'.[24]

We find similar themes regarding childhood in Edward Carpenter's writings. Even more stridently than Morris, Carpenter presents the childhood stage as a prelapsarian age of natural goodness and spontaneous creativity and freedom. Like Morris, too, and as with Walter Benjamin, he equates the particular experience of childhood with socialism and the socialist future. In a chapter on 'The New Morality' in *Civilisation: Its Cause and Cure and Other Essays* which was first published in 1889, Carpenter looked forward to a day when the individual and the collective would be freed from the 'hard and cramping rules' imposed by bourgeois morality and convention. Clearly, an adult life defined by the bourgeois moral code represented a 'fallen' condition for Carpenter. Indifferent to the suffering and needs of the poor, 'pharisaical', self-centred, self-interested and materialistic, this was a false morality that 'runs and trickles through all of modern society, poisoning the well-springs of affection'.[25] The 'new morality', on the other hand, which had its counterpart in Eastern philosophy and which was being taken up by 'Modern Socialism', was to be a morality 'without a code', which had its basis in an 'organic, almost physiological morality of the common life'.[26] Happily free 'from limiting formulae', this morality of the 'common life', this 'sense of organic unity, of the common welfare, the instinct of Humanity or of general helpfulness' was 'perhaps the most fundamental fact of existence' for Carpenter.[27] More significantly from the point of view of our concerns in this chapter is that Carpenter believed that this alternative morality of the 'common life' was woven into the very 'Being' of children. Just as significantly Carpenter was of the view, as was Walter Benjamin writing later in the context of an ever-accelerating modernity, that the modern adult needed to rediscover these 'lost' virtues of childhood which the bourgeois morality of formulae had so callously repressed in the adult condition. 'It will mean,' said Carpenter, 'the liberation of a thousand and one instincts, desires and capacities which since our childhood's days have lain buried within us, concealed and ignored because we have thought them wrong or unworthy, when really all they have wanted has been recognition....'[28]

In later writings, Carpenter expanded on these thoughts on childhood. Following Wordsworth, he believed that the child was infused with the 'divine' and that 'Heaven lies about us in our infancy'. Carpenter traced the child's genius back to the very earliest age of humankind, back to that original Golden Age of innocence and purity and to the primitive beings who inhabited that world. According to Carpenter, the child was the privileged custodian of inherited gifts. The child entered the world possessing:

> vast stores of sub-conscious memory, derived from its ancestral inheritances; we all admit that a certain grace and intuitive insight and even prophetic quality, in the child-nature, are due to the harmonization of these racial inheritances in the infant, even before it is born.[29]

In Carpenter's thinking, the original Golden Age and the experience of childhood melded. The earliest time for Carpenter, invoking the childhood metaphor, was humankind's 'child-stage', while primitive man he saw as gloriously child-like in the way he interacted with the world. In this conception, primitive man and the child of the modern world share important characteristics. Both are vigorous and careless in outlook, both delight in mimetic play and mimetic ritual and both possess that mimetic gift to render their surroundings more magical and immediate. Here, once again, the themes of adult redemption and the need to 'return to origins' run through contemporary socialist thinking. To know and value the child's experience, even the child of the modern age, was to in some way magically inhabit that earliest time when innocence and goodness reigned, to be in the presence of those instincts which prevailed at the time of the earlier paradise.

Edward Carpenter's child then, as with Walter Benjamin, inhabited a world that was pre-bourgeois and pre-modern to the extent that he believed it contained traces of the earliest paradise. This was a superior world which, moreover, contained the seeds of a finer life to come. Carpenter thus saw in the figure of the child, as did Benjamin, a key to the socialist future. To Carpenter, children were not only capable of magically re-enchanting their surroundings, but they had an almost natural instinct for fellowship. The child was therefore held up as a repository of latent socialist values, a precious vessel containing all the positive virtues of innate goodness and kindness thought to be intrinsic to the development of a true socialist character. This tendency to idealise the child's qualities along these lines was not confined to Carpenter and William Morris. It seemed to run like a thread through much of the socialist thinking and writing of this period, as just a few examples from *The Clarion* will show. According to one *Clarion* contributor writing in 1895, children were

> the loveliest, the purist, the most helpless of created beings,... whose humours are too subtle for the keenest observers, whose pathos is too delicate for the finest poet, whose innocence and gaiety are a reproof unanswerable to them that preach the black doctrine of inherited sin.[30]

Writing the same month, another *Clarion* writer sacralised childhood, contending that children come to us from God and are 'full of the fun and the grace which keep the world young'.[31] Yet another *Clarion* contributor wrote of the child's 'higher capabilities' and those 'possibilities of nobility latent within him'.[32] The children's world was truly magical, for C. Allen Clarke writing in another edition of the *Clarion*, as in the mimetic rapport they had with nature:

> We'll go where the lark learns music,
> Where the brooklets babble low,
> In that world of pretty visions,
> Where the business folk ne'er go,
> We'll try and find where the insects
> Get their magic humming tops,
> Where the butterflies' wings are painted
> With colours not bought in shops.
> And let sour men call us foolish,
> And think that they are very wise
> Because they can see nothing
> When there's a whole world in our eyes.[33]

At other moments, the child was immersed in an enchanting world of fairy tales beyond the disenchanted spaces of the adult bourgeois world:

> We'll visit the elves and fairies,
> In the children's part of earth;
> Far sweeter than jingle of money
> Is the music of their mirth.
> We'll help Jack slay the Giants,
> Or up the beanstalk climb,
> In those brave big days of wonder
> In 'Once upon a time'.[34]

But these contemporary socialist writings on children usually contained a lament for time passing. The later years, as the childhood years passed, would be marked by loss and subtraction as the onset of 'maturity' and the pressure to conform to the modern bourgeois world and its codes acted to shatter the hopes of the earliest time. For Edward Carpenter, the erosion of that natural harmony between the infant and the virtues derived from the ancestral past began early. 'After birth,' he lamented, 'the impact of the outer world serves rather to break up and disintegrate this harmony than to confirm and strengthen it.'[35] C. Allen Clarke contrasted the beauty of the child's experience with that of the Victorian bourgeois adult:

> They struggle, and hurry, and worry,
> For a fortune of fiddle-de-dee,
> And a Ghost with a Sharp Scythe mocks them
> – But that they cannot see.[36]

As we have seen then, the notion that corrupted adulthood could be redeemed by returning to the purity and creativity of childhood was a feature of modernist thinking *and* featured in the thoughts of leading socialists of the revival period. This theme is present as well in the projects of child rescue that socialists vigorously engaged in during the revival years. In late Victorian Britain, many proletarian children remained cruelly exploited and thus were in need of rescue. Although matters had improved since the more widespread abuses of the early to mid-nineteenth century, the proletarian child still tended to move in a world marked by extreme poverty and poor health. This was an environment, particularly in the urban centres, of overcrowding, industrial pollution, mean slums and dirt. Again, although the very worst abuses of child labour in factories had ended by the late Victorian period, children remained subject to an exploitative labour market. This can be seen with the half-time system, whereby the existing law granted children part-time exemption from schooling in order to work to supplement the household wage. Child labour, said the socialist Fred Brocklehurst in 1894, with the half-time exemption system at the heart of things, 'is the physical and moral curse of this country'.[37] 'Upon no ground of expediency, justice or health,' he continued, 'can we defend the modern Moloch practice of offering up child life upon the alter of our industrial supremacy.'[38] For many socialists of the period, the cause of saving proletarian children from the evils of poverty, debilitating illnesses and capitalist exploitation was at the heart of their socialist belief. This was certainly the case with the ILP activist Margaret McMillan. As Carolyn Steedman has shown, McMillan pursued this project with missionary zeal during the revival decades and beyond. Leading the child out of 'slumdom' and back to the 'garden of childhood' where they naturally belonged helped define and give meaning to McMillan's socialist faith.[39] She was highly active in projects to enhance the proletarian child's health, development and emotional well-being. Supported by her sister, Rachel, she was a pioneer of nursery education in England. She also worked to develop progressive educational programmes, which sought to provide a broader and more humane education for children beyond mere preparation for the unskilled capitalist labour market. She also threw herself into the campaign for free school meals, which became reality under the 1906 Provision of School Meals Act, and for regular medical inspections for school children.

Margaret McMillan was not alone in this social mission. The project of child rescue became a life-long devotion for many of her socialist contemporaries, like her sister Rachel, Katherine Bruce Glasier and Mary Chignell.[40] The urge to rescue the proletarian child from corrupt capitalism was felt by male socialists, too. It was a desire to save the children which initially drew Robert Blatchford to socialism, and he would later throw open the columns of *The Clarion* to contributors, like Margaret McMillan, who wished to promote the cause of child rescue.[41] At one stage during his editorship of *The Clarion*, Blatchford even wrote a weekly article for the children himself.[42] Like Margaret McMillan and other contemporary socialist writers on childhood, he was not averse to sentimentalising, even sacralising the child-figure in his writings. Daughters, he remarked, move 'in grace and helpfulness through the household, bringing sunshine and melody' with their presence and 'dropping kind words and endearments' from their lips.[43] Keir Hardie, too, was moved by the children's plight. He even penned fairy tales with a socialist message in the ILP newspaper *The Labour Leader*, in an effort to provide spiritual uplift to the working-class child.[44]

Socialist efforts to safeguard the child even took an organisational form. The socialist revival would see extraordinary efforts to build socialist children's organisations, with an aim to ward off outside influences, threats and other perils associated with Victorian modern life. The first such organisation to be created was the army of Labour Crusaders in April 1894 under the auspices of the ILP and its newspaper *The Labour Leader*. With a membership open to 'lads and lassies' under 16 years of age, the Crusader army moved in a magical fairy tale world of brave 'Knights' and 'Dames', and cruel 'Giants'.[45] Spurred on by Keir Hardie and other *Labour Leader* writers, the little socialist Knights and Dames were urged to go forth to fight these cruel Giants, who represented 'Capital', 'Greed', 'Ignorance', 'Competition', 'Monopoly' and 'Hunger'.[46] By February 1896, over 1200 children had been recruited to the Crusader army.[47] The Crusader organisation sought through fairy tales, didactic instruction and other means to heighten the child's natural moral sensibilities by promoting the ethic of social sympathy. The appeal, therefore, an orientation consistent with the contemporary socialist belief in the purity of childhood origins, was to the child's innate capacity for kindness and compassion. Sympathy, moreover, generated a spirit of community and co-operation and built bonds of loyalty. As a Crusader columnist wrote, 'sympathy brings us together and unites us, and enables us to conquer where, alone and without sympathy we might fail'.[48]

The Cinderella Clubs were of a different order to the Crusader army. They were initially inspired by Robert Blatchford, the first Club making its appearance in Manchester in October 1889. Cinderella Clubs then spread to other industrial centres in Britain during the revival years. Blatchford's *Clarion* comrade, Alex M. Thompson, estimated that there were eventually 33 branches of the Cinderella Society in Britain.[49] Whereas the Crusader organisation tended to focus on the children of ILP activists, the Cinderella movement sought to spread its goodwill to the masses of slum-children in the industrial towns. There was a further difference. While the principal aim of the Crusader movement was to cultivate the child's ethical outlook, the Cinderella groups worked to bring out the joy in the child. As Blatchford explained it, 'my idea was not to teach or lecture the child, but to amuse them'.[50] Throughout the 1890s and beyond, the socialist-inspired Cinderella Clubs organised parties and games, field trips, summer outings and Christmas pantomimes for 'outcast' children. Cinderella children were also the beneficiaries of philanthropic gifts of toys and much welcomed meals.

Another quite remarkable socialist-inspired children's organisation that sprang up during the revival years was the Socialist Sunday School movement. The original idea for this movement can be traced to 1892 when a former Sunday school teacher and SDF member Mrs Mary Grey founded a Sunday school in Battersea for the teaching of socialist ideals and morals to children.[51] Though the idea took a while to catch on, by 1895 the movement sprang to life in earnest through the efforts of Lizzie Glasier of the Glasgow Women's Labour Party and others to establish a network of Socialist Sunday Schools throughout the country. The movement would eventually establish a strong presence in Glasgow, Edinburgh, Yorkshire, Lancashire and London. Indeed, by 1907, London boasted over 20 Socialist Sunday Schools.[52] By 1912 there were around 96 schools spread around the country, catering for an estimated 4540 children. From 1901, the Sunday school movement published its own monthly newspaper, the *Young Socialist*. Even more vigorously than the Crusaders, the Socialist Sunday Schools sought to nurture the child's natural moral sensibilities by encouraging the ethic of social sympathy and co-operative solidarity. At Socialist Sunday School gatherings, the children would sing socialist and labour hymns, familiarise themselves with the socialist catechism, recite the Socialist Ten Commandments and listen to sermons stressing the higher ethical standards of a co-operative and socialist way of life.[53]

There is an unmistakeable modernist element within these various efforts at child rescue. By saving the child from predatory capitalism, whether by exposing industrial cruelties through impassioned journalism, participating in progressive projects to improve the child's health and development or by offering a 'sheltering sky' in the socialist children's groups, the adult rescuer helped to reclaim the child for childhood. Through such efforts, the purity of childhood was maintained and the life of the child was regenerated. But so too was the adult regenerated in turn. By returning to the spirit of this earliest time, by empathising with the childhood experience and going to the aid of the most vulnerable and innocent in society, adult rescuers found that they had discovered the 'divine' within themselves. In a related sense, the adult rescuer would also be awakened into the higher consciousness of socialist political consciousness by engaging in acts of child rescue and restoring the child to the full bloom of childhood. Thus the rescue work of Margaret McMillan, as Carolyn Steedman recognised, showed that 'it was possible to take a dirty, malnourished, swollen-eyed child and make it healthy and beautiful. The people were thus to be awakened to a sense of how they had been robbed, promoted into political consciousness by their children.'[54] The wider socialist movement itself also felt the benefits of engaging with the childhood experience and the child's world. Through the regenerated child, the child restored to the glory of childhood, the socialist revival became infused with the spirit, vitality and virtues of childhood, and was thus regenerated in turn. Lizzie Glasier, one of the driving forces behind the Socialist Sunday School movement, certainly recognised as much. Glasier, who hoped to raise 'a great army of little socialist pioneers', was convinced that with the children assisting, the work of socialist propaganda 'will go on with more cheerfulness and courage [and] the rugged paths on the road to socialism will be less wearisome to tread'.[55] With the 'resolute children' in the vanguard, she continued, in one of those metaphoric flights of fancy common to the rhetoric of the socialist revival, 'a wider expanse of vision will open up to our view. More speedily will we emerge from under the dark shadow of competitive commercialism into the sunlit land of freedom.'[56] At this point, and by way of summing up this discussion, we should be reminded of one of the essential elements of the modernist origin myth that we referred to earlier in this chapter, namely the notion that to return to, or re-enter, the time and purity of origin helped to regenerate life, whether this involved the life of an individual, community or even an entire age.[57] To broaden the scope of the origin myth, the life that was regenerated in this case was the life of a political project, namely the socialist mission to bring into being a new world which would rediscover the harmony, bliss and goodness which prevailed at the 'beginning' or in the earliest time of life, the time of childhood.

7
Fabian Modernism

We have looked at a number of versions of socialist modernism in this book up to now. It remains to consider one other version, one very different in content, scope and purpose to the other varieties of socialist modernism we have observed in the socialist project of the late Victorian and Edwardian decades. This alternative version of socialist modernism was not concerned with the notion of an inward spiritual experience, utopian millenarian fantasies, eschatological visions of a coming Kingdom of socialism or romantic myths concerning a retrievable 'Golden Age'. Rather, it was a species of modernism informed by what Roger Griffin has called 'scientistic' currents of thought within contemporary culture, politics and society.[1] In harbouring its own particular vision of future socialism and strategy as to how to arrive there, we need to see this scientistic variant of modernism as similar in kind to the 'heroic modernism' that became quite popular in a later period of modernism, just before and after the Great War. This was a strain of modernism with its own particular profile and characteristics, a type of modernism that owed many of its most aggressive impulses and even some of its assumptions to the prevailing 'grand narrative' of modernisation–modernity. Indeed, this scientistic version of modernism would embrace a vision of the future as equally 'Faustian' as the one that featured in the modernisation–modernity 'grand narrative'. Of all the tendencies within the socialist revival, it was the Fabian group that was most wedded to this scientistic modernist agenda. Before we go on to examine this relationship between Fabianism and scientistic modernism, it is important to point out that whereas Fabian scientistic modernism certainly shared characteristics with heroic modernism it also revealed traces of 'social modernism' in its makeup. This was due to the strong health component informing many of the assumptions and aims of the Fabian scientistic project. This health preoccupation can be traced to certain powerful currents within contemporary society, not least a perception within certain intellectual and cultural circles that the nation was succumbing to a corrosive process of economic decline and associated 'race' degeneration, and that something urgent needed to be done about it. It is to all of the above matters that we shall now turn.

The Fabians were not always inclined towards a scientistic view of politics and society. During its first three years of life, from its foundation in 1883–6, the Fabian Society's doctrine revealed spiritual influences. The Fabians were, after all, a breakaway group from the avowedly spiritual Fellowship of the New Life. Even after the split, spiritually inclined socialists could be found in Fabian ranks, including Edward Pease, Frank Podmore, William Clarke, Annie Besant and Percival Chubb. Indeed, Chubb remained a member of both the Fabians and the Fellowship of the New Life. There were other influences, too, namely Anarchist and SDF Marxist influences. During these early years of life the Fabians were, in the words of George Bernard Shaw, 'just as Anarchist as the Socialist League and just as insurrectionary as the Federation (SDF)', believing that their aim was 'to bring about a tremendous smash-up of existing society, to be succeeded by complete Socialism'.[2] All this began to change, however, after 1886. For Shaw, the years 1886–7 marked the moment when the Fabians 'came to their senses'. At this point, awareness set in amongst leading Fabians 'as to the advisability of setting to work by the ordinary political methods and having done with Anarchism and vague exhortations to Emancipate the Workers'.[3] The events which triggered this turn towards pragmatism centred on the emotive issue of unemployment. Unemployment rates were particularly high during the years 1885–7, as the British economy still struggled to cope with the effects of the economic downturn which had begun c.1873. Supporting the unemployed and highlighting their plight became a high-point of socialist agitation during the first decade of the socialist revival. The two years of agitation between 1886 and 1887 saw hunger marches, riots, mass protest rallies at Hyde Park on 8 February 1886, Trafalgar Square on 13 November 1887 and Hyde Park again on 20 November 1887, and high-profile arrests and trials of socialist celebrities, including the leader of the SDF Henry Mayers Hyndman. There were even activist deaths, which culminated in the martyrdom of the 41-year-old Law clerk Alfred Linnell. Three people were killed during the 'Bloody Sunday' disturbances of 13 November, while Linnell was killed during the 20 November protest against the behaviour of the police on 'Bloody Sunday'. His funeral on 18 December 1887 was a highly charged, emotional affair attended by tens of thousands of mourners and sympathetic onlookers. It was also a highly choreographed spectacle. Linnell's open hearse was inscribed with the words 'Killed in Trafalgar Square', while the red flag, the Irish green flag and the red, yellow and green flag of the Radicals flew over the coffin. Many of the leading figures in the new socialist movement were present, including Herbert Burrows, Frank Smith, John Burns, Eleanor Marx, Annie Besant and William Morris. Morris was one of the pall-bearers, composed a 'Death Song' for the occasion and delivered a moving open-air speech at the funeral.

Despite the high-octane drama of the 1886 and 1887 events, the aggressive police tactics, arrests and deaths imparted a sobering lesson in state power, which convinced leading Fabians of the futility of head-on, quasi-revolutionary collisions with a powerful and well-entrenched capitalist power. At this point in the development of home-grown socialism, we thus see the growth of an awareness on the part of the Fabians that a measure of political pragmatism and an engagement with strategic thinking and electoral politics was required if socialist ideals were to achieve some realisation in political policies and practice. Hand in hand with this turn towards pragmatism went a condemnation of the 'insurrectionist' tendencies and revolutionary rhetoric associated with groups such as Hyndman's SDF. As George Bernard Shaw put it later in 1892, reflecting on the 'Bloody Sunday' reversal, 'the police received the blessing of Mr Gladstone; and Insurrectionism, after a two years' innings, vanished from the field and has not since been much heard of'.[4]

From 1886–7 onwards, then, and into the 1890s, a distinctly Fabian socialist doctrine began to take shape. This doctrine had distinct and significant modernist elements within it, and it will be the task of the remaining sections of this chapter to bring these elements to the fore. Before we look more closely at this doctrine from the perspective of modernism, however, mention should be made of another important conjuncture that would give impetus to the Fabian effort to fashion a different conception of socialism and socialist strategy. If the events of 1886–7 convinced Fabians that there was to be no dramatic, decisive revolutionary rupture with the liberal-capitalist present and socialists were there for the 'long haul', then the events of 1895–7 brought even more evidence of this 'fact'. Stanley Pierson has pinpointed the years 1895–7 as a quite decisive moment in the development of contemporary socialism. As a consequence of the events of these years, even socialists outside of the Fabian group began to move towards a more active engagement with strategic issues and to think about more pragmatic and constructive ways to facilitate change towards socialism.[5] There were a number of reasons for this shift in mindset, according to Pierson. Firstly, Britain's political climate was altering in ways which made it more difficult for socialist ideas to flourish. At this point, and particularly after the Tory and Liberal-Unionist landslide at the General Election of 1895, socialists were faced with a powerful Conservative resurgence, as well as the emotional counter-appeal of populist Social-Imperialism.[6] Secondly, Pierson contends that an improving economic situation after 1896, as the economy began to come out of the 'Long Depression', worked to dilute much of the economic and social distress which had driven many into the socialist camp. Thirdly, Pierson claims that the extraordinary advances that socialism had made during the 1880s and through to the mid-1890s and beyond had taken a heavy toll on socialist bodies and spirits. These exertions resulted in many of the movement's key activists succumbing to physical and mental exhaustion and even death, tragic premature death in some cases. William Morris, *The Clarion*'s Edward Fay, Tom Maguire, Caroline Martyn, the London dockers' leader Tom McCarthy, Samuel Washington, the Manchester ILP activist Edward Pankhurst, Eleanor Marx and Edward Aveling all passed away during the years 1896–8.[7] To these reasons, we should add the stalling of New Unionism after its initial surge in the early part of the decade, as well as the Progressives on the London County Council after their earlier successes.[8]

The 'sobering' experiences of 1886–7 and 1895–7, then, would give real impetus to the Fabian project to steer socialists towards an alternative, more pragmatic political strategy, as well as a more pragmatic understanding of socialism. As mentioned and as we will see below, there would be quite distinct modernist elements within this project. Before we look at this modernist component, it would be useful to identify certain key features of the Fabian approach at the more general level of political ideology and tactics. As previously mentioned, following the setback of 1886–7 Fabians would repudiate all forms of 'insurrectionary' phraseology and methods, whether of the type seen in the 'direct action' confrontations with the state during the 'Bloody Sunday' disturbances, or as expressed through more extreme, violent forms of revolutionary rhetoric. Indeed, Fabians would have no truck with the Marxist theory of value, the Marxist 'melodrama' of the 'class war', the doctrine of proletarian revolution, nor any notion of change in society occurring as a result of a cataclysmic upheaval. For leading Fabians, socialist minds should be bent towards the albeit long-term task of forming a 'Collectivist political party' that could win the support of 'educated' workers, left-leaning Radicals and dis-affected Liberals, which would press for socialistic measures on a wide range of political fronts. In the meantime, prior to the arrival of the 'Collectivist party', strenuous efforts should be made to 'perme-ate' mainstream political parties, particularly the Liberal Party, with socialistic ideas.

As mentioned, there were significant modernist elements within the Fabian project. Unlike the other, more spiritual, mythological, religious, mystical and even occultist forms of socialist modernism we have been considering in this book up to now, Fabian modernism was heavily underpinned by a 'scientistic' vision to create a new and better world. As with their modernist contemporaries within areas of the socialist revival, Fabians were optimists who believed that the future course of historical development could be shaped in a way that would bring real and lasting social benefits to those hitherto excluded from the wealth produced by society. In the Fabian modernist utopia, however, modern science and technology, ideally in strategic alliance with the state, would play a central role. To some extent, Fabian opti-mism and scientism was informed by modernist sentiments of a kind which anticipated the 'heroic modernism' that became popular in a later period of modernism just before the Great War, but particu-larly after the carnage of that conflict. As well as striving to clean up the 'filth' and squalor that blighted life for many in the mod-ern world, post-War heroic modernists like Le Corbusier and Walter Gropius were driven by an urge to improve the lot of humankind by bringing a sense of order and clarity into the chaos of modern life.[9] In their endorsement of more rational systems of architecture and daily living, realised through a style of architecture that was geo-metric, logical, simple, precise and 'clean', Le Corbusier and Gropius believed that they were pointing the way towards a better future for all. Modern technology and industrial methods would help facili-tate the passage to this 'brave new world'. Heroic modernists like Le Corbusier and Gropius made creative use of modern industrial mate-rials in their designs and generally endorsed the rationalist heritage of technology and science through their approach and ethos. In peering into the future through their imagined technological utopias, heroic modernists were tacitly endorsing the logic of the technological and industrial changes associated with the processes of modernisation and modernity. Indeed, heroic modernism would be more reconciled to the prevailing 'grand narrative' of modernisation–modernity than other forms of modernism. In other words, it was a form of modernism which felt itself impelled to accept the logic and universality of modernisation–modernity and was thus more prepared than other versions of modernism to work with the grain of mainstream technological, industrial and economic processes. Put another way, if the spiritual, mythological, religious, mystical and occultist forms of socialist modernism we have looked at in past chapters indicated a desire to escape from the blight of 'progress' and mainstream 'history', then heroic modernism was indicative of an urge to collaborate with the project of progress and history. Even more than this, heroic modernists were prepared to accelerate this project, forever forward into an open, boundless, though always technological future.

If Fabian scientistic modernism anticipated post-War heroic modernism, it also shared characteristics with another intellectual tradition which aligned itself closely to the modernisation–modernity agenda and the Enlightenment rationalist project. To identify this tradition, we need to gaze backwards to the era of Saint-Simonian socialism of the first half of the nineteenth century. As with the Fabians, Henri de Saint-Simon and the zealous Saint-Simonian disciples who spread the faith after the prophet's death in 1825 propounded a highly optimistic vision of the future. The Saint-Simonian future, moreover, as with the heroic modernist future we have just been looking at, was a 'scientistic utopia' that, if realised, would produce a social transformation of epic and universal proportions. Saint-Simonians were passionate about the transformative potential of science, technology and industry. This passion was underpinned by a positivist belief in the power of these iconic symbols of the modern world to unleash dormant capacities of growth within society and thereby facilitate the passage to a new age of prosperity and social justice which catered for all, including the hitherto excluded masses. As with the positivism that underpinned later Fabian thinking, there would be a sort of remorseless inevitability to this ascent to a higher plane. As articulated in his 1813 essay on *The Science of Man* in 1813, Saint-Simon claimed that fields of scientific knowledge moved in a definite and progressive order from a more infant stage to a higher, 'positive' stage, as when alchemy gave way to the higher stage of chemistry.[10] For Saint-Simon, history had progressed to a stage where the 'science of man' should now proceed to its own 'positive' stage. Saint-Simon's friend and ex-pupil Auguste Comte later spread the positivist 'gospel', claiming that humankind was progressing towards a higher, 'positive' future, having passed through two earlier, more simple phases – the 'theological' and the 'metaphysical'.[11] One should note here the assumption that there existed within the historical process certain irresistible tendencies which were propelling it forward to a higher stage of development. As we will see below, teleological assumptions of a similar nature were present in the Fabian conception of historical progress.

There was a further aspect to this Saint-Simonian vision of the future which, again, resurfaced in Fabian scientistic modernism. This was the belief in the capacity of enlightened engineers and scientists to steer society towards this higher stage of development. In both the Saint-Simonian and Fabian scientistic utopias, these 'industrious' engineers and scientists were elevated to the status of a secular 'priesthood', a new meritocratic elite who would help bring about the transition to the more advanced industrial and social arrangement. They were deemed to be able to perform this vital role because of their heightened sense of public duty and visionary perspective, the latter enabling them to see beyond traditional obstacles to the enormous potential inherent in modern science, technology and industry. The Faustian elements in the Saint-Simonian project are unmistakeable. The Saint-Simonian intellectuals who followed in the footsteps of the prophet, many of whom were engineers and scientists, embraced a truly Faustian vision of the future. We can see this vision at work in the determination of these industrious, mostly young, intellectuals to break out of the constraints of the present and carve out a more rational, supposedly superior future. The projects of the Saint-Simonian elite could be truly spectacular in ambition and scale, whether these involved punching a canal through the Isthmus of Suez or constructing elaborate networks of railways across France and other parts of Europe. Concerned less with short-term profit, they were often long-range and 'heroic' in their stated intention to bring about a more comprehensive social transformation. These projects also aimed to unlock dormant productive capacity within the economy and society, as well as harness the power of modern science and technology to this agenda. All this was, of course, deemed to have wider social benefits. The Saint-Simonian Faustian project was innovative in other ways. As Marshall Berman points out, it aimed at a novel synthesis of public and private spheres, with the former, the 'Faustian public planner', usually assuming the leading role in planning and directing the effort towards the attainment of the project's rational goals.[12]

Fabian scientistic modernism shared characteristics with both the traditions we have just been looking at. As with the Saint-Simonians and the post-War heroic modernists, Fabian modernists were excited by the future and their agenda was aggressively orientated towards it. There was also a distinct Faustian dimension to Fabian optimism about the future. As we will see, Fabians believed in aggressive conscious forward planning, and the capacity of enlightened elites to steer society towards a higher stage of development. Like all true Faustians, Fabian modernists were captivated by the power and potential of modern science, technology and industry, believing that these potent instruments of the modern world would help carve out a brave new future that would bring economic and social benefits for all. These various traditions converged in another related sense. In their quest to secure this better future, Fabian socialists, as with the Saint-Simonianians and post-War heroic modernists, were more than willing to accommodate their agenda to the dominant 'grand narrative' of modernisation–modernity. Because leading Fabians frequently demonstrated a willingness to embrace Enlightenment rationalist assumptions concerning technological, scientific, industrial and economic progress, there was no immediate, decisive break with the trajectory of the changes wrought by the modernisation process as a whole, nor indeed the existing framework of the modern capitalist mode of production and economy. Take the following stark judgement of Sidney Webb made in 1899:

> .... But if we are to clear up our ideas, and apply our socialist principles to the practical problems of life, we must definitely make up our mind between contrary ideals. If our aim is the transformation of England into a Social-Democracy, we must frankly accept the changes brought about by the Industrial Revolution, the factory system, the massing of population in great cities, [and] the elaborate differentiation and complication of modern civilisation ....[13]

Thus, rather than seeking to flee from the terrors of capitalist 'progress', which was the response of many of their modernist contemporaries within the socialist revival, Fabian modernists felt it necessary to enter into collaboration with this project, if only to try to steer it in a socialist or 'collectivist' direction.

If there were defects in this arrangement, then Fabians were optimistic that the imperfections associated with the capitalist mode of production could be eliminated over time. This optimism flowed from the deeply held conviction that the future course of historical development was heading in a socialist direction. It is at this point that we encounter another intellectual influence on Fabian modernism. As well as revealing strains of positivism in its modernist perspective on science, technology, industry and the future, we can also discern the influence of Darwinism and Social-Darwinism on Fabian modernism. Fabians perceived society in evolutionary terms as a relatively self-regulating organism that over time was gradually, but naturally, progressing towards a higher form of social organism. This model of change rested on the optimistic belief that the tendency of the evolving organism was in the preferred direction, that is, towards the public, socialised organisation of production, which they perceived to be more rational and 'efficient' than the current privatised capitalist system of production. In this Fabian historical teleology the emergence of a socialistic or 'collectivist' organism seemed to be almost determined in advance, the outcome of the irresistible surge of social tendencies within the historical process which was compelling modern societies to discard the increasingly anachronistic mode of organising life associated with *laissez-faire* 'individualism'. As Sidney Webb put it:

> In this direction, too, [i.e. towards the Collectivist future] is the mighty sweep and tendency of social evolution. Without our knowledge, even against our will, we in England have already been carried far by the irresistible wave. What Canute will dare to set a limit to its advance? One option we have, and one only.[14]

In this Fabian conception of 'evolutionary socialism', the socialist future it seems was being brought about by 'natural necessity'. As we will see below, however, this did not mean that Fabians were fully reconciled to the theory of 'natural selection'. Indeed, they were more than willing to propose measures to help expedite the evolutionary process.

In time, and certainly by the early 1900s, this tendency to view the world through the lens of evolutionary Social-Darwinism inclined Fabian modernism towards a more authoritarian approach to national affairs. It is at this point as well, with Fabianism revealing its links with Darwinian thinking, that Fabian modernism took on a distinctly social modernist hue. To understand these developments within Fabianism more fully, we need to look more closely at Fabian organicism, that is, the predilection to view society as a 'social organism'. As with other late Victorian and Edwardian Social-Darwinists, Fabians tended to view society through a biological perspective. This idea that there was an association between biology and social life was, as Greta Jones informs us, already beginning to interest intellectuals in Britain and elsewhere by the mid-nineteenth century.[15] After *The Origins of Species* was published in 1859, the temptation to draw comparisons between social life and biology and see 'analogies between social processes and living organisms' became even more widespread in intellectual and political circles.[16] More specifically, for our purpose in seeking to more fully understand the appearance of strains of authoritarianism and social modernism within Fabianism, this would lead not only to the proliferation of organic analogies as a means of understanding society but also to the tendency to view social problems from the perspective of biological health and treatment.

As we have seen, for Sidney Webb and other leading Fabians the nation was a biological organism similar in its workings and laws of development to organic life forms in the natural world, which was gradually ascending to a higher form of social organisation. It was socialism or 'collectivism' which represented this more advanced form of social organisation that, in time, was destined to lift society to a higher stage of evolutionary development. This being said, Fabian optimism about the future course of historical development was tempered by anxiety, because the same evolutionary challenges and perils which governed life in the natural world applied also to the social world. According to Darwinian theory, an incessant competitive struggle for existence was being waged in the natural world, and only those species that were capable of adapting to this hostile environment would survive and thus go on to reproduce according to these laws of 'natural selection'. Similar evolutionary mechanisms were at work in the social and political world, for Social-Darwinists, including Fabian Social-Darwinists. As in nature, the socio-political environment, extending to the international arena, was severe, ruthlessly competitive and favoured the 'fittest'. In order to ensure survival in such an environment, and ultimately allow the nation to progress in an evolutionary sense, it was deemed necessary to ensure that the social organism was as healthy or efficient as possible. This meant that the evolving organism of society was not to be completely left to its own devices as the laws of 'natural selection' implied, even if social evolution seemed to be pointing in a collectivist direction. Rather, there should be some intervention in the evolutionary process to help facilitate the nation's quest for 'social fitness' and thus expedite the trend towards the collectivist future. For Sidney Webb and other Fabians, intervention usually meant state intervention. This meant strengthening the framework and authority of the state and enhancing its presence in national life. With their attempt to ensure that the state secured the nation's fitness and efficiency and guided its fortunes in a hostile world, Fabian Social-Darwinists therefore moved some way from Darwin's original idea concerning natural selection. Rather, the planned intervention of the external agency of the state would replace the more random, unmediated operations of Darwinian natural selection.

Their rather pessimistic Social-Darwinist take on the world, coupled with anxiety about the nation's 'biological health', led some Fabians to flirt with quite authoritarian solutions to contemporary social and political problems. We can see this tilt towards a more authoritarian approach, for example, when Sidney and Beatrice Webb formed the 'Co-efficients' in November 1902. As with the Saint-Simonians before them, Fabian modernists favoured elites. They were convinced that the goal of national efficiency and modern progress imposed a pressing obligation on society to cultivate a new meritocracy of technicians, administrators and other 'experts', an elite of professionals who possessed the vision, know-how and will to drive society to its next stage of development. The Co-efficients, a small, select dining club of 'experts' committed to promoting the cause of efficiency in all areas of national and imperial life, were formed with this aspiration in mind.[17] One of the most striking features of the Co-efficient group, given the professed socialist beliefs of its founders, was its curious political composition. In their determination to expedite their national efficiency agenda, the Webbs demonstrated that they were not too particular about the political company they kept. Their experts were drawn from across the political spectrum, and included elements from the contemporary Social-Imperialist Radical Right. Leopold Amery, a supporter of Joseph Chamberlain's protectionist Social-Imperialism, was a member of the group, as was the Liberal-Imperialist and geo-political strategist Halford J. Mackinder. Others were the Liberal-Imperialist barrister Richard Haldane, the

Liberal-Imperialist Carlyon Bellairs and the diehard Tory Leopold Maxse. Maxse was the editor of the *National Review*, and was obsessed about the German economic and military threat to the British Empire. The former British High Commissioner to South Africa and influential Tariff Reform protectionist Viscount Milner joined the group at a later date. So, too, did the Liberal-Imperialist and editor of *Monthly Review* Henry Newbolt.[18] As with the Webbs, the bulk of these Co-efficient experts believed that the nation's affairs in troubled times were best served by a strong, efficiently organised, interventionist state. Even more interesting, however, given the Fabian involvement in the group, was the anti-democratic orientation of a number of the Co-efficients.[19] Leopold Maxse and Lord Milner harboured a deep distrust of parliamentary democracy and government, while Halford Mackinder also had concerns.[20] The intended longer-term aim of the Co-efficients to create a new party of 'National Efficiency' comprising all the talents regardless of class and political affiliation, as well as its strident endorsement of a robust imperialism, also betrayed the group's rightist, even authoritarian, leanings.

To a large extent, these more extreme approaches to perceived national problems were a consequence of that tendency within Social-Darwinism to see analogies between the nation-state and living biological organisms. Once the nation was cast in this way, as a social organism menaced by threats to its health from within and without, as with other living organisms in nature, social and political problems began to be viewed increasingly through the lens of biological health, treatment and cure. It is no surprise then that during these years sociologists, political commentators and others often used medical language and metaphors to diagnose social and political problems, with some behaving 'like doctors attempting to cure certain ills which had arisen in the body politic'.[21] Thus, the prominent urban theorist and Social-Darwinist fellow traveller Patrick Geddes saw the cure of adverse social conditions in Britain's cities 'in terms of the treatment of an organic disease which if left untouched would be fatal to the organism itself'.[22] This tendency to represent social problems as medical ones requiring a prognosis, treatment and cure encouraged the quite strident forms of interventionism in society, of the type proposed by the Fabians.[23]

We can see this more strident interventionism at work in another area of Fabian thinking. As Roger Griffin states, Social-Darwinism 'encouraged the subliminal social anxieties fuelled by modernity to be "biologized" into the conviction that civilisation was being destroyed from within by the forces of physiological "degeneracy" and racial decay'.[24] It is at this point that Social-Darwinist organicism merged with the so-called 'science' of eugenics. Eugenicists were obsessed about health and the nation's supposedly degenerating social stock, and promoted aggressive schemes of social reform to address this. As for the claim that eugenics had a scientific basis, eugenicists maintained that their views were supported by the science of Darwinian evolutionary biology and by scientific knowledge concerning heredity. In terms of the latter, eugenicists believed that individual characteristics and behaviour were determined by heredity rather than environmental factors, a view apparently given the stamp of scientific approval by the German biologist August Weismann's theory of the 'germ plasm'.[25] For Weismann, the 'germ plasm' was a hereditary substance passed from generation to generation and was the sole agent of inheritance. In claiming that 'germ cells' were the agent of heredity, as well as being immune from environmental influences, Weismann was rejecting the Lamarckian theory that acquired characteristics could be inherited.

The significance of these views on biological heredity for eugenicists is that they heightened fears concerning Britain's supposedly deteriorating social stock. Britain's cities and the urban poor became the main the focus of these fears. The later half of the nineteenth century saw a dramatic increase in urbanisation and urban populations, along with a corresponding fear of the expansion of the demoralised 'danger classes' who populated the urban slums or 'residuum'.[26] For their part, eugenicists believed that Britain's cities were home to vast hordes of the physically and mentally 'unfit' with a tendency towards pathological behaviour, and that their numbers were multiplying due to unrestrained procreation. It was hereditary weakness rather than environmental factors which inclined the urban poor towards pathological behaviour, such as crime and alcoholism, and mired them in poverty, according to eugenicists. Politically motivated eugenicists believed that this urban blight was sapping national vitality and that something dramatic needed to be done to ensure the nation's survival in an inhospitable world. Convinced that degenerate behaviour was genetically transmitted rather than environmentally induced, their prognosis was to press for a regulatory system of selective breeding to discourage or inhibit the reproduction of the 'unfit', while simultaneously encouraging an increase in the birth rate of the supposedly physically and mentally healthier types in society. Taking all these ingredients into account – the *angst* concerning degeneration, the urge to regenerate the national organism, the promotion of social measures to create a healthier population and the attempt to mobilise science and an interventionist reform-minded state to help socially engineer this project – eugenics needs to be seen 'as a form of social modernism in its own right'.[27] Eugenics was social modernist in a further sense. Its perverse health agenda was aggressively orientated towards the future, believing that future progress would only come about through the introduction of social schemes which not only re-adjusted the relative fertility rates of society's weaker and stronger elements, but which worked to 'eliminate' the unfit.[28]

As some scholars have pointed out, eugenics was not the preserve of Fascism, Nazism, the Radical Right, Social-Imperialism or other variants of right-wing thinking. Left-wing thinkers also held strong eugenicist views, including leading Fabians.[29] There were certainly strands of thinking within eugenics which would have appealed to Fabians. These include the modernist orientation of eugenics towards the future, the belief that scientific knowledge should underwrite policy, the social modernist concern about the condition of the urban poor and the equally social modernist belief in state action to bring about social improvement. The efficiency element within eugenics, namely the attempt by eugenicists to efficiently manage the fertility rates of human beings and indeed entire social groups, also interested the Fabians. The Fabians were also of the view that the professional middle-class 'expert' was best placed to administer the affairs of an efficient modern society, and some Fabians certainly identified with eugenic proposals to encourage middle-class procreation. George Bernard Shaw was one Fabian who believed that a modern society should seek to multiply its 'highest types'. It was imperative that society breed exceptional individuals for Shaw, because the conscious striving of these creative 'will-to-achievement' types, or 'Supermen', would further evolution and help shape it in the preferred direction. Shaw favoured granting mothers who displayed the appropriate virtues an endowment to assist and encourage the bearing of a healthy child:

> If a woman can, by careful selection of a father, and nourishment of herself, produce a citizen with efficient senses, sound organs, and a good digestion, she should clearly be secured a sufficient

reward for that natural service to make her willing to undertake and repeat it.[30]

As for the denizens of the 'residuum', it was necessary to check their numbers in order to stave off national disaster:

> Our only hope, then, is in evolution. We must replace the man by the Superman .... The only fundamental and possible socialism is the socialization of the selective breeding of Man: in other terms, of human evolution. We must eliminate the Yahoo, or his vote will wreck the commonwealth.[31]

Shaw was evidently no admirer of mass democracy, or society's lower orders which he contemptuously referred to as 'tinkers'. The 'tinkers' were 'riff-raff' for Shaw, 'and to hand the country over to riff-raff is national suicide, since riff-raff can neither govern nor will let any-one else govern except the highest bidder of bread and circuses'.[32] The social modernist orientation of Shaw's thinking is apparent for all to see, as in his desire to utilise the modern state as an instrument of eugenicist social improvement. His recommendations in this area were often bizarre, as in his proposal to set up a 'State Department of Evolution' with a Cabinet seat granted to its chief.[33] He also suggested the establishment of a special Chartered Company 'for the improve-ment of human live stock'.[34] It should not surprise us to find that Shaw lectured for the Eugenics Education Society.[35]

Eugenics as social modernism is even more evident in Sidney Webb's thinking. Webb believed that eugenics was progressive and could be used to address social ailments and help produce a better, healthier society. Like other eugenicists, he worried about the ris-ing birth-rate in the 'residuum', as well as the declining birth-rate amongst 'the more prudent, foreseeing and self-restrained sections of the community'.[36] It was vital therefore to find ways to raise fer-tility rates amongst those of virtue within society. 'In order to put a stop to the adverse selection that is at present going on', he wrote in 1907, 'we must encourage the thrifty, foreseeing, prudent and self-controlled parents to remove the check which, often unwillingly enough, they at present put on their natural instincts and love of children.'[37] The state was to play a positive role in this enterprise. State aid in the form of an 'endowment of motherhood' should be granted to those child-rearing mothers who conformed to the appro-priate profile. The endowment would comprise unlimited medical provision and free meals on demand for mothers, as well as a free supply of milk to their infants. On occasions, Webb's social eugenics would lapse into racial eugenics, as when he contemplated the prospect of Britain 'gradually falling to the Irish and the Jews', or even 'the Chinese', on account of 'alien' immigration and unfettered procreation habits in the residuum.[38] If Sidney Webb tended to favour positive social eugenics, his Fabian colleague H.G. Wells demonstrated an inclination to embrace the most rabid forms of negative eugenics. It was the state's right to ensure, he asserted, that those wishing to have children were 'above a certain minimum of personal efficiency', demonstrated 'a certain minimum of physical development' and were free 'of any transmissible disease'.[39] At times, his eugenicist social modernism went even further. The state needed to resort 'to a kind of social surgery', he urged, to prevent certain types from spawning offspring. These were the 'mildly incompetent, the spiritless and dull, the poorer sort who are ill', indeed all those who remain 'idiots and lunatics', drunkards, 'perverse and incompetent', or are 'tainted with certain foul and transmissible diseases'.[40] As for the 'social surgery', it stopped short of 'lethal chambers' for adults, but did include killing 'all deformed and monstrous and evilly diseased births' and quarantining those 'degenerate' adults 'who spoil the world for others' on special islands patrolled by guards.[41]

The Fabians' particular brand of modernism would incline them towards authoritarianism and interventionism in another sense. The Fabians were just as determined to erase 'inefficiency' within the contemporary socialist movement, as they were to eliminate inefficiency in national life. As with their stance towards perceived problems in national life, this intolerance of socialist 'inefficiency' stemmed mainly from the Fabians' scientistic and rational interpretation of socialism. This intolerance moreover would have implications for the future course and character of socialism in Britain beyond the revival years. Because of the relevance of this for wider questions relating to socialist modernism within the revival, as well as the future course of British socialism, this issue will form part of the deliberations in the Conclusion to this book.

Conclusion

This book started out with a distinct aim. Its aim was to attempt to 'go beyond' established historiographical frameworks and offer a fresh perspective on the socialist revival of the late Victorian and Edwardian decades. This involved exploring the socialist revival, and indeed the very nature of British socialism itself during these important years of its development, from the standpoint of modernism. In reconceptualising an important segment of the recent history of British socialism in this way, in establishing a relationship between the socialist revival and modernism, this book has identified with a 'maximalist' reading of modernism. In other words, modernism has been interpreted as a wide-ranging project and aspiration extending beyond the concerns of the artistic and literary avant-garde to embrace political and social movements for change which sought to forge a new world and mode of existence beyond modernity based on a more transcendental or spiritual conception of life.

The modernist components within the socialist revival were palpable, as the various chapters in this monograph sought to show. The particular historical conjuncture of the late Victorian and Edwardian era itself was interpreted as a distinctly modernist moment. For many of the legions of new socialist converts who entered the socialist camp, liberal-capitalist modernity had arrived at the terminus of a long era of development and domination and history was now poised on the cusp of profound and radical change. To the fellowship socialist Edward Carpenter, it had:

> become obvious that the existing order of things – in Government, Law, Finance, Industry, Commerce, Morality, Religion, the Capitalist Wage system, the Rivalry of nation with nation, the

administration and cultivation of the Land, and so forth – could not continue much longer. In each one and all of these matters we have been heading towards an *impasse*, a block, a point at which further progress in the old direction must cease, and a new departure begin.[1]

This was, moreover, an undecided future which spawned visions of alternative scenarios of tomorrow to that of the narrow, 'pre-given' Enlightenment-dominated model of the future promoted by the advocates of capitalist 'progress'. This modernist moment was alive with competing or differential temporalities, whereby the future was imagined by socialists as an exciting realm of possibility, at once open and charged with hope and latent with the prospect of more humane relationships and spiritual life beyond liberal-capitalist modernity and its decadent Victorian values. As for those complex ideological configurations within the socialist revival, with their fusing of seemingly paradoxical and contradictory themes, these have been interpreted as wonderfully erratic modernist montages. This was 'politics in a new key', to borrow Carl Schorske's splendid description of the new modernist politics that emerged in *fin de siècle* Vienna, kaleidoscopes of new political forms and expressions which were perfectly attuned to the modernist moment of *fin de siècle* Britain with its seismic economic, social, political and cultural convulsions and tantalising glimpses of alternative futures.[2]

Modernist innovation and novelty of form can also be seen in those fascinating fusions of the material and the spiritual that permeated the socialism of these years, as in the mystical monist socialism of those such as the Bolton socialist James William Wallace and Edward Carpenter, who experienced in 'cosmic consciousness' a mystical union with a higher reality. To downplay or ignore the interpenetration of the material with the spiritual in the socialist ideological makeup would have been to seriously misunderstand the nature of British socialism during the late Victorian and Edwardian years. During these decades, there was a widespread fascination in Britain and elsewhere with spiritual matters, as seen in the interest in mysticism, occultism, the fourth dimension and Emersonian transcendentalism, which manifested itself as a reaction to Enlightenment rationalism, modernisation and the de-sacralising tendencies of Victorian materialism and culture.[3] This engagement with spiritual concerns did not signal a desire to retreat from the modern world but, on the contrary, was a distinctly modern or modernist reaction to some of the central issues thrown up by the processes of modernisation–modernity. It would be naive to think, as the previous chapters sought to show, that the new socialist movement of the *fin de siècle* would somehow have remained untouched or unaffected by this turn towards the spiritual within the wider society and culture.

The reaction to modernity and progress, the attempt to craft new and more meaningful life in the context of a new beginning beyond the alienation, philistinism and decadence of Victorian and Edwardian capitalism, assumed other forms as well. As this book showed, visions of a different type of future could be glimpsed or evoked through aesthetics, myth, religious symbolism, metaphoric imagery, dreams and utopian imagining. These various, quite exotic elements within the socialist ideological makeup were thus also interpreted as so-many forms, manifestations and expressions of modernism. The utopian communities set up by socialists and other radicals during these decades also exhibited distinctly modernist characteristics. We saw this in the wonderful eclecticism on display in the political profile of these community experiments. We also observed it in their spatial profiles, as socialist communitarians sought to carve out new spaces and spatial relationships beyond the mainstream of capitalist space. The relationship between modernism and these community schemes is even more apparent when we identified the latter as radical experiments in social modernism. This book identified a further component of modernism within the socialist revival. This emanated from the socialist engagement with the childhood experience, bearing in mind the importance of childhood for the modernist quest to magically re-enchant a world that was becoming increasingly disenchanted and de-spiritualised as a result of the combined pressures of modernisation, modernity and capitalist progress.

Modernism and British Socialism has allowed us to explore and appreciate the creativity, richness, heterogeneity and breadth of both the socialist revival and modernism. Given the former, we should conclude this study of modernism and British socialism by asking why the luxuriant forms of socialist modernism we have been looking at in this book failed to endure as a more long-lasting presence within the socialist project. This is all the more surprising when we take into account the evangelical fervour of socialism during the revival years, its incredible openness and tolerance of diversity, its strong spiritual basis, its imaginative views on lifestyle and its capacity to present captivating utopian visions of a glorious new dispensation bathed in the perfection which prevailed during the earliest time. Even during the euphoric decades of the socialist revival itself, these imaginative, often exotic and always transcendent renderings of socialism were rarely in the ascendant. How should we account for this, as well as the failure of these particular 'narratives' and modes of socialist modernism to endure as a more lasting presence within British socialism? To answer these questions, we need to return to the other narrative of socialist modernism that we looked at in Chapter 7, Fabian modernism.

We saw in that discussion the Fabian obsession with 'efficiency' and the tendency to view social problems from the perspective of biological health and treatment, which inclined the Fabian project to adopt an authoritarian approach in certain matters relating to national life. This obsession with efficiency inclined Fabianism towards authoritarianism in another sense, which has a bearing on the questions just posed. This other strand of authoritarianism within Fabian modernism needs some explaining because it had implications for the way the socialist project developed in Britain. The Fabians demonstrated a will and determination during the revival years to eliminate inefficiency within the socialist project, as well as in national life. They contrived to do this by seeking to erase 'difference' within the socialist movement. In other words, they sought to render socialism homogenous by erasing all spiritual, religious, romantic, mystical and utopian, both imagined and applied, influences from contemporary socialist thinking and practice. They set about this task with the same ruthless sense of logic they showed when confronting other perceived areas of inefficiency in society and political life, as well as when challenging 'insurrectionist' tendencies within the socialist movement. To understand this intolerance towards socialist 'inefficiency', we need to take a further look at the nature of Fabian modernism.

It was the Fabians' scientist and rational interpretation of socialism, particularly their orientation towards a heroic future imagined as technologically advanced and efficient, which made them highly suspicious of those conceptions of socialism they deemed to be backward-looking or nostalgic. As Sidney Webb remarked of those who envisaged a socialist arrangement as comprising associations of small-scale independent producers, free of overseers, the 'wage system' and the disciplinary frameworks of modern industrialisation, of the type that had characterised the pre-modern, pre-capitalist economy:

> To listen to their interpretation one would imagine that they suppose us to contemplate a reversion to a mythical time when every man worked as an independent producer, and enjoyed the whole product of his individual labour. I need hardly say that socialism involves nothing of the sort.[4]

Fabians were equally dismissive of aesthetic interpretations of socialism of the kind which featured in that strain of 'aesthetic modernism' within the socialist project. They were particularly dismissive of those who believed that the socialist cause could be seriously advanced by propaganda which presented an 'aesthetically-heightened' image of future socialism. Thus, socialism for George Bernard Shaw, if it was to 'gain serious attention nowadays, must come into the field as political science and not as sentimental dogma'.[5] In other words, those conceptions of socialism which sought to 'dramatise' the socialist message 'either in an artistic or religious form to arouse popular sympathy and enchain popular attention' must eventually give way to a more rational, scientific exposition of the socialist case along the lines articulated by the Fabian group.[6] Or, to present it another way, Fabian intellectuals exhibited a disdain for those self-styled artists and poets within the socialist movement who preferred to place aesthetics, as David Harvey would have put it, 'above science, rationality and politics'.[7] Shaw was even more dismissive of religious dramatisations of socialism. These were the 'religious illusions' of socialism for Shaw, namely those various expressions of socialist utopian modernism which took a religious form as in the eschatological myth of the coming socialist Kingdom. This intolerance towards these alternative, 'softer' versions of socialist modernism was further reinforced by the Fabian belief that socialism needed to continue along the path of progress or modern industrial development if it was to evolve into the dominant form of socio-economic organisation in society. Thus Shaw asserted that 'the data of Collectivism [i.e. socialism] are to be found in Blue Books, statistical abstracts, reports, records and observations of the actual facts and conditions of industrial life, not in dreams, ideals, prophecies and revelations'.[8]

The Fabians' scientistic interpretation of socialism made them intolerant of those 'soft' forms of socialist social modernism practised in the small-scale utopian communities as well. Sidney Webb was particularly scathing of those who believed that socialism should be built on a foundation of local community experiments. The Fabian Society, he wrote in 1899, 'had but little sympathy with schemes for the regeneration of mankind by the establishment of local Utopias, whether in Cumberland or Chile', nor did it have faith 'in the recuperative qualities of spade husbandry or in any devices for dodging the Law of Rent'.[9] Utopian schemes had a 'static' character, for Webb, writing earlier in 1889. As such, they were a form of arrested development that ignored the laws of social evolution by assuming that a perfected state had already been arrived at 'without need or possibility of future organic alteration'.[10] Such assumptions were, of course, profoundly unscientific and naive to Webb. In its hostile attitude towards these small-scale efforts at utopia-building, Fabianism demonstrated it was reactionary in an additional, related sense. By opposing the differential, place-bound counter-spaces of the community schemes, it was setting its face against the impulse towards spatial heterogeneity within the socialist revival. In so doing, the Fabians were tacitly endorsing the particular spatial logic of contemporary capitalism. Indeed the Fabian modernists favoured a model of progress which worked towards the production of a 'technicist, scientific and intellectualised representation of space' which would have been highly compatible with the trajectory of capitalist development.[11]

For socialists who yearned for a more just society but wondered how it would come about, Fabian modernism had much to recommend it. While many would have baulked at the more authoritarian forms of social modernism as expressed through Fabian eugenics, the heroic modernism of Fabianism would have had a strong appeal. As we have seen, Fabianism was highly optimistic about the future and had a definite vision of what this future would look like. The Fabian future would be an unambiguously modernist utopia involving science, technology, modern industrial methods and rational planning which, according to its advocates, would bring about a genuine social transformation. All this would be overseen by a highly 'efficient' state machine and a new meritocratic class of enlightened intellectuals working on behalf of the public good. The Fabian group also felt that it knew how best to arrive at this highly rational future. It mocked those efforts to achieve socialism via class-war 'insurrectionism' or the small-scale local utopias. As with their understanding of socialism, Fabian political strategy was pragmatic, rational and shorn of sentimentality. Socialism will come, said George

Bernard Shaw, 'by prosaic instalments of public regulation and public administration enacted by ordinary parliaments, vestries, municipalities, parish councils, school boards and the like'.[12] In short, 'the lot of the socialist is to be one of dogged political drudgery'.[13] For the Fabians, this approach was highly logical and entirely in keeping with their evolutionary perspective which was premised on the understanding of history as a relatively pre-determined process. In other words, they felt that the laws and direction of social evolution impelled them to work with the grain of modern industrial and political development. To do otherwise was unscientific and profoundly naive.

All this being said, the Fabian effort to infuse socialism with greater 'efficiency', to render the socialist project more scientific, rational and pragmatic and ensure it did not stray from the narrow pathway of 'growth and accumulation' demanded by mainstream history and progress, contrived to kill something fundamental within British socialism. This was that aspiration to dream within the socialist revival, of imagining at arriving at other worlds and places in a future as yet undefined, open and full of radical possibilities. This was not the narrow pre-determined 'scientistic' future of Fabian modernism, or indeed of the project of modernisation, modernity and capitalist progress. Rather, in these other 'softer' narratives of socialist modernism, the future was undecided and indeterminate, a product of multiple perspectives and full of quirky 'ambivalence' to borrow Zygmunt Bauman's term.[14] This was 'that sense of beyond' which W.H.G. Armytage recognised as 'the motive power' of British socialism at crucial stages of its development and which endowed it 'with a heart'.[15] In their determination to bring socialism 'back down to earth', make it more relevant to mainstream processes, Fabianism subverted and closed off these alternative understandings of socialism and diverted the socialist aspiration for change along a narrowly scientistic and materialistic path. Once socialist doctrine had been cast so narrowly in this way by the self-appointed Fabian guardians of British socialism, it seemed unavoidable that much of the creativity and hope which had bloomed so abundantly during the revival years, and which expressed itself through the various forms of socialist modernism featured in this book, would fade away or find itself pushed to the 'eccentric' margins of the socialist project in Britain.

Notes

Introduction

1. William Jupp, *Wayfarings: A Record of Adventure and Liberation in the Life of the Spirit* (London: Headley Bros., 1918), p. 60.
2. E.P. Thompson has claimed that during the 1870s the number of socialists may have numbered as little as 20. See Edward P. Thompson, *William Morris: From Romantic to Revolutionary* (London: Lawrence and Wishart, 1955), p. 276.
3. The latter is mentioned in George Bernard Shaw, 'The Fabian Society: Its Early History', *Fabian Tract No. 41* (February 1892), p. 7.
4. These Christian Socialist bodies are discussed in Peter D'A. Jones, *The Christian Socialist Revival, 1877–1914. Religion, Class and Social Conscience in Late Victorian England* (Princeton: Princeton University Press, 1968).
5. Keith Laybourn, *The Rise of Socialism in Britain, c.1881–1951* (Sutton: Gloucestershire, 1997), pp. 32, 34.
6. See Lena Wallis, *The Life and Letters of Caroline Martyn* (Glasgow: Labour Leader, 1898). Caroline Martyn died in July 1896 at the age of just 29. She became one of the first socialist martyrs of the revival era.
7. On Carpenter, see Chushichi Tsuzuki, *Edward Carpenter, 1844–1929: Prophet of Human Fellowship* (Cambridge: Cambridge University Press, 1980); Edward Carpenter, *My Days and Dreams* (London: Allen and Unwin, 1916).
8. Annie Besant, *Annie Besant, An Autobiography* (London: T. Fisher Unwin, 1893), pp. 317–8.
9. See Chapter 2.
10. Examples of this earlier literature would include Henry Pelling, *The Origins of the Labour Party, 1880–1900* (Oxford: Clarendon Press, 1965) and G.D.H. Cole, *A Short History of the British Working Class Movement, 1789–1947* (London: Allen and Unwin, 1948).
11. See, for example, Eugenio Biagani and Alistair Reid, eds, *Currents of Radicalism: Popular Radicalism, Organised Labour and Party Politics in Britain, 1850–1914* (Cambridge: Cambridge University Press, 1991).
12. Stanley Pierson was particularly instrumental in promoting this concept. See Stanley Pierson, *British Socialists: The Journey from Fantasy to Politics* (Cambridge, Mass.: Harvard University Press, 1979); Stanley Pierson, *Marxism and the Origins of British Socialism. The Struggle for a New Consciousness* (Ithaca: Cornell University Press, 1973).

13. Examples include: Stephen Yeo, 'A New Life: The Religion of Socialism in Britain, 1883–1896', *History Workshop* 4 (1977): pp. 5–56; and Eric Hobsbawm, *Primitive Rebels. Studies in Archaic Forms of Social Movement in the 19th and 20th Century* (Manchester: Manchester University Press, 1959).

14. See, for example, James Hinton, *Labour and Socialism: A History of the British Labour Movement 1867–1974* (Brighton: Wheatsheaf Harvester, 1983); John Callaghan, *Socialism in Britain Since 1884* (Oxford: Blackwell, 1990). Thus, in an otherwise exemplary survey of British socialism, Callaghan devotes just a couple of sentences to the subject of 'ethical socialism' on page 6 of his book.

15. Roger Griffin, *Modernism and Fascism. The Sense of a Beginning under Mussolini and Hitler* (London: Palgrave Macmillan, 2007); Modris Eksteins, *The Rites of Spring* (Boston: Houghton Mifflin, 1989); and Marshall Berman, *All That Is Solid Melts into Air. The Experience of Modernity* (London: Verso, 1981).

16. Griffin, *Modernism and Fascism*, pp. 61–4.

1   Defining Modernism

1. Frederic Jameson, *A Singular Modernity. Essays on the Ontology of the Present* (London: Verso, 2002), p. 99.
2. Marshall Berman, *All That Is Solid Melts into Air. The Experience of Modernity* (London: Verso, 1981), p. 16.
3. Jameson, *A Singular Modernity*, pp. 141–4.
4. Roger Griffin, *Modernism and Fascism. The Sense of a Beginning under Mussolini and Hitler* (London: Palgrave Macmillan, 2007), pp. 45–6.
5. David Harvey, *The Condition of Postmodernity: An Enquiry into the Origins of Cultural Change* (Oxford: Blackwell, 1989); Jameson, *A Singular Modernity*.
6. Georg Simmel, ed., 'The Metropolis and Mental Life', in Georg Simmel, ed., *On Individuality and Social Forms* (Chicago: University of Chicago Press, 1971).
7. Anthony Giddens, *The Consequences of Modernity* (Cambridge: Polity, 1990), p. 37.
8. Harvey, *The Condition of Postmodernity*, pp. 27–8.
9. Zygmunt Bauman, *Modernity and Ambivalence* (Oxford: Polity Press, 1991), p. 7.
10. Griffin, *Modernism and Fascism*, p. 49.
11. Bauman, *Modernity and Ambivalence*, pp. 10–11.
12. Reinhart Koselleck, 'The Eighteenth Century As the Beginning of Modernity', in Reinhart Koselleck, ed., *The Practice of Conceptual History. Timing History, Spacing Concepts* (Stanford: Stanford University Press, 2002), p. 161.

13. Peter Osborne, 'Modernity Is a Qualitative, Not a Chronological, Category', *New Left Review* 1/ 192 (March–April 1992): pp. 65–84.
14. Koselleck, 'The Eighteenth Century', p. 168.
15. Doreen Massey, *For Space* (London: Sage, 2005), p. 68.
16. Harvey, *The Condition of Postmodernity*, pp. 229–30.
17. Helga Nowotny, *Time: The Modern and Postmodern Experience* (Cambridge: Polity, 1994), p. 18.
18. Giddens, *The Consequences of Modernity*, pp. 16–21.
19. Roger Friedland and Deirdre Boden, eds, *NowHere: Space, Time and Modernity* (Berkeley: University of California Press, 1994), pp. 28–9.
20. Malcolm Bradbury and James McFarlane, 'The Name and Nature of Modernism', in Malcolm Bradbury and James McFarlane, eds, *Modernism, 1890–1930* (Harmondsworth: Penguin, 1976), pp. 26–7.
21. Griffin, *Modernism and Fascism*, p. 53.
22. See Chapter 4.
23. Harvey, *The Condition of Postmodernity*, pp. 205–11.
24. This 'alternative' space is discussed in Chapter 5.
25. Griffin, *Modernism and Fascism*, pp. 122–4, 131.
26. Griffin, *Modernism and Fascism*; Jameson, *A Singular Modernity*; Karl-Heinz Bohrer, *Suddenness: On the Moment of Aesthetic Appearance* (New York: Columbia University Press, 1994).
27. Jameson, Ibid., p. 192.
28. Griffin, *Modernism and Fascism*, p. 63.
29. Harvey, *The Condition of Postmodernity*, p. 273.
30. Berman, *All That Is Solid*, p. 15.
31. Hugo von Hofmannsthal. Cited in James McFarlane. 'The Mind of Modernism', in Bradbury and McFarlane, eds, *Modernism*, p. 71.
32. Bradbury and McFarlane, 'The Name and Nature of Modernism', p. 49.
33. McFarlane, 'The Mind of Modernism', pp. 78–9.
34. Griffin, *Modernism and Fascism*, p. 62.

2 The Spiritual and Epiphanic Modernism of British Socialism

1. Frederic Jameson, *A Singular Modernity. Essays on the Ontology of the Present* (London: Verso, 2002), p. 136.
2. Holbrook Jackson, *The Eighteen Nineties. A Review of Art and Ideas at the Close of the Nineteenth Century* (London: Grant Richards, 1913), pp. 30, 31.
3. Perry Anderson, 'Marshall Berman: Modernity and Revolution', in Perry Anderson, *A Zone of Engagement* (London: Verso, 1992), pp. 25–55.
4. The other one of Anderson's three co-ordinates was the 'codification of a highly formalised academicism' in the arts, which provided a set of 'high'

cultural values against which critical modernist art could measure itself. Ibid., pp. 34–5.

5. Ibid., p. 36.
6. Edward Carpenter, *My Days and Dreams* (London: Allen and Unwin, 1916), pp. 247–8.
7. Annie Besant, *Modern Socialism* (London: Freethought, 1890), p. 4.
8. Splendidly discussed by Stephen Kern, *The Culture of Time and Space, 1880–1918* (Cambridge, Mass.: Harvard University Press, 1983).
9. Frank Kermode, *The Sense of an Ending: Studies in the Theory of Fiction* (Oxford: Oxford University Press, 1967).
10. Roger Griffin, *Modernism and Fascism. The Sense of a Beginning under Mussolini and Hitler* (London: Palgrave Macmillan, 2007), 104–14.
11. William Jupp, *Wayfarings: A Record of Adventure and Liberation in the Life of the Spirit* (London: Headley Bros., 1918), p. 70.
12. Ibid., p. 83.
13. Cited in Ibid., p. 86.
14. Ibid., p. 62.
15. Mentioned in Jupp, *Wayfarings*, pp. 86–7.
16. Ibid., pp. 62–3.
17. See Mark Bevir, 'British Socialism and American Romanticism', *The English Historical Review*, 110, 438 (September 1995): pp. 878–901.
18. Cited in Lena Wallis, *The Life and Letters of Caroline Martyn* (Glasgow: Labour Leader, 1898), p. 60.
19. Fenner Brockway, *Towards Tomorrow* (London: Hart-Davis, MacGibbon, 1977), pp. 24–5.
20. Ibid.
21. Jupp, *Wayfarings*, p. 97.
22. Chester Armstrong, *Pilgrimage from Nenthead: An Autobiography* (London: Methuen, 1938), pp. 146–7.
23. Ibid., p. 149.
24. Wallace's illumination featured in Richard Maurice Bucke's celebrated account of cosmic consciousness. See Richard Maurice Bucke, *Cosmic Consciousness: A Study in the Evolution of the Human Mind* (Philadelphia: Innes and Sons, 1901), pp. 332–42.
25. James William Wallace, 'Walt Whitman and Religion'. Lecture delivered to Progressive League, Bolton, 28 March 1915. Cited in Paul Salveson, *Loving Comrades. Lancashire's Links to Walt Whitman* (Bolton: WEA, 1984), p. 5.
26. John Johnston and James William Wallace, *Visits to Walt Whitman in 1890–1891* (London: Allen and Unwin, 1917), p. 19.
27. Edward Carpenter, *Civilisation: Its Cause and Cure and Other Essays* (New York: Charles Scribner's Sons, 1921; first edition 1889), pp. 1–62.
28. Ibid., pp. 3–4.
29. Ibid., pp. 29, 56.
30. Ibid., p. 55.

31. Edward Carpenter, *From Adam's Peak to Elephanta* (London: Swan Sonnenschein, 1892), p. 243.
32. Carpenter, *Civilisation*, p. 56.
33. Ibid., p. 4.
34. Ibid., p. 55.
35. Ibid., p. 13.
36. Ibid., p. 55.
37. See Carpenter, *My Days and Dreams*, pp. 111–13.
38. Jameson, *A Singular Modernity*, pp. 131–7.
39. Ibid., p. 136.
40. Jackson, *The Eighteen Nineties*, p. 24.
41. Jupp, *Wayfarings*, p. 60.
42. Jackson, *The Eighteen Nineties*, p. 132.
43. See Bevir, 'British Socialism'.
44. Carpenter, *Civilisation*, p. 57.
45. Linda Henderson, 'Mysticism as the "Tie That Binds": The Case of Edward Carpenter and Modernism', *Art Journal*, 46, 1 (Spring 1987): pp. 29–37.
46. Cited in Bucke, *Cosmic Consciousness*, 249. These meditations by Carpenter on cosmic consciousness first appeared in the May 1894 edition of *The Labour Prophet*.
47. Mercea Eliade, *The Myth of the Eternal Return: Or, Cosmos and History* (Princeton: Princeton University Press, 1954), pp. 35–6, 141–2.
48. See George Lansbury, *My Life* (London: Constable, 1928), pp. 6–9.
49. Ibid., p. 7.
50. See Stanley Pierson, *Marxism and the Origins of British Socialism. The Struggle for a New Consciousness* (Ithaca: Cornell University Press, 1973), pp. 162, 171.
51. Percy Redfern, *Journey to Understanding* (London: Allen and Unwin, 1946), p. 41.
52. Alex Owen, *The Place of Enchantment: British Occultism and the Culture of the Modern* (Chicago: University of Chicago Press, 2004), p. 25.
53. Redfern, *Journey*, p. 41.
54. Ibid.
55. Joy Dixon, *Divine Feminine. Theosophy and Feminism in England* (Baltimore: Johns Hopkins University Press, 2001), pp. 136, 177–9, 185–90.
56. See Alfred Orage, *Consciousness: Animal, Human and Superman* (London: Theosophical Society, 1907); see also Florence Farr, 'Superman Consciousness', *The New Age* (6 June 1907): p. 92; and Owen, *The Place of Enchantment*, pp. 132–5.
57. Owen, *The Place of Enchantment*, p. 24.
58. Carpenter, *From Adam's Peak*, p. 245.
59. See Linda Henderson, *The Fourth Dimension and Non-Euclidean Geometry in Modern Art* (Princeton: Princeton University Press, 1983).
60. *The Labour Prophet*, August 1892, p. 4.

61. John Trevor, *My Quest for God* (London: Labour Prophet, 1897), pp. 181–2.
62. Ibid., p. 185.
63. Ibid., p. 187.
64. Ibid., p. 242.
65. *The Labour Prophet*, March 1892, p. 4.
66. Ibid., p. 203.
67. Trevor, *My Quest for God*, p. 271.

3   Socialist Utopian Modernism: The Myths of the Kingdom and the Golden Age

1. John Trevor, *My Quest for God* (London: Labour Prophet, 1897), p. 192; Holbrook Jackson, *The Eighteen Nineties. A Review of Art and Ideas at the Close of the Nineteenth Century* (London: Grant Richards, 1913), p. 24.
2. Ibid., p. 31.
3. See, for example, *The Clarion*, 4 May 1895, p. 138. Entitled the 'Dream of Hope', the article has an Angel appearing in a daydream to a metal foundry piece-worker. The 'Angel of Truth' proceeded to offer the weary worker a vision of hope via a sumptuous image of a 'Garden of Pleasure' to set against the real world of sulphurous fumes and unbearable heat that pervaded his place of work.
4. Ernst Bloch, *The Principle of Hope*, Vol. 2 (Cambridge, Mass.: MIT Press, 1995), pp. 794, 820–7.
5. *The Clarion*, 27 April 1895, p. 133.
6. *Labour Leader*, 4 May 1895, p. 7.
7. Robert Tressell, *The Ragged Trousered Philanthropists* (London: Granada, 1965), pp. 583–4. Noonan wrote the book under the pen name of 'Robert Tressell' in 1906–8. It was first published in 1914.
8. Letter of 24 March 1887, which is reprinted in Margaret McMillan, *The Life of Rachel McMillan* (London: J.M. Dent, 1927), p. 30.
9. Frederic Jameson, *Archaeologies of the Future. The Desire Called Utopia and Other Science Fictions* (London: Verso, 2005), pp. 15–6.
10. David Harvey, *The Condition of Postmodernity: An Enquiry into the Origins of Cultural Change* (Oxford: Blackwell, 1989), p. 273.
11. Ernst Bloch, *The Principle of Hope*, Vol. 1 (Cambridge, Mass.: MIT Press, 1995), pp. 117–22.
12. Ibid., p. 119.
13. Percy Redfern, *Journey to Understanding* (London: Allen and Unwin, 1946), p. 19.
14. J. Keir Hardie, *From Serfdom to Socialism* (London: George Allen, 1907), p. 44.
15. *Fabian Tract No. 42* (January 1892; reprinted July 1899): p. 15.
16. George Lansbury, *My Life* (London: Constable, 1928), p. 287.

17. Ibid., p. 285.
18. See Norman Cohn, *The Pursuit of the Millennium. Revolutionary Millenarians and Mystical Anarchists of the Middle Ages* (London: Paladin, 1970).
19. Bloch, *The Principle of Hope*, Vol. 2, pp. 502, 508.
20. See Eric Voegelin, *The New Science of Politics* (Chicago: University of Chicago Press, 1952).
21. Cited in Stanley Pierson, *Marxism and the Origins of British Socialism. The Struggle for a New Consciousness* (Ithaca: Cornell University Press, 1973), p. 261.
22. Frank Kermode, *The Sense of an Ending: Studies in the Theory of Fiction* (Oxford: Oxford University Press, 1967), pp. 96–8.
23. Ibid., pp. 104–15; Mircea Eliade, *Myth and Reality* (London: Allen and Unwin, 1964), pp. 72–4.
24. Bloch, *The Principle of Hope*, Vol. 3 (Cambridge, Mass.: MIT Press, 1995), p. 1196.
25. George Bernard Shaw, 'Illusions of Socialism', in Edward Carpenter, ed., *Forecasts of the Coming Century: By a Decade of Writers* (Manchester: The Labour Press, 1897), p. 157.
26. Cited in Pierson, *Marxism*, p. 226. See also, Tom Barclay, *Memoirs and Medleys: The Autobiography of a Bottle-washer* (Leicester: E. Backus, 1934).
27. Rowland Kenney, *Westering: An Autobiography* (London: J. M. Dent, 1939), pp. 36–7.
28. John Trevor, 'Our First Principle', *Labour Prophet Tracts* (London: Labour Prophet, 1895), p. 37.
29. Mark Bevir, 'The Labour Church Movement, 1891–1902', *The Journal of British Studies*, Vol. 38, 2 (April 1999): pp. 217–45.
30. Trevor, 'Our First Principle', p. 41.
31. Joachim of Fiore, *Liber de Concordia Novi ac Veteris Testamenti*, cited in Melvin Lasky, *Utopia and Revolution* (London: Macmillan, 1977), p. 22.
32. Edward Carpenter, *My Days and Dreams* (London: Allen and Unwin, 1916), p. 206.
33. John Trevor, *My Quest for God* (London: Labour Prophet, 1897), pp. 242–3, 235–6.
34. Ibid., p. 242.
35. A point emphasised by Roger Griffin. See Roger Griffin, *Modernism and Fascism. The Sense of a Beginning under Mussolini and Hitler* (London: Palgrave Macmillan, 2007), pp. 71–81.
36. Harvey, *The Condition of* Postmodernity, pp. 30, 34.
37. James McFarlane, 'The Mind of Modernism', in Malcolm Bradbury and James McFarlane, eds, *Modernism, 1890–1930* (Harmondsworth: Penguin, 1976), pp. 82–3.
38. Eliade, *Myth and Reality*, pp. 1–19.
39. Ibid., p. 30.

40. Mircea Eliade, *The Sacred and the Profane: The Nature of Religion* (New York: Harcourt, Brace and World, 1959), p. 94.
41. Ibid., p. 106.
42. Eliade, *Myth and Reality*, pp. 64–9.
43. Quoted in R.J. Campbell, J. Keir Hardie and John Bruce Glasier, *The New Theology and the Social Movement* (London: ILP, 1907), p. 9.
44. Hardie, *From Serfdom*, pp. 103–4.
45. Mercea Eliade, *The Myth of the Eternal Return: Or, Cosmos and History* (Princeton: Princeton University Press, 1954), 132.
46. Hardie, *From Serfdom*, p. 104.
47. Annie Besant, *The Evolution of Society* (London: Freethought, 1886), p. 24.
48. McMillan, *The Life of Rachel McMillan*, p. 30.
49. See Morris's 1867 poem 'The Life and Death of Jason'; and Edward Carpenter, *Pagan and Christian Creeds: Their Origin and Meaning* (New York: Harcourt, Brace and Company, 1920), which has a chapter on 'The Myth of the Golden Age', pp. 137–53.
50. See Pierson, *Marxism*, p. 226. Glasier provided a lengthy defence of the Golden Age myth in two editions of the *Labour Leader*, on 29 April and 6 May 1920.
51. Ibid.
52. Ibid.
53. Ovid, *Metamorphoses* (London: Penguin, 1955), p. 32.
54. Bloch, *The Principle of Hope*, Vol. 2, pp. 490–1; Cohn, *The Pursuit,* p. 188.
55. Cohn, Ibid., p. 198.
56. Harry Levin, *The Myth of the Golden Age in the Renaissance* (Oxford: Oxford University Press, 1972), pp. 16–7.
57. Bloch, *The Principle of Hope*, Vol. 2, p. 483.
58. H.G. Wells, *A Modern Utopia* (Lincoln: University of Nebraska Press, 1967; first published 1905).
59. William Morris, *News from Nowhere* (London: Reeves and Turner, 1891).
60. Robert Blatchford, *The Sorcery Shop: An Impossible Romance* (London: Clarion Press, 1909).
61. Ibid., pp. 15–6.
62. Ibid., p. 17.
63. John C. Kenworthy, *From Bondage to Brotherhood* (London: Walter Scott, 1901), pp. 48–55. *Brotherhood*, 26 August 1887, p. 219.
64. *Brotherhood*, 26 August 1887, p. 219.
65. Ibid.
66. Edward Carpenter, *Civilisation: Its Cause and Cure and Other Essays* (New York: Charles Scribner's Sons, 1921; first edition 1889).
67. Ibid., p. 49.
68. Ibid., p. 43.

4 Experiments in Social Modernism: The Communities of Hope

1. For the remainder, see Chapter 1.
2. Cited in Walter H.G. Armytage, *Heavens Below. Utopian Experiments in England, 1560–1960* (London: Routledge, 1961), p. 293.
3. New Fellowship, *The New Fellowship* (London: Thornton Heath, 1890), p. 10. The Fellowship's fondness for colonies is also mentioned in Ernest Rhys, *Everyman Remembers* (London: J.M. Dent, 1931), pp. 2–3.
4. Alfred Higgins, *A History of the Brotherhood Church* (Stapleton: Brotherhood Church, 1982), provides a valuable history of the Church.
5. Nellie Shaw, *Whiteway: A Colony on the Cotswolds* (London: C.W. Daniel, 1935), p. 20.
6. Ibid., pp. 24–5.
7. Ibid., pp. 31–2.
8. Percy Redfern, *Journey to Understanding* (London: Allen and Unwin, 1946), p. 94.
9. Ashingdon and Wickford are mentioned in Dennis Hardy, *Utopian England: Community Experiments, 1900–1945* (London: E and FN Spon, 2000), p. 175.
10. Ibid., pp. 23–4. See also Jan Marsh, *Back to the Land: The Pastoral Impulse in England From 1880 to 1914* (London: Quartet, 1982), pp. 115–18.
11. Hardy, *Utopian England*, p. 24.
12. See Shaw, *Whiteway*
13. Ibid., p. 60.
14. Ibid., p. 59.
15. Ibid.
16. Redfern, *Journey*, p. 97.
17. Marsh, *Back to the Land*, pp. 101–2.
18. The Blackburn Colony is discussed in Redfern, *Journey*, pp. 96–7. See Hardy, *Utopian England*, p. 175, for the Leeds group.
19. Hardy, Ibid., pp. 177–8.
20. Paul Salveson, *Loving Comrades: Lancashire's Links to Walt Whitman* (Bolton: Worker's Educational Association, 1984), p. 1.
21. Hardy, *Utopian England*, pp. 169–70. Mirfield is also mentioned in Redfern, *Journey*, p. 120.
22. There is a glowing endorsement of the Starnthwaite Mill Colony by Katherine St John Conway in *The Labour Prophet*, August 1892, p. 61.
23. See *The Clarion*, 11 June 1892, p. 2. The disquiet is mentioned in Stanley Pierson, *Marxism and the Origins of British Socialism. The Struggle for a New Consciousness* (Ithaca: Cornell University Press, 1973), p. 220.
24. *Freedom. A Journal of Anarchist Communism*, March 1896, p. 69.

25. Nigel Todd, *Roses and Revolutionists. The Story of the Clousden Hill Free Communist and Co-operative Colony* (London: Peoples Publications, 1986), provides a valuable account of this Colony.

26. See Henry Thoreau, *Walden* (London: Walter Scott, 1886; first edition 1854cc).

27. See Edward Carpenter, *My Days and Dreams* (London: George Allen and Unwin, 1916), pp. 111–13.

28. Henry Salt, *Seventy Years among Savages* (London: Allen and Unwin, 1921), p. 74.

29. Stephen Winsten, *Salt and His Circle* (London: Hutchinson, 1951), p. 54.

30. Dugald Semple, *Joy in Living: An Autobiography* (Glasgow: William MacLellan, 1957), pp. 13–6.

31. Hardy, *Utopian England*, pp. 112–28.

32. Ibid., p. 128.

33. See, for instance, Marsh, *Back to the Land*; Armytage, *Heavens Below*; Hardy, *Utopian England*; and Dennis Hardy, *Alternative Communities in Nineteenth Century England* (London: Longman, 1979).

34. Shaw, *Whiteway*, pp. 26–30.

35. Ibid., p. 21.

36. Ibid., p. 22.

37. See, for example, Roger Griffin, *Modernism and Fascism. The Sense of a Beginning under Mussolini and Hitler* (London: Palgrave Macmillan, 2007), pp. 141–6; Francis Stoner Saunders, *Hidden Hands. A Different History of Modernism* (London: Channel 4 Publications, 1995), pp. 11–7; Christopher Wilk, 'The Healthy Body Culture', in Christopher Wilk, ed., *Modernism: Designing a New World, 1914–1939* (London: V & A Publications, 2006), pp. 249–95.

38. Saunders, Ibid., p. 11.

39. Ibid.

40. *The Labour Prophet*, August 1892, p. 57.

41. Griffin, *Modernism and Fascism*, p. 144.

42. *The New Fellowship*, p. 11.

43. 'The New Religion', *The Scout*, No. 8, Vol. 1 (November 1895): pp. 212–3.

44. *The Clarion*, 4 June 1892, p. 2.

45. Edward Carpenter, *Civilisation: Its Cause and Cure and Other Essays* (New York: Charles Scribner's Sons, 1921; first published 1889), p. 44.

46. See Shaw, *Whiteway*, pp. 73, 109.

47. See Hardy, *Alternative Communities*, p. 185.

48. Winsten, *Salt*, p. 546.

49. See Julia Twigg, 'The Vegetarian Movement in England, 1847–1981: A Study in the Structure of Its Ideology' (Unpublished PhD Thesis, University of London, 1981).

50. Robert Blatchford, *Merrie England* (London: Clarion Publications, 1893), p. 16.

51. Unwin's socialism, it should be said, was more keenly felt.

52. Salt, *Seventy Years*, p. 79.
53. Henry Salt, *Animals' Rights* (London: G. Bell & Sons, 1892). See also Henry Salt, *The Logic of Vegetarianism: Essays and Dialogues* (London: Ideal Publishing Union, 1899).
54. *Brotherhood*, 6 May 1887, p. 35.
55. Ibid.
56. *Brotherhood*, August 1888, pp. 25–6.
57. Shaw, *Whiteway*, p. 58.
58. Armytage, *Heavens Below,* p. 313.
59. Henry Nevinson, *Changes and Chances* (London: Nisbet and Co., 1923), p. 129.
60. Ibid., p. 130.
61. *Brotherhood*, September 1888, p. 57 and *Labour Leader*, 16 March 1895, p. 12.
62. Griffin, *Modernism and Fascism*, p. 141.
63. Carpenter, *Civilisation*, pp. 44–5.
64. Joseph Burtt, Preface to Shaw, *Whiteway*, p. 5.
65. Semple, *Joy in Living*, p. 148.

5 Contesting Abstract Space

1. David Harvey, *The Condition of Postmodernity: An Enquiry into the Origins of Cultural Change* (Oxford: Blackwell, 1989), p. 216.
2. Phil Hubbard, Rob Kitchin and Gill Valentine, eds, *Key Thinkers on Space and Place* (London: Sage, 2004), p. 2.
3. Émile Durkheim, *The Elementary Forms of Religious Life* (London: Allen and Unwin, 1915).
4. Zygmunt Bauman, *Liquid Modernity* (London: Polity, 2000), p. 112.
5. Ibid., p. 114.
6. Ibid.
7. Harvey, *The Condition of Postmodernity*, p. 232.
8. One just has to think of the Acts of Union with Scotland in 1707 and Ireland in 1801 which served to pull these territories of the 'Celtic fringe' into the mainstream.
9. Harvey, *The Condition of Postmodernity*, p. 253.
10. Henri Lefebvre, *The Production of Space* (Oxford: Blackwell, 1991), pp. 49–52.
11. Ibid., p. 370.
12. See Rob Shields, *Lefebvre, Love, and Struggle: Spatial Dialectics* (London: Routledge, 1999), p. 147.
13. Doreen Massey, *For Space* (London: Sage, 2005).
14. Ibid., p. 68.
15. Bauman, *Liquid Modernity*, pp. 12–13.

16. Anthony Giddens, *The Consequences of Modernity* (Cambridge: Polity, 1990), pp. 16–21.
17. Roger Friedland and Deirdre Boden, eds, *NowHere: Space, Time and Modernity* (Berkeley: University of California Press, 1994), p. 6.
18. Michel Foucault, *Discipline and Punish. The Birth of the Prison* (New York: Vintage, 1979), p. 138.
19. Lefebvre, *The Production of Space*, p. 33.
20. Sometimes referred to as 'spaces of representation' in the literature on Lefebvre. See, for example, Shields, *Lefebvre*, pp. 164–70.
21. Ibid., p. 45.
22. Thomas Gieryn, 'A Space for Place in Sociology', *Annual Review of Sociology*, Vol. 26 (2000): p. 476.
23. Lefebvre, *The Production of Space*, p. 341.
24. Ibid., pp. 341–2.
25. Andrew Merrifield, 'Place and Space: A Lefebvrian Reconciliation', *Transactions of the Institute of British Geographers*, Vol. 18, No. 4 (1993): p. 521.
26. Harvey, *The Condition of Postmodernity*, p. 239.
27. Stephen Kern, *The Culture of Time and Space, 1880–1918* (Cambridge, Mass.: Harvard University Press, 1983), pp. 131–80.
28. Ibid., pp. 141–3.
29. Harvey, *The Condition of Postmodernity*, p. 272.
30. Ibid., p. 273.
31. Jan Marsh, *Back to the Land: The Pastoral Impulse in England From 1880 to 1914* (London: Quartet, 1982), p. 98.
32. Joseph Burtt, cited in Nellie Shaw, *Whiteway: A Colony on the Cotswolds* (London: C.W. Daniel, 1935), p. 6.
33. The absence of fencing at Wickford is mentioned in Dennis Hardy, *Alternative Communities in Nineteenth Century England* (London: Longman, 1979), p. 199.
34. Cited in Ibid., p. 190.
35. Shaw, *Whiteway*, p. 67.
36. Hardy, *Alternative Communities*, p. 183.
37. Shaw, *Whiteway*, p. 112.
38. Ibid., p. 54.
39. See Julia Twigg, 'The Vegetarian Movement in England, 1847–1981: A Study in the Structure of its Ideology' (unpublished PhD thesis, University of London, 1981).
40. See also, Lefebvre, *The Production of Space*, p. 315.
41. Shaw, *Whiteway*, p. 158.
42. Tim Cresswell, *Place* (Oxford: Blackwell, 2004), p. 9.
43. Hardy, *Alternative Communities*, p. 196.
44. Harvey, *The Condition of Postmodernity*, pp. 272–3.
45. See Chapter 3.

46. Lefebvre, *The Production of Space*, pp. 357, 349 and Shields, *Lefebvre*, p. 164.
47. Edward Carpenter, *Civilisation: Its Cause and Cure and Other Essays* (New York: Charles Scribner's Sons, 1921; first published 1889), p. 48.
48. Ibid., pp. 48–9.
49. Ibid., pp. 49–50.
50. Robert Blatchford, *Dismal England* (London: Walter Scott, 1899), p. 27.
51. Ibid., p. 107.
52. Robert Blatchford, *Merrie England* (London: Clarion Publications, 1893), p. 16.
53. Ibid.
54. Ibid., p. 18.
55. Ibid., pp. 16, 18.
56. Robert Blatchford, *The Sorcery Shop: An Impossible Romance* (London: Clarion Press, 1909), p. 188.
57. Ibid., p. 83.
58. Ibid., pp. 16, 19.
59. Ibid., pp. 195–6.
60. William Jupp, *The Religion of Nature and of Human Experience* (London: Philip Green, 1906), pp. 176–7.
61. Mentioned in James Leatham, *Glasgow in the Limelight* (Turriff: Deveron Press, 1923), p. 40.
62. William Morris, *News from Nowhere* (London: Routledge and Kegan Paul, 1970; first published 1891), pp. 35, 58.
63. Ibid., p. 62.
64. W.H.G. Armytage, *Heavens Below. Utopian Experiments in England, 1560–1960* (London: Routledge, 1961), p. 307.
65. See Chapter 3.
66. Carpenter, *Civilisation*, p. 43.

6 The Return to Origins: Modernism, Socialism and Childhood

1. Roger Griffin, *Modernism and Fascism. The Sense of a Beginning under Mussolini and Hitler* (London: Palgrave Macmillan, 2007), pp. 104–14.
2. Friedrich Nietzsche, *Thus Spoke Zarathustra: A Book for All and None* (Cambridge: Cambridge University Press, 2006; first published 1883 and 1885).
3. Ibid., p. 17.
4. Cassandra Laity and Nancy Gish, *Gender, Desire, and Sexuality in T.S. Eliot* (Cambridge: Cambridge University Press, 2004), p. 132.
5. Griffin, *Modernism and Fascism*, p. 152.

6. See Mircea Eliade, *Myth and Reality* (London: Allen and Unwin, 1964), p. 79.

7. Jonathan Fineberg, *The Innocent Eye: Children's Art and the Modern Artist* (Princeton: Princeton University Press, 1997); Jonathan Fineberg, *Discovering Child Art: Essays on Childhood, Primitivism, and Modernism* (Princeton: Princeton University Press, 2001).

8. Friedrich Nietzsche, *Beyond Good and Evil* (Harmondsworth: Penguin, 1990; first published 1886), p. 94.

9. See Walter Benjamin, *Berlin Childhood Around 1900* (Cambridge, Mass.: Belknap Press, 2006).

10. Carlo Salzani, 'Experience and Play: Walter Benjamin and the Prelapsarian Child', in Andrew Benjamin and Charles Rice, eds, *Walter Benjamin and the Architecture of Modernity* (Melbourne: re.press, 2009), pp. 175–98.

11. Ibid., pp. 179–80.

12. Walter Benjamin, 'The Mimetic Faculty', in Walter Benjamin, *One Way Street and Other Writings* (London: Verso, 1985), p. 160.

13. Dan Mellamphy and Nandita B. Mellamphy, 'What's the Matter With Materialism? Walter Benjamin and the New Janitocracy', *Janus Head*, 11(1) (2009): p. 172.

14. Walter Benjamin, 'One Way Street', in Benjamin, *One Way Street*, p. 74.

15. Salzani, 'Experience and Play', p. 184.

16. Ibid., p. 185.

17. Walter Benjamin, *The Arcades Project* (Cambridge, Mass.: Belknap Press, 1999), p. 361.

18. Ibid.

19. William Morris, *News from Nowhere* (London: Routledge and Kegan Paul, 1970; first published 1891), p. 87.

20. Ibid.

21. Ibid., p. 116.

22. Ibid., pp. 21–6.

23. See William Morris and E. Belfort Bax, 'Socialism from the Root Up', *Commonweal* (30 October 1886): pp. 242–3.

24. Cited in Stanley Pierson, *Marxism and the Origins of British Socialism. The Struggle for a New Consciousness* (Ithaca: Cornell University Press, 1973), p. 86.

25. Edward Carpenter, *Civilisation: Its Cause and Cure and Other Essays* (New York: Charles Scribner's Sons, 1921; first published 1889), p. 235.

26. Ibid., pp. 233, 237–8.

27. Ibid., p. 227.

28. Ibid., p. 238.

29. Edward Carpenter, *Pagan and Christian Creeds: Their Origin and Meaning* (New York: Harcourt, Brace and Company, 1920), p. 173.

30. *The Clarion*, 2 February 1895, p. 37.

31. *The Clarion*, 9 February 1895, p. 45.

32. *The Clarion*, 13 April 1895, p. 120.
33. *The Clarion*, 6 April 1895, p. 109.
34. Ibid.
35. Carpenter, *Pagan and Christian Creeds*, p. 174.
36. *The Clarion*, 6 April 1895, p. 109.
37. *The Labour Leader*, 29 September 1894, p. 10.
38. Ibid.
39. Carolyn Steedman, *Childhood, Culture and Class in Britain: Margaret McMillan, 1860–1931* (New Brunswick: Rutgers University Press, 1990).
40. Ibid., p. 60.
41. Ibid., p. 153.
42. The first of these articles appeared in *The Clarion*, 30 November 1895, p. 381.
43. *The Clarion*, 17 December 1892, p. 4.
44. See, for example, *The Labour Leader*, 13 October, 1894, p. 11, and 27 October, 1894, p. 11.
45. See *The Labour Leader*, 2 June 1894, p. 7, and 30 June 1894, p. 11.
46. See *The Labour Leader*, 13 October, 1894, p. 11, and 27 October, 1894, p. 11.
47. Figure mentioned in *The Labour Leader*, 1 February 1896, p. 37.
48. *The Labour Leader*, 16 June 1894, p. 7.
49. Alex M. Thompson, *Here I Lie: The Memorial of an Old Journalist* (London: Routledge, 1937), p. 138.
50. Robert Blatchford, *My Eighty Years* (London: Cassell, 1931), p. 190.
51. Fred Reid, 'Socialist Sunday Schools in Britain, 1892–1939', *International Review of Social History*, 2 (1966): pp. 20–1.
52. Ibid., p. 27.
53. There is an interesting account of Socialist Sunday School activities in Alice Foley, *A Bolton Childhood* (Manchester: Workers' Educational Association, 1973), pp. 67–73.
54. Steedman, *Childhood, Culture and Class*, p. 181.
55. *The Labour Leader*, 25 May 1895, p. 4.
56. Ibid.
57. See Eliade, *Myth and Reality*, p. 79.

7 Fabian Modernism

1. Roger Griffin, *Modernism and Fascism. The Sense of a Beginning under Mussolini and Hitler* (London: Palgrave Macmillan, 2007), pp. 146–51.
2. George Bernard Shaw, 'The Fabian Society: Its Early History', *Fabian Tract No. 41* (February 1892), p. 4.
3. Ibid., p. 12.
4. Ibid., p. 10.

5. Stanley Pierson, *Marxism and the Origins of British Socialism. The Struggle for a New Consciousness* (Ithaca: Cornell University Press, 1973), pp. 246–57.
6. The Conservatives and their Liberal-Unionist allies gained 411 seats in the 1895 General Election, giving them an overall majority of 152. Their Liberal opponents lost around 100 seats, their heaviest electoral defeat of the century.
7. Pierson, *Marxism*, p. 247.
8. Alan M. McBriar, *Fabian Socialism and English Politics, 1884–1914* (Cambridge: Cambridge University Press, 1962), p. 83.
9. For a flavour of Le Corbusier's and Gropius's thinking, see Le Corbusier, *My Work* (London: Architectural Press, 1961); *Towards a New Architecture* (London: Architectural Press, 1946); and Walter Gropius, *Architecture and Design in the Age of Science* (New York: Spiral Press, 1952); *Apollo in the Democracy: The Cultural Obligation of the Architect* (New York: McGraw-Hill, 1968).
10. For an intelligent account of Saint-Simon and the Saint-Simonians, see James Billington, *Fire in the Hearts of Men: Origins of the Revolutionary Faith* (New Brunswick: Transaction, 1999; first published 1980), pp. 210–21.
11. Ibid., p. 216.
12. Marshall Berman, *All That Is Solid Melts into Air. The Experience of Modernity* (London: Verso, 1981), pp. 72–5.
13. Sidney Webb, 'Socialism: True and False', *Fabian Tract No. 51* (July 1899): p. 10.
14. Sidney Webb, 'English Progress towards Social Democracy', *Fabian Tract No. 15* (1890): p. 15.
15. Greta Jones, *Social Darwinism and English Thought: The Interaction between Biological and Social Theory* (Brighton: Harvester Press, 1980), p. 1.
16. Ibid., pp. 4–9.
17. Bernard Semmel, *Imperialism and Social Reform. English Social-Imperial Thought* (London: Allen and Unwin, 1960), pp. 64–82.
18. Ibid. Sir Edward Grey and Bertrand Russell were other members of the group.
19. It should be noted that other Fabians, apart from the Webbs, participated in the Co-efficient group. William Reeves, later to be appointed Director of the London School of Economics, was a group member, as was H.G. Wells. George Bernard Shaw was admitted to the group shortly before it wound up in 1908.
20. See Thomas Linehan, *British Fascism 1918–39: Parties, Ideology and Culture* (Manchester: Manchester University Press, 2000), pp. 20–1.
21. Jones, *Social Darwinism*, p. 59.
22. Ibid.
23. Ibid., p. 60.
24. Griffin, *Modernism and Fascism*, p. 149.

25. Weismann published his findings in *The Germ Plasm: A Theory of Heredity* in 1892.
26. Lydia Morris, *Dangerous Classes: The Underclass and Social Citizenship.* (London: Routledge, 1994), pp. 19–22.
27. Griffin, *Modernism and Fascism*, p. 148.
28. See Donald MacKenzie, 'Eugenics in Britain', *Social Studies of Science*, Vol. 6, No. 3/4 (September 1976): p. 503.
29. See MacKenzie, 'Eugenics in Britain', pp. 499–532; Diane Paul, 'Eugenics and the Left', *Journal of the History of Ideas*, Vol. 45, No. 4 (October–December 1984), pp. 567–90; Michael Freeden, 'Eugenics and Progressive Thought: A Study in Ideological Affinity', *The Historical Journal*, Vol. 22, No. 3 (September 1979): pp. 645–71.
30. George Bernard Shaw, *Man and Superman: A Comedy and a Philosophy. The Revolutionist's Handbook and Pocket Companion* (Harmondsworth: Penguin, 1931; first published 1903), p. 246.
31. Ibid., pp. 244–5.
32. Ibid., p. 248.
33. Ibid., p. 245.
34. Ibid.
35. Paul, 'Eugenics and the Left', p. 568.
36. Sidney Webb, 'The Decline in the Birth Rate', *Fabian Tract No. 131* (March 1907): p. 17.
37. Ibid., p. 18.
38. Ibid., p. 17.
39. H.G. Wells, *A Modern Utopia* (Lincoln: University of Nebraska Press, 1967; first published 1905), pp. 183–4.
40. Ibid., pp. 141–2.
41. Ibid., pp. 143–7.

Conclusion

1. Edward Carpenter, *My Days and Dreams* (London: Allen and Unwin, 1916), p. 311.
2. Carl Schorske, *Fin-de-siècle Vienna. Politics and Culture* (Cambridge: Cambridge University Press, 1981), pp. 116–80.
3. This fascination is dealt with most convincingly by Alex Owen, *The Place of Enchantment: British Occultism and the Culture of the Modern* (Chicago: University of Chicago Press, 2004).
4. Sidney Webb, 'Socialism: True and False', *Fabian Tract No. 51* (July 1899): p. 17.
5. George Bernard Shaw, 'The Illusions of Socialism', in Edward Carpenter, ed., *Forecasts of the Coming Century: By a Decade of Writers* (Manchester: The Labour Press, 1897), pp. 150–1.

6. Ibid.
7. David Harvey, *The Condition of Postmodernity: An Enquiry into the Origins of Cultural Change* (Oxford: Blackwell, 1989), p. 18.
8. Shaw, 'The Illusions of Socialism', p. 156.
9. Webb, 'Socialism: True and False', p. 4.
10. Sidney Webb, 'Historic', in George Bernard Shaw, ed., *Fabian Essays in Socialism* (London: The Fabian Society, 1889), p. 31.
11. This was also the space of heroic modernism and Le Corbusier. See Henri Lefebvre, *The Production of Space* (Oxford: Blackwell, 1991), p. 43.
12. Shaw, 'The Illusions of Socialism', p. 161.
13. Ibid.
14. Zygmunt Bauman, *Modernity and Ambivalence* (Oxford: Polity Press, 1991.
15. W.H.G. Armytage, *Heavens Below. Utopian Experiments in England, 1560–1960* (London: Routledge, 1961), p. 433.

Select Bibliography

Primary sources

General works

Adams, Maurice. *The Ethics of Social Reform* (London: W. Reeves, 1887).

Bax, Ernest Belfort. *The Ethics of Socialism* (London: Swan Sonnenschein, 1893).

Bax, Ernest Belfort. *The Religion of Socialism* (London: Swan Sonnenschein, 1890).

Benjamin, Walter. *The Arcades Project* (Cambridge, Mass.: Belknap Press, 1999).

Benjamin, Walter. *Berlin Childhood Around 1900* (Cambridge, Mass.: Belknap Press, 2006).

Benjamin, Walter. *One Way Street and Other Writings* (London: Verso, 1985).

Besant, Annie. *The Evolution of Society* (London: Freethought, 1886).

Besant, Annie. *Modern Socialism* (London: Freethought, 1890).

Besant, Annie. *Why I Became a Theosophist* (London: Freethought, 1889).

Bland, Edith Nesbit (ed.). *Essays by Hubert Bland* (London: Max Goschen, 1914).

Blatchford, Robert. *Dismal England* (London: Walter Scott, 1899).

Blatchford, Robert. *Merrie England* (London: Clarion Publications, 1893).

Blatchford, Robert. *The Sorcery Shop: An Impossible Romance* (London: Clarion Press, 1909).

Campbell, R. J., Hardie, J. Keir and Glasier, John Bruce. *The New Theology and the Social Movement* (London: ILP, 1907).

Carpenter, Edward. *Civilisation: Its Cause and Cure and Other Essays* (New York: Charles Scribner's Sons, 1921; first edition 1889).

Carpenter, Edward (ed.). *Forecasts of the Coming Century: By a Decade of Writers* (Manchester: The Labour Press, 1897).

Carpenter, Edward. *From Adam's Peak to Elephanta* (London: Swan Sonnenschein, 1892).

Carpenter, Edward. *Pagan and Christian Creeds: Their Origin and Meaning* (New York: Harcourt, Brace and Company, 1920).

Conway, Katharine St. John and Glasier, John Bruce. *The Religion of Socialism: Two Aspects* (Manchester: Labour Press Society, 1890).

Glasier, John Bruce. *William Morris and the Early Days of the Socialist Movement* (London: Longmans, Green, 1921).

Hardie, J. Keir. *From Serfdom to Socialism* (London: George Allen, 1907).

Hyndman, Henry Mayers. *The Text-book of Democracy: England for All* (Brighton: Harvester, 1881).

Jackson, Holbrook. *The Eighteen Nineties. A Review of Art and Ideas at the Close of the Nineteenth Century* (London: Grant Richards, 1913).

Johnston, John and Wallace, James William. *Visits to Walt Whitman in 1890–1891* (London: Allen and Unwin, 1917).

Joynes, James Leigh. *The Socialist Catechism* (London: W. Reeves, 1886).

Jupp, William. *The Religion of Nature and of Human Experience* (London: Philip Green, 1906).

Kenworthy, John Coleman. *Tolstoy: His Life and Works* (London: Walter Scott, 1902).

Leatham, James. *Socialism and Character* (London: Twentieth Century Press, 1897).

Le Corbusier. *Towards a New Architecture* (London: Architectural Press, 1946).

Lees, Edith. *Attainment* (London: Alston Rivers, 1909).

Macdonald, J. Ramsay. *The Socialist Movement* (London: Williams and Norgate, 1911).

McMillan, Margaret. *The Life of Rachel McMillan* (London: J.M. Dent, 1927).

Maude, Aylmer. *The Teaching of Tolstoy* (Manchester: Albert Broadbent, 1900).

Morris, May. *William Morris: Artist, Writer, Socialist* (Oxford: Blackwell, 1936).

Morris, William. *News from Nowhere* (London: Reeves and Turner, 1891).

Morris, William and Bax, Ernest Belfort. *Socialism: Its Growth and Outcome* (London: Swan Sonnenschein, 1893).

Nietzsche, Friedrich. *Beyond Good and Evil* (Harmondsworth: Penguin, 1990; first published 1886).

Nietzsche, Friedrich. *Thus Spoke Zarathustra: A Book for All and None* (Cambridge: Cambridge University Press, 2006; first published 1883 and 1885).

Orage, Alfred. *Consciousness: Animal, Human and Superman* (London: Theosophical Society, 1907).

Pease, Edward. *The History of the Fabian Society* (London: A.C. Fifield, 1916).

Quelch, Harry. *The Social Democratic Federation* (London: Twentieth Century Press, 1907).

Rowley, Charles. *Social Politics* (Manchester: John Heywood, 1885).

Salt, Henry. *Animals' Rights* (London: G. Bell & Sons, 1892).

Semple, Dugald. *Joys of the Simple Life* (London: G. Bell & Sons, 1915).

Thoreau, Henry. *Walden* (London: Walter Scott, 1886; first edition 1854).

Tressell, Robert. *The Ragged Trousered Philanthropists* (London: Granada, 1965; first edition 1914).

Shaw, George Bernard (ed.). *Fabian Essays in Socialism* (London: The Fabian Society, 1889).

Shaw, George Bernard. 'The Fabian Society: Its Early History', *Fabian Tract No. 41* (February 1892): pp. 1–30.

Shaw, George Bernard. *Man and Superman: A Comedy and a Philosophy. The Revolutionist's Handbook and Pocket Companion* (Harmondsworth: Penguin, 1931; first published 1903).

Trevor, John. *My Quest For God* (London: Labour Prophet, 1897).

Wells, H. G. *A Modern Utopia* (Lincoln: University of Nebraska Press, 1967; first published 1905).

Autobiographical books

Armstrong, Chester. *Pilgrimage from Nenthead: An Autobiography* (London: Methuen, 1938).

Barclay, Tom. *Memoirs and Medleys: The Autobiography of a Bottle-Washer* (Leicester: E. Backus, 1934).

Barnes, George. *From Workshop to War Cabinet* (London: Herbert Jenkins, 1924).

Bax, Ernest Belfort. *Reminiscences and Reflexions of a Mid and Late Victorian* (London: Allen and Unwin, 1918).

Besant, Annie. *Annie Besant, An Autobiography* (London: T. Fisher Unwin, 1893).

Blatchford, Robert. *My Eighty Years* (London: Cassell, 1931).

Brockway, Fenner. *Towards Tomorrow* (London: Hart-Davis, MacGibbon, 1977).

Carpenter, Edward. *My Days and Dreams* (London: Allen and Unwin, 1916).

Clunie, James. *The Voice of Labour: The Autobiography of a House Painter* (Dunfermline: A. Romanes, 1958).

Clynes, John Robert. *Memoirs* (London: Hutchinson, 1937).

Edwards, Wil Jon. *From the Valley I Came* (London: Angus and Robertson, 1956).

Foley, Alice. *A Bolton Childhood* (Manchester: Workers' Educational Association, 1973).

Gosling, Harry. *Up and Down Stream* (London: Methuen, 1927).

Haddow, William. *My Seventy Years* (Glasgow: Robert Gibson, 1943).

Jupp, William. *Wayfarings: A Record of Adventure and Liberation in the Life of the Spirit* (London: Headley Bros., 1918).

Kenney, Rowland. *Westering: An Autobiography* (London: J. M. Dent, 1939).

Kirkwood, David. *My Life of Revolt* (London: George Harrap, 1935).

Lansbury, George. *My Life* (London: Constable, 1928).

Leatham, James. *Glasgow in the Limelight* (Turriff: Deveron Press, 1923).

Meek, George. *George Meek, Bath Chair-Man by Himself* (London: Constable, 1910).

Nevinson, Henry. *Changes and Chances* (London: Nisbet and Co., 1923).

Paton, John. *Proletarian Pilgrimage: An Autobiography* (London: Routledge, 1935).

Quelch, Lorenzo. *An Old-Fashioned Socialist: An Autobiography* (Reading: Lorenzo Quelch Memorial Group, 1992).

Redfern, Percy. *Journey to Understanding* (London: Allen and Unwin, 1946).

Rhys, Ernest. *Everyman Remembers* (London: J.M. Dent, 1931).

Rowley, Charles. *Fifty Years of Work Without Wages* (London: Hodder and Stoughton, 1912).

Salt, Henry. *Seventy Years Among Savages* (London: Allen and Unwin, 1921).

Semple, Dugald. *Joy in Living: An Autobiography* (Glasgow: William MacLellan, 1957).

Shaw, Nellie. *Whiteway: A Colony on the Cotswolds* (London: C.W. Daniel, 1935).

Stonelake, Edmund. *The Autobiography of Edmund Stonelake* (Glamorgan: Mid-Glamorgan County Council, 1981).

Thompson, Alex, M. *Here I Lie: The Memorial of an Old Journalist* (London: Routledge, 1937).

Tillett, Ben. *Memories and Reflections* (London: John Long, 1931).

Toole, Joseph. *Fighting Through Life* (London: Rich and Cowan, 1935).

Turner, Ben. *About Myself 1863–1930* (London: Humphrey Toulmin, 1930).

Published letters

Wallis, Lena. *The Life and Letters of Caroline Martyn* (Glasgow: Labour Leader, 1898).

Newspapers, journals and pamphlets

Brotherhood
The Clarion
Commonweal
Fabian Tracts
Freedom. A Journal of Anarchist Communism
Humanity
Justice
Labour Leader
Labour Prophet
New Age
The New Order
The Scout
Seed-Time
Teddy Ashton's Journal
Workmen's Times

Other

Bucke, Richard Maurice. *Cosmic Consciousness: A Study in the Evolution of the Human Mind* (Philadelphia: Innes and Sons, 1901).

Secondary literature

Articles and chapters in edited volumes

Anderson, Perry. 'Marshall Berman: Modernity and Revolution', in Perry Anderson, *A Zone of Engagement* (London: Verso, 1992), pp. 25–55.

Antliff, Mark. 'The Fourth Dimension and Futurism: A Politicized Space', *The Art Bulletin* 82, 4 (December 2000): pp. 720–33.

Bevir, Mark. 'British Socialism and American Romanticism', *The English Historical Review* 110, 438 (September 1995): pp. 878–901.

Bevir, Mark. 'The Labour Church Movement, 1891–1902', *The Journal of British Studies* 38, 2 (April 1999): pp. 217–45.

Freeden, Michael. 'Eugenics and Progressive Thought: A Study in Ideological Affinity', *The Historical Journal* 22, 3 (September 1979): pp. 645–71.

Henderson, Linda Dalrymple. 'The Fourth Dimension and Non-Euclidean Geometry in Modern Art: Conclusion', *Leonardo* 17, 3 (1984): pp. 205–10.

Henderson, Linda Dalrymple. 'Mysticism as the "Tie That Binds": The Case of Edward Carpenter and Modernism', *Art Journal* 46, 1 (Spring 1987): pp. 29–37.

MacKenzie, Donald. 'Eugenics in Britain', *Social Studies of Science* 6, 3/4 (September 1976): pp. 499–532.

Osborne, Peter. 'Modernity is a Qualitative, Not a Chronological, Category', *New Left Review* 1, 192 (March–April 1992): pp. 65–84.

Paul, Diane. 'Eugenics and the Left', *Journal of the History of Ideas* 45, 4 (October–December 1984): pp. 567–90.

Weiler, Peter. 'William Clarke: The Making and Unmaking of a Fabian Socialist', *Journal of British Studies* 14 (November 1974): pp. 77–108.

Yeo, Stephen. 'A New Life: The Religion of Socialism in Britain, 1883–1896', *History Workshop* 4 (1977): pp. 5–56.

General works

Anderson, Perry. *A Zone of Engagement* (London: Verso, 1992).

Armytage, Walter H.G. *Heavens Below. Utopian Experiments in England, 1560–1960* (London: Routledge, 1961).

Bauman, Zygmunt. *Liquid Modernity* (London: Polity, 2000).

Bauman, Zygmunt. *Modernity and Ambivalence* (Oxford: Polity Press, 1991).

Benjamin, Walter. *Berlin Childhood around 1900* (Cambridge, Mass.: Belknap Press, 2006).

Berger, Peter. *The Homeless Mind: Modernization and Consciousness* (Harmondsworth: Penguin, 1974).

Berman, Marshall. *All That Is Solid Melts into Air. The Experience of Modernity* (London: Verso, 1981).

Biagani, Eugenio and Reid, Alistair (eds). *Currents of Radicalism: Popular Radicalism, Organised Labour and Party Politics in Britain, 1850–1914* (Cambridge: Cambridge University Press, 1991).

Billington, James. *Fire in the Hearts of Men: Origins of the Revolutionary Faith* (New Brunswick: Transaction, 1999; first published 1980).

Bloch, Ernst. *The Principle of Hope, Vols. 1–3* (Cambridge, Mass.: MIT Press, 1995).

Bohrer, Karl-Heinz. *Suddenness: On the Moment of Aesthetic Appearance* (New York: Columbia University Press, 1994).

Bradbury, Malcolm and McFarlane, James (eds). *Modernism, 1890–1930* (Harmondsworth: Penguin, 1976).

Buck-Morss, Susan. *The Dialectics of Seeing: Walter Benjamin and the Arcades Project* (Cambridge, Mass.: MIT Press, 1991).

Callaghan, John. *Socialism in Britain since 1884* (Oxford: Blackwell, 1990).

Childs, Peter. *Modernism* (London: Routledge, 2000).

Cohn, Norman. *The Pursuit of the Millennium. Revolutionary Millenarians and Mystical Anarchists of the Middle Ages* (London: Paladin, 1970).

Cole, G.D.H. *A Short History of the British Working Class Movement, 1789–1947* (London: Allen and Unwin, 1948).

Cresswell, Tim. *Place* (Oxford: Blackwell, 2004).

Dixon, Joy. *Divine Feminine. Theosophy and Feminism in England* (Baltimore: Johns Hopkins University Press, 2001).

Eksteins, Modris. *The Rites of Spring* (Boston: Houghton Mifflin, 1989).

Eliade, Mircea. *Myth and Reality* (London: Allen and Unwin, 1964).

Eliade, Mercea. *The Myth of the Eternal Return: Or, Cosmos and History* (Princeton: Princeton University Press, 1954).

Eliade, Mircea. *The Sacred and the Profane: The Nature of Religion* (New York: Harcourt, Brace and World, 1959).

Fenn, Richard. *The End of Time. Religion, Ritual, and the Forging of the Soul* (London: SPCK, 1997).

Fineberg, Jonathan. *Discovering Child Art: Essays on Childhood, Primitivism, and Modernism* (Princeton: Princeton University Press, 2001).

Fineberg, Jonathan. *The Innocent Eye: Children's Art and the Modern Artist* (Princeton: Princeton University Press, 1997).

Foucault, Michel. *Discipline and Punish. The Birth of the Prison* (New York: Vintage, 1979).

Fremantle, Ann. *This Little Band of Prophets: The Story of the Gentle Fabians* (London: Allen and Unwin, 1960).

Friedland, Roger and Boden, Deirdre (eds). *NowHere: Space, Time and Modernity* (Berkeley: University of California Press, 1994).

Giddens, Anthony. *The Consequences of Modernity* (Cambridge: Polity, 1990).

Griffin, Roger. *Modernism and Fascism. The Sense of a Beginning under Mussolini and Hitler* (London: Palgrave Macmillan, 2007).

Hannam, June and Hunt, Karen. *Socialist Women, 1880s to 1920s* (London: Routledge, 2001).

Hardy, Dennis. *Alternative Communities in Nineteenth Century England* (London: Longman, 1979).

Hardy, Dennis. *Utopian England: Community Experiments, 1900–1945* (London: E & FN Spon, 2000).

Harvey, David. *Spaces of Hope* (Edinburgh: Edinburgh University Press, 2000).

Harvey, David. *The Condition of Postmodernity: An Enquiry into the Origins of Cultural Change* (Oxford: Blackwell, 1989).

Henderson, Linda. *The Fourth Dimension and Non-Euclidean Geometry in Modern Art* (Princeton: Princeton University Press, 1983).

Higgins, Alfred. *A History of the Brotherhood Church* (Stapleton: Brotherhood Church, 1982).

Hinton, James. *Labour and Socialism: A History of the British Labour Movement 1867–1974* (Brighton: Wheatsheaf Harvester, 1983).

Hobsbawm, Eric. *Primitive Rebels. Studies in Archaic Forms of Social Movement in the 19th and 20th Century* (Manchester: Manchester University Press, 1959).

Howell, David. *British Workers and the Independent Labour Party 1881–1906* (Manchester: Manchester University Press, 1983).

Hubbard, Phil, Kitchin, Rob and Valentine, Gill. (eds). *Key Thinkers on Space and Place* (London: Sage, 2004).

Jameson, Frederic. *Archaeologies of the Future. The Desire Called Utopia and Other Science Fictions* (London: Verso, 2005).

Jameson, Frederic. *A Singular Modernity. Essays on the Ontology of the Present* (London: Verso, 2002).

Jones, Greta. *Social Darwinism and English Thought: The Interaction between Biological and Social Theory* (Brighton: Harvester Press, 1980).

Jones, Peter D'A. *The Christian Socialist Revival, 1877–1914. Religion, Class and Social Conscience in Late Victorian England* (Princeton: Princeton University Press, 1968).

Kermode, Frank. *The Sense of an Ending: Studies in the Theory of Fiction* (Oxford: Oxford University Press, 1967).

Kern, Stephen. *The Culture of Time and Space, 1880–1918* (Cambridge, Mass.: Harvard University Press, 1983).

Kertzer, David. *Rituals, Politics and Power* (New Haven: Yale University Press, 1988).

Koselleck, Reinhart. *The Practice of Conceptual History. Timing History, Spacing Concepts* (Stanford: Stanford University Press, 2002).

Laity, Cassandra and Gish, Nancy. *Gender, Desire, and Sexuality in T.S. Eliot.* (Cambridge: Cambridge University Press, 2004).

Lasky, Melvin. *Utopia and Revolution* (London: Macmillan, 1977).

Laybourn, Keith. *The Rise of Socialism in Britain, c.1881–1951* (Sutton: Gloucestershire, 1997).

Lefebvre, Henri. *The Production of Space* (Oxford: Blackwell, 1991).

Levin, Harry. *The Myth of the Golden Age in the Renaissance* (Oxford: Oxford University Press, 1972).

MacKenzie, Norman and MacKenzie, Jeanne. *The First Fabians* (London: Weidenfeld and Nicolson, 1977).

Marsh, Jan. *Back to the Land: The Pastoral Impulse in England From 1880 to 1914* (London: Quartet, 1982).

Massey, Doreen. *For Space* (London: Sage, 2005).

McBriar, Alan M. *Fabian Socialism and English Politics, 1884–1914* (Cambridge: Cambridge University Press, 1962).

Morris, Lydia. *Dangerous Classes: The Underclass and Social Citizenship* (London: Routledge, 1994).

Nowotny, Helga. *Time: The Modern and Postmodern Experience* (Cambridge: Polity, 1994).

Owen, Alex. *The Place of Enchantment: British Occultism and the Culture of the Modern* (Chicago: University of Chicago Press, 2004).

Pelling, Henry. *The Origins of the Labour Party, 1880–1900* (Oxford: Clarendon Press, 1965).

Pierson, Stanley. *British Socialists: The Journey From Fantasy to Politics* (Cambridge, Mass.: Harvard University Press, 1979).

Pierson, Stanley. *Marxism and the Origins of British Socialism. The Struggle for a New Consciousness* (Ithaca: Cornell University Press, 1973).

Rowbotham, Sheila and Weeks, Jeremy. *Socialism and the New Life: The Personal and Sexual Politics of Edward Carpenter and Havelock Ellis* (London: Pluto, 1977).

Salveson, Paul. *Loving Comrades. Lancashire's Links to Walt Whitman* (Bolton: Worker's Educational Association, 1984).

Saunders, Francis. *Hidden Hands. A Different History of Modernism* (London: Channel 4 Publications, 1995).

Schorske, Carl. *Fin-de-siècle Vienna. Politics and Culture* (Cambridge: Cambridge University Press, 1981).

Semmel, Bernard. *Imperialism and Social Reform. English Social-Imperial Thought* (London: Allen and Unwin, 1960).

Shields, Rob. *Lefebvre, Love, and Struggle: Spatial Dialectics* (London: Routledge, 1999).

Simmel, Georg. *On Individuality and Social Forms* (Chicago: University of Chicago Press, 1971).

Steedman, Carolyn. *Childhood, Culture and Class in Britain: Margaret McMillan, 1860–1931* (New Brunswick: Rutgers University Press, 1990).

Thompson, Edward P. *William Morris: From Romantic to Revolutionary* (London: Lawrence and Wishart, 1955).

Todd, Nigel. *Roses and Revolutionists. The Story of the Clousden Hill Free Communist and Co-operative Colony* (London: Peoples Publications, 1986).

Tsuzuki, Chushichi. *Edward Carpenter, 1844–1929: Prophet of Human Fellowship* (Cambridge: Cambridge University Press, 1980).

Voegelin, Eric. *The New Science of Politics* (Chicago: University of Chicago Press, 1952).

Waters, Chris. *British Socialists and the Politics of Popular Culture, 1884–1914* (Manchester: Manchester University Press, 1990).

Wilk, Christopher (ed.). *Modernism: Designing a New World, 1914–1939* (London: V & A Publications, 2006).

Winsten, Stephen. *Salt and his Circle* (London: Hutchinson, 1951).

Worley, Matthew (ed.). *The Foundations of the British Labour Party: Identities, Cultures and Perspectives, 1900–39* (Farnham: Ashgate, 2009).

Zieleniec, Andrzej. *Space and Social Theory* (London: Sage, 2007).

Unpublished PhD theses

Twigg, Julia. 'The Vegetarian Movement in England, 1847–1981: A Study in the Structure of Its Ideology' (University of London, 1981).

Index

Adams, Maurice, 29
aesthetic evocations of socialism, 4,
    5, 8, 46, 49, 63, 94, 96, 136
ambivalence, 12–13, 138
    see also Bauman, Zygmunt
anarchism, 2, 4, 62, 69, 117
    Tolstoyan anarchism, 68
    see also utopian communities
Anderson, Perry, 26–7
apocalyptic thinking, 26, 28, 52, 57,
    58, 88
    see also eschatological thinking;
        millenarianism
Armstrong, Chester, 32
Arts and Crafts movement,
    71, 92
Ashbee, Charles, 71
autonomous reason, 11–12
    see also reflexivity
Aveling, Edward, 119

Barclay, Tom, 52
Bauman, Zygmunt, 12–13, 80, 82,
    138
'Becoming', concept of, 9, 21, 47,
    56, 57, 59
'Being', concept of, 20–21, 24, 33–4,
    35, 41, 47, 56, 57, 77–8, 105,
    109
Bellamy, Edward, 45
    Looking Backward, 2000–1987
        (1888), 45
Benjamin, Walter, 103–6, 108, 109,
    110
    mimetic faculty, 104, 106, 109
Berman, Marshall, ix, 6, 11, 21, 122
Besant, Annie, 3–4, 27, 38, 59, 75,
    117, 118

Blatchford, Robert, 1, 2, 45, 61, 62–3,
    68, 73, 74, 76, 94–5, 112, 113–4
    Dismal England (1899), 94
    Merrie England (1893), 45, 76, 94–5
    The Sorcery Shop (1909), 45, 62–3
Blavatsky, Madame Helena, 4
Bloch, Ernst, 45, 47–8, 52, 60, 61
'Bloody Sunday' disturbances (13
    November 1887), 118, 119
Bohrer, Karl-Heinz, 20
British Socialist Party, 2
Brocklehurst, Fred, 112
Brockway, Fenner, 31–2
Brotherhood, 63, 67
Burns, John, 118
Burrows, Herbert, 39, 76, 118
Burtt, Joseph, 78

capitalism, 4, 10–11, 18, 27, 37, 46,
    61, 81–2, 83, 86, 106, 137
    Manchester school economics, 27
Carlyle, Thomas, 2, 72
Carpenter, Edward, 3, 19, 26, 33–5,
    37–8, 39–40, 54, 55, 59, 63–4,
    69, 70, 75, 76, 77–8, 93–4, 97,
    108–10, 111, 132–3
Chesterton, G.K., 2, 45
    The Napoleon of Notting Hill
        (1904), 45
Chignell, Mary, 112
childhood, 8, 98–115, 134
    half-time system, 112
    see also socialist children's
        movement
Christian Socialist Society, 1
Christian Socialist League, 2
Chubb, Percival, 117
Church Socialist League, 2

cities, 18, 73, 74, 95–6, 128
Clarion movement, 1, 4, 65
  Clarion, The, 2, 110, 112
Clarke, C. Allen, 110, 111
Clarke, William, 117
Co-efficient group, 126–7
  see also Fabians
Cohn, Norman, 60
Cole, G.D.H., 2
Communist Party of Great Britain
  (CPGB), 2
Conway, Katherine St John (later
  Glasier), 70, 76, 112
Co-operative movement, 39, 77
  see also Owenite co-operative
  experiments
cosmic consciousness, 32–5, 37–8,
  39, 54, 55, 133
  see also space, 'fourth dimension'
  of space; superman
  consciousness
cosmological socialism, 6, 34, 35
Cubism, 87

Dada, 17, 93
Darwinism, 124–6
  The Origins of Species (1859), 125
  see also Social-Darwinism
decadence, 6, 18, 22, 44, 58–9, 99,
  101
  Victorian decadence, 28, 134
Dickens, Charles, 2
dysgenic living, 18, 73, 78, 88
  see also cities
distanciation, 16–17, 83
  see also Giddens, Anthony
dream visions of socialism, 4, 23, 45,
  49, 59, 62, 93, 95–6, 138, 144
Duchamp, Marcel, 40
Durkheim, Émile, 80

Eagle Street socialists, 33
Edwardian Age, 1, 24, 58
Eksteins, Modris, ix, 6
Eliade, Mircea, 38, 52, 56, 57, 58

Eliot, T.S., 17, 19, 52, 55, 101
  The Waste Land (1922), 101
Emerson, Ralph Waldo, 3, 31, 36, 72
Emersonian immanentism, 3, 31,
  36–7, 41, 53, 55, 133
Enlightenment, 10, 11–12, 13–16,
  20, 22, 25, 80, 81, 106, 133
  Enlightenment rationalism, 19,
  20, 121, 123, 133
eschatological thinking, 44, 49–55,
  57, 101
  see also apocalyptic thinking;
  millenarianism
ethical socialism, 5
eugenics, 128–31
  see also Social-Darwinism
Eugenics Education Society, 130

Fabians, 1, 6, 65, 116–31, 135–8
  see also Co-efficient group;
  modernism, Fabian
  modernism; positivism;
  Saint-Simonian socialism;
  scienticism; Social-Darwinism
Faustian project, 13, 16, 80, 106,
  116, 122–3
Fay, Edward, 119
Fellowship of the New Life, 1, 4,
  29–30, 32, 36, 63, 67, 74, 117
  see also Seed-Time
fellowship socialism, 30–1, 36, 62
fin de siècle phenomena, 27, 43, 51
First Industrial Revolution, 27
Foster, Fred, 92
Foucault, Michel, 83–4, 90
Fourier, Charles, 106, 108
French Revolution, 10
Freudian unconscious, 48

Geddes, Patrick, 127
General Election of 1895, 119
George, Henry, 2
Giddens, Anthony, 12, 16, 18, 83
Glasier, John Bruce, 59, 95
Glasier, Lizzie, 114, 115

'God consciousness', 40–2, 54–5
    see also Trevor, John
Great Depression, 27
Griffin, Roger, 6, 7, 10, 18, 20, 22, 28, 74, 77, 98, 101, 116, 127
Gropius, Walter, ix, 19, 120
Grey, Mary, 114
    see also Socialist Sunday Schools
Guild of St Matthew, 3
Guild Socialism, 2

Hammersmith Socialist Society, 2
Hardie, Keir, 45, 49, 58, 59, 68, 69, 113
Harvey, David, 10, 12, 15, 18, 21, 47, 79, 87, 89, 92, 136
Headlam, Stewart, 49
health and hygiene, 18, 63, 73, 94, 72–8, 115, 117, 127–9
    see also modernism, social modernism; utopian communities
Humanity, 76
Hyndman, Henry Mayers, 1, 6, 117, 118

Independent Labour Party (ILP), 2, 65, 70, 77, 113
    The Labour Leader, 113
individualism, 10, 17, 24, 124
intuition, 19, 55

Jackson, Holbrook, 25–6, 36, 44
Jameson, Frederic, 9, 10, 20, 25, 36, 47
Jefferies, Richard, 2
Joachim of Fiore, 50, 53–4
Joyce, James, 19, 20, 52, 55
Joynes, Jim, 76
Jupp, William, 29–30, 32, 36, 76, 95

Kandinsky, Wassily, ix, 19, 37, 102
Kenney, Annie, 39
Kenney, Rowland, 52, 53

Kenworthy, J.C., 63, 67, 68, 72
    see also utopian communities
Kermode, Frank, 27, 51–2
Kern, Stephen, 87
Kingsley, Charles, 1
Klee, Paul, 19, 102
Koselleck, Reinhart, 14
Kropotkin, Prince Peter, 2, 68, 70, 71, 72

Labour Army, 1, 3
Labour Church, 1, 3, 39, 40–2, 52–3, 54–4
Labour Party, 1, 2, 5, 114
Labour Representation Committee (LRC), 2
Lamarckian theory, 128
Lansbury, George, 38, 50, 68
Lawrence, D.H., 37
Lefebvre, Henri, 81, 84–5, 86, 93
    see also space
Le Corbusier, 19, 55, 120
Letchworth Garden City, 76
    Howard, Ebenezer, 76
    Unwin, Raymond, 76
liberalism, 10
Liberal Party, 120
'life force', concept of, 31–2
    see also Shaw, George Bernard
liminoidality, ix, 28, 98
    liminoid moment, 28, 43, 44, 46, 47
Linnell, Alfred, 118

MacDonald, Ramsay, 51
Mackinder, Halford J., 126, 127
McFarlane, James, 21, 22, 55
McMillan, Margaret, 39, 49, 112, 115
McMillan, Rachel, 46, 59
machine and machine age, 19
Maguire, Tom, 119
Malevich, Kazimir, 40
Mann, Thomas, 17
Mann, Tom, 76
Martyn, Caroline, 2–3, 31, 119

Marx, Eleanor, 118, 119
Marx, Karl, 2
    Marxism, 2, 38, 39, 52
Massey, Doreen, 15, 82
    see also space
materialism, 10, 17, 24, 26, 28, 96,
    133
Matisse, Henri, 19, 102
Maxse, Leopold, 127
metaphoric evocations of socialism,
    8, 45–6, 115
metaphysical truths, ix, 13, 20–1, 29,
    35, 100
millenarianism, 49–57
    see also apocalyptic thinking;
        eschatological thinking;
        myth, of the Kingdom
modernisation, xii, 8, 9–11, 15, 18,
    28, 62, 79–81
modernism
    aesthetic modernism, 6, 7, 8,
        17–18, 20, 94, 136
    artistic modernism, 17, 20, 40, 55,
        93, 102–3
    definition of, 17–23
    epiphanic modernism, 7, 20,
        24–42 *passim*
    Fabian modernism, 116–31
        passim, 135–8
    heroic modernism, 7, 8, 116,
        120–1, 123, 137
    maximalist concept of, ix, 6, 17,
        132
    programmatic modernism, 22
    social modernism, 7, 8, 65–78
        passim, 117, 125–6, 127–31,
        see also utopian communities;
        vegetarianism
    utopian modernism, 7, 8, 43–64
        passim, 136
modernity, ix, xi, xii, 8, 11–17, 18,
    19, 25, 28, 43, 44, 46, 65, 73, 99,
    100, 106, 116, 121, 127–8, 138
    and space, 80–8
    and time, 13–16, 25, 100, 102

Mondrian, Piet, 19
Montefiore, Dora, 39
Morris, William, 2, 19, 45, 59, 61,
    71, 72, 92, 96, 107–8, 118, 119
    A Dream of John Ball (1888), 45
    News From Nowhere (1891), 45, 96,
        107–8
Munch, Edvard, 19
mysticism, 3, 4, 19, 55, 133
myth
    of the Golden Age, 8, 59–64, 96,
        102, 109
    of the Kingdom, 8, 49–55, 57–9
    of Merrie England, 61

naturism, 30–32, 35, 40, 74–5, 77–8,
    91, 93
    see also social modernism
Nevinson, Henry, 77
New Age journal, 2, 25
new beginning, 4, 45, 59, 98,
    99–100, 107, 134
    see also fin de siècle phenomena
New Unionism, 119
Nietzsche, Friedrich, ix, xii, 22, 39,
    99–100, 103
    Beyond Good and Evil (1886), 103
    Thus Spoke Zarathustra (1883), 99
Noonan, Robert (Robert Tressell), 46
    The Ragged Trousered Philanthropists
        (1914), 46
'Not-Yet-Conscious' 48, 62
    see also Bloch, Ernst
Nowotny, Helga, 16

occultism, xii, 3, 133
Orage, Alfred, 2, 25, 39
Osborne, Peter, 14
Owenite co-operative experiments, 1

Pankhurst, Edward, 119
Peasants' Revolt (1381), 60
Pease, Edward, 39, 117
Picasso, Pablo, ix, 19, 55, 102
Pierson, Stanley, 119

place, 82, 87, 89, 92, 137
  see also space
Podmore, Frank, 39, 76, 117
positivism, 10
Pound, Ezra, 19, 52
primitivism, 19, 35
  primitive consciousness, 34–5, 54
prophets, 41, 54, 59, 99
Protestant non-conformism, 2, 4

Radicalism, 51
rebirth, 1, 33, 35, 39, 52, 56, 58, 77,
  78, 98
Redfern, Percy, 39, 49, 76
reflexivity, 12, 14, 34, 54, 104
regeneration, 28–9, 30, 45, 56, 58,
  98, 102
religion of socialism, 5, 74
religious symbolism, 5, 134
revitalisation movement, 24, 28, 65
ritual, 89, 109
  May Day ritual, 45–6
Romanticism, British, 2
Romanticism, American, 4, 30–31
Ruskin, John, 2, 66, 71, 95

sacralisation, 101
Saint-Simonian socialism, 121–3
Salt, Henry, 70–71, 75, 76
Schorske, Carl, 133
scienticism, 116–17, 120–1, 131, 138
Scottish Labour Party, 1
Second Industrial Revolution, 26,
  27, 43, 88
Seed-Time, 29, 67
Semple, Dugald, 71, 76, 78
sexual emancipation, 74, 90
Shaw, George Bernard, 31, 52, 117,
  118, 129–30, 136
Shaw, Nellie, 67, 68, 72, 76, 91
  see also utopian communities
simple-life socialism, 70–1, 75–6, 77,
  91–2, 93, 95
  see also naturism; modernism,
    social modernism

Smith, Frank, 2, 118
Smith, Thomas, 68
  see also utopian communities
Snowden, Philip, 57
Social-Darwinism, 124–8
Social Democratic Federation (SDF),
  1, 6, 52, 117, 118
socialist children's movement
  Cinderella Clubs, 113–14
  Labour Crusader army, 113, 114
  Socialist Sunday Schools, 114, 115
  see also childhood
Social-Imperialism, 119, 126,
  129
Socialist Labour Party, 2
Socialist League, 1, 2, 6, 65, 117
Socialist Party of Great Britain, 2
Socialist Sunday Schools, 114, 115
Socialist Union, 1
space
  capitalist 'abstract' space, 80–3,
    84–7
  disciplinary spaces, 83–4, *see also*
    Foucault, Michel
  Euclidean space, 87, 97
  'fourth dimension' of space,
    39–40, 97, 133
  natural space, 80–1
  sacred space, 97
  socialist space, 88–97
  spatial architecture, 91–2, 95
  see also place
Stacy, Enid, 70
Steedman, Carolyn, 112, 115
Stravinsky, Igor, 19
Strindberg, August, 21
superman consciousness, 39
Surrealism, 17, 93

Theosophy, xii, 3–4, 19, 38–9, 55
Thompson, Alex, M., 45, 113
Thoreau, Henry, 2, 66, 70, 92, 95

time
    Enlightenment concept of time,
        13–16
    epiphanic time, 20, 25, 32–5,
        37–8, 40
    see also distanciation; *fin de siècle*
        phenomena
Tolstoy, Leo, x, 2, 38, 67, 68, 69,
    71, 76
transcendentalism, 31, 36, 44, 133
Trevor, John, 1, 40–2, 44, 52–3, 54–5

universal consciousness, 31–3, 34,
    41, 55
see also Emersonian immanentism
utopian imagining, 4, 22–3, 46–9,
    134
see also 'Not-Yet-Conscious'
utopian communities
    Ashingdon Colony, 68, 74, 91, 92
    Blackburn Brotherhood Colony,
        69, 91
    Broad Campden Colony, 71
    Brotherhood Church Community
        of Hackney, 67
    Brotherhood Circle of Derby, 69
    Brotherhood Workshop in Leeds,
        69, 90
    Chipping Campden Colony, 71
    Clousden Hill Colony, 69, 70, 74,
        77, 90, 91
    Croydon Brotherhood Church, 72
    Daisy Hill Colony, 69

Mayland Colony, 68, 74, 91
Millthorpe, 35, 70, 71, 74, 75, 91
Mirfield Community, 69
Norton Colony, 69, 74, 75, 90, 91
Purleigh Colony, 68, 74, 90, 91
Starnthwaite Mills Colony, 69, 70,
    74, 91
Totley farm Colony, 66, 74, 89
Walden Pond, 66, 92, 95,
    see also Thoreau, Henry
Whiteway Colony, 68–9, 74, 75,
    76, 78, 89–90, 91, 92
Wickford Colony, 68, 74, 90, 91

vegetarianism, 72, 74, 75–7
    see also modernism, social
        modernism
Victorianism, 24, 27, 30, 36, 38

Wallace, James William, 32–3, 133
Wallace, John Bruce, 63, 67, 76, 77
    see also utopian communities
Webb, Beatrice, 68, 76
Webb, Sydney, 68, 130–31
Weismann, August, 128
Wells, H.G., 45, 62, 76, 131
    A Modern Utopia (1905), 45
Whitman, Walt, 2, 30, 31, 32–3
Wordsworth, William, 109
Workers' Cry, The, 2

Yeats, William Butler, 17, 19, 21, 52,
    108